1965

W9-DFF-769

THE MAGIC MOUNTAIN

UNIVERSITY OF NORTH CAROLINA
STUDIES IN THE GERMANIC LANGUAGES
AND LITERATURES

Publication Committee

FREDERIC E. COENEN, EDITOR

WERNER P. FRIEDERICH
JOHN G. KUNSTMANN

GEORGE S. LANE
HERBERT W. REICHERT

For other volumes in this series see page 184.

Foreign Sales through:
Librairie E. Droz
8 Rue Verdaine
Geneva, Switzerland

NUMBER FORTY-NINE

UNIVERSITY
OF NORTH CAROLINA
STUDIES IN
THE GERMANIC LANGUAGES
AND LITERATURES

THE MAGIC MOUNTAIN

A Study of Thomas Mann's Novel
Der Zauberberg

By

Hermann J. Weigand

CHAPEL HILL
THE UNIVERSITY OF NORTH CAROLINA PRESS
1964

TO

EWALD A. BOUCKE

PREFACE

In an age when novels are turned out and hastily read by the hundred year after year, it may seem a futile undertaking to devote a whole volume to the study of one of them. It would certainly be pedantic to do so, if Thomas Mann's "Zauberberg" were just an ordinary novel; but critics of all shades—and violently hostile voices are by no means lacking in the chorus of comment—are agreed that the "Zauberberg" is one of the most significant literary landmarks of our age. Superlatives, like prayer, had perhaps better be reserved for the privacy of one's chamber; but I do not think it exceeds the bounds of due restraint to say that for many readers the "Zauberberg" (and the personality that stands behind it) has pointed the way to a new faith in life, to a quickened consciousness of things really mattering, and to a more exacting attitude towards one's own sphere of activity, however humble or restricted.

This study lays no claim to finality or exhaustiveness. In many respects it is a groping attempt to deal with a very complex theme capable, doubtless, of much better co-ordination. If I were to choose a motto for this book, it would be Hans Castorp's apology: "I would rather make a stab at things in the hope of expressing something difficult half-way than always be spouting excellent platitudes." I do not believe I need to apologize for taking the reader's familiarity with the immediate content of the "Zauberberg" for granted. Many topics, however, have only been casually touched upon that might well have deserved fuller treatment—it would have been tempting, for instance, to devote a whole chapter to the "Zauberberg" as a work of symbolical autobiography.

All quotations from the German in the body of this book are offered in the original, with an English version alongside for the convenience of the reader. (Published translations have been consulted where readily available. In most such cases I have adopted their text verbatim, reserving, however, the liberty to make any changes that seemed warranted in the interest of greater fidelity to the original.) There is something awkward about this procedure, but any other course would have involved paying too great a price for smoothness. A more word-conscious stylist than Thomas Mann probably never lived; and the tissue of themes in the "Magic

Mountain" is to a unique degree a tissue of "magic words with indefinitely ramified associations". No translation can hope to keep intact this tissue of magic words. In any two languages a given number of key words, corresponding in a fairly exact way as to their primary meanings, will tend to diverge more and more in expanding the range of their associated content. That is one of several reasons why any really adequate translation of the "Zauberberg" is an impossibility. Anyone who has read it only in English cannot help missing in large measure this functioning of its language after the manner of the musical "Leitmotiv", by which device echoes of the themes already developed constantly fall upon the ear and tend to keep the growing totality of the content ever present in consciousness or just below its threshold. It is necessary to recognize this situation frankly, although this reflects no discredit upon Mrs. Lowe-Porter's painstaking and often felicitous rendering.

The notes at the back of this volume are of two kinds. There are page references to passages alluded to or quoted in the text. As distinguished from these checks, such notes as contribute additional explanatory data or more detailed discussion are designated by numbers enclosed in circles.

To Miss Helen MacAfee, Managing Editor of the "Yale Review", and to my colleague, Professor Karl Young, both of whom read my manuscript, I am deeply indebted for many thoughtful suggestions. I also gratefully acknowledge the generous contribution toward the costs of publication on the part of the local Committee administering the funds of the General Education Board for the promotion of the humanities.

This study is dated, of course, by the fact that it was written without the benefit of hindsight afforded by the second half of Thomas Mann's literary career. Even so, it is still regarded by students as the most searching interpretation of one of the world's literary masterpieces. Thomas Mann himself gave it the stamp of his approval in the Princeton essay included in both the German and the American editions of *The Magic Mountain*. Except for the correction of a few misprints, this edition is an exact reproduction of the original.

HERMANN J. WEIGAND

New Haven, Connecticut
June, 1964

CONTENTS

"Der geduldige Künstler, der in langem
Fleiss den figurenreichen, so vielerlei
Menschenschicksal im Schatten einer Idee
versammelnden Romanteppich, 'Maja'
mit Namen, wob. . . ."

THOMAS MANN'S NOVEL

THE MAGIC MOUNTAIN

DER ZAUBERBERG

I. CLASSIFICATION

Let us begin our analysis of the "Zauberberg" by a brief attempt to group it with other novels that are related to it in scope, theme, and design. Of all forms of literary art the novel comes closest to embracing the whole of life in its span, and the number of possible classes that can be set up with regard to its subject matter alone is as great as the number of aspects of life itself. That task we may leave to the cataloguer, confining ourselves here to the pursuit of a few leads that may help our approach to the "Zauberberg" as a living work of art.

First of all, the "Zauberberg" presents itself as a pedagogical novel. It is repeatedly styled so in its own pages. We may as well be warned from the outset, however, that there is the same flavor of ironic modesty about this designation as there is about Thomas Mann's frequent reference to his hero as a simple young man, a youth without guile. The literary *genre* of the pedagogical novel, as known to histories of literature, is always concerned with a very specific sort of education,—an education that sets out to mould the plastic personality of a child along lines determined by its educators; and the process of education is pronounced complete when the youthful personality has come to conform dependably to the moral pattern that represents the educator's ideal. In the "Zauberberg", true enough, we have two educators, educating at cross purposes to each other, each coveting the mastery over Hans Castorp, like God and the Devil in the medieval mysteries fighting for the possession of the human soul; the pedagogical point of the novel, however, consists in the fact that the hero steers his course between the two, without committing himself to the orthodoxy of either. While deriving enormous stimulation

3

from their exhortations, warnings, and disputes, he dodges all direct
attempts to force him into the rôle of a disciple. Hans Castorp
develops, not according to the lines of a pattern imposed from without, but according to an inner law of his own personality that becomes manifest by degrees. We are in reality dealing, then, with a
novel of self-development rather than with a pedagogical novel, except in the wider sense in which Hans Castorp himself formulates
the principle of his "pedagogy", when he says to Clavdia in one of
those rare moments of ultra-clear consciousness:

"Du weisst wohl nicht, dass es etwas wie die alchimistisch-hermetische
Pädagogik gibt, Transsubstantiation,
und zwar zum Höheren, Steigerung
also, wenn du mich recht verstehen
willst. Aber natürlich, ein Stoff, der
dazu taugen soll, durch äussere Einwirkungen zum Höheren hinaufgetrieben und -gezwängt zu werden, der
muss es wohl im voraus ein bisschen in
sich haben." [1]

"You, of course, do not know that
there is such a thing as alchemistic-
hermetic pedagogy, transsubstantiation, from lower to higher, ascending
degrees, if you understand what I
mean. But of course matter that is
capable of taking those ascending
stages by dint of outward pressure
must have a little something in itself
to start with."

Hans Castorp has it *in sich*—to an extraordinary degree, in fact.
And this established, the "Zauberberg" reveals its affiliation with
that aristocratic and exclusive group among the novels of self-
development which constitutes Germany's most distinctive contribution to the world's fiction. I am referring, of course, to the
Bildungsroman. Goethe's "Wilhelm Meister", Keller's "Grüner
Heinrich", Stifter's "Nachsommer", Thomas Mann's "Zauberberg"—these most outstanding representatives of the type all focus
upon a quest of *Bildung* that transcends any specific practical aims.
Bildung—a term quite inadequately renderable by "culture"—we
might define as the approach to a totality of integrated human experience, provided we stress the integration. This result is always
but a by-product of the hero's conscious activities. He may see as
his goal a brilliant career on the stage like Wilhelm Meister, only to
discover, years later, that he lacked the fundamental qualifications
for success; he may be buffeted about like Keller's artist-apprentice
Heinrich, and return home, after years of struggle and hardship, a
complete failure, as measured by all specific worldly standards; or

again, like another Heinrich, the hero of Stifter's I-novel, he may be spared all violent shock and noisy commotion in the tranquil if eager scientific exploration of his physical environment in all its aspects; he may finally, like Hans Castorp, sacrifice all prospects of a practical career to the pursuit of a quixotic passion. In each case the by-product of these strivings, struggles, pursuits, and passions is something infinitely richer than the specific result coveted, altogether regardless of success or failure, and each author could dismiss his hero with the valedictory that stands at the end of "Wilhelm Meisters Lehrjahre": "Du kommst mir vor, wie Saul der Sohn Kis', der ausging, seines Vaters Eselinnen zu suchen, und ein Königreich fand" ("You appear to me like Saul, the son of Kis, who went out to seek his father's she-asses, and found a kingdom"). The keynote of the true *Bildungsroman* is, thus, an affirmative attitude toward life as a whole.

If the by-product of Wilhelm Meister's adventurings can be formulated as *Lebenskunst*, if the upshot of the disappointments of Keller's hero is spiritual freedom, if the studious pursuits of Stifter's Heinrich blend into polyphonic harmony,—what is the incidental yield of Hans Castorp's hermetic existence? It is the development of genius! Genius, present in the germ as an element of his native endowment, is awakened and nurtured by a series of highly abnormal factors. Thomas Mann's irony scores its most surprising point, perhaps, in the transformation of this simple young man into a genius in the realm of experience. Perhaps it takes a long time for it to dawn upon the reader that this is what has been happening—it certainly takes Hans Castorp long enough to find out, but no false modesty keeps him from acknowledging the fact, once discovered. We remember his telling Clavdia about the alchemistic-hermetic pedagogy, as involving transsubstantiation, *Steigerung*, and his emphasizing that for this pedagogy to take effect, the subject exposed to its workings "must have a little something in itself to start with". And he continues:

"Und was ich in mir hatte, das war, ich weiss es genau, dass ich von langer Hand her mit der Krankheit und dem

"And what I had in me, as I quite clearly know, was that from long ago, even as a lad, I was familiar with ill-

Tode auf vertrautem Fusse stand . . . denn der Tod, weisst du, ist das geniale Prinzip. . . . Zum Leben gibt es zwei Wege: Der eine ist der gewöhnliche, direkte und brave. Der andere ist schlimm, er führt über den Tod, und das ist der geniale Weg!" [2]

ness and death . . . for death, you know, is the principle of genius. . . . There are two paths to life: one is the regular one, direct, honest. The other is bad, it leads through death— that is the way of genius."

There is no ambiguity about this self-appraisal, nor can there be any doubt but that it coincides with Thomas Mann's own version, as we shall see when we come to analyze the factors involved in the awakening of Hans Castorp's genius.

It accords with the character of the "Zauberberg" as a *Bildungs-roman* that the hero is repeatedly styled "ein Bildungsreisender" [3] (a cultural traveller). In a spirit of irony, of course;—this designation being patterned to suggest the familiar commercial traveller—and this irony is in line with the traditions of the German *Bildungsroman* and derives its sanction from the prototype of the class, from "Wilhelm Meister" itself. The host of Goethe's contemporaries who bent their efforts to producing variations of the Wilhelm Meister theme were equally keen in exploiting its comic possibilities. Thus Tieck, himself the author of a variation of the Meister theme, introduces, in the prologue of his "Kaiser Oktavianus", a *Bildungsreisender* whose plodful musings on what is in store for him include the following pedestrian lines:

"Manches Glück wird mir begegnen,

Auch mag's manchmal Schläge regnen,

Meist folgt Morgen auf das Heute.

Jeder führt etwas im Schilde,

Und umsonst ist nichts auf Erden,

Darum acht' ich nicht Beschwerden,

Wenn ich mich nur etwas bilde." [4]

"Good fortune will smile on me now and then,

Occasionally I may come in for a drubbing;

For the most part Tomorrow follows Today.

Every day has something or other in store,

And you get nothing for nothing on earth.

For that reason I'll make light of hardships

If only I acquire a little 'Bildung'."

And one thinks, of course, of the frank travesty of the ideal of *Bildung* in Heine's "Bäder von Lucca", where we make the acquaintance of the self-styled Marchese Christophoro di Gumpelino and his valet

Hirsch Hyazinth, the little shrimp of a lottery agent who accompanies his master on his ludicrous tour of Italian galleries and cathedrals solely "der Bildung wegen". Thomas Mann's irony, it goes without saying, is of a different sort, and it will be taken up in a separate chapter.

Viewed from another angle, the "Zauberberg" belongs in the class of novels of unilinear development, as opposed to the novel of multiple strands of action. Most of Wassermann's novels, for example, represent the latter type. Thus his "Gänsemännchen", and his "Christian Wahnschaffe" even more so, trace the lives of a veritable host of characters that have their own experiences and their own fates. It is only at salient points of the action that they become linked with the development of the central hero; and after they have effected their contribution to his experience, it is just as likely as not that they again become detached from the line of the hero's life and continue to move in orbits of their own, where the reader glimpses them from time to time before they lose themselves on the periphery. This type of novel, if the looseness of its unity is to be something other than a bewildering jumble, has very definite problems of organization to cope with, and Wassermann's way of handling these problems makes one of the most fascinating elements of his technique. The closest conceivable unity, on the other hand, is represented by the type of the I-novel, where the content of the narrative is filtered through the medium of the narrator's personality in its entirety. The "Zauberberg" steers a middle course between these two types. Although we are introduced to approximately one hundred men and women in its pages, Hans Castorp dominates the action from start to finish; his personality makes itself felt in every scene. We never for a moment lose sight of the fact that it is Hans Castorp's experience which the author is transmitting to us; not a single incident is developed which does not affect him directly, and not one is included but for the reason of its effect upon him.[5] The principle of unity is, then, the unity of the hero's experiences. But there is a second angle to the case. While the author identifies himself with his hero in the most far-reaching way, he is at the same time distinctly present in the novel over and above the hero. The author is Hans Castorp plus ever-present resources of insight and conscious interpretation that transcend the normal level of Hans Castorp's experience. Only in those rare moments of *Steigerung* when it is given to Hans Castorp to turn an x-ray beam of intuition upon himself, is the merging of the two personalities absolutely complete.

This dual author's rôle involves recognition of the fact that the "Zauberberg" is a psychological novel. The author frequently comments on his hero's behavior and subjects it to searching analysis. And the behavior of this apparently simple young man is a most intricate business, for it harbors ever so many elements that have to put on the shrewdest of disguises in order to slip by the alert "censor" that guards the threshold of consciousness. We encounter in Hans Castorp all that complex functioning of the subconscious forces of the self on which the genius of Freud has trained the searchlight of psychological study. We sense the omnipresence of the libido as the psychic fluidum, impregnating Hans Castorp's behavior, coloring his every gesture, act, and utterance. But it would be an unfair distortion of the antecedents of Thomas Mann's psychology to stop at the name of Freud. His ready assimilation of Freud's discoveries is largely due to the fact that Nietzsche's pioneer work in tracing the genealogy of morals had been one of the great formative influences of his youth. Nor can we afford to forget how largely Ibsen and Hebbel and Kleist intuitively anticipated the principles of modern psychoanalysis.

All the foregoing attempts to classify the "Zauberberg" have turned on the hero-author relationship. But this relationship, enormously important though it is, is far from exhausting the significance of the "Zauberberg". The reader who has allowed himself to be engrossed by Hans Castorp's story to the exclusion of everything else is certain to feel that he has missed a great deal. He may even confess to being puzzled as to what it is all about. It is well to emphasize, therefore, that, in addition to several other things, the "Zauberberg" is a symbolic novel. The hero, the secondary characters grouped about him, the *milieu* of Haus Berghof—they are all charged with a meaning over and above what is visible on the surface, and it is this aspect of things that may make the reader who found pure delight in following the saga of the Buddenbrook family, leave the "Zauberberg" in bewilderment,—the more so as, to the superficial view, both novels are couched in the same naturalistic manner and excel in the same meticulously accurate portrayal of the characters and their environment. No doubt, this difference between "Buddenbrooks" and the "Zauberberg" is fundamental, and while it is partly to be accounted for by a revolutionary change in temper of the literary age, it is equally indicative of the course of Thomas Mann's own development. It will be one of our most interesting tasks to pursue the implications of the symbolic principle in detail. At this point I can only outline the symbolic relation that obtains between the concrete elements of the "Zauberberg" and the more general phenomena they aim to encompass. But lest I be accused of manufacturing a symbolic perspective which the author did not even remotely dream of, it is well to make clear once for all that such an approach has the author's authoritative sanction. In one of those passages of the "Zauberberg" where the author speaks in his own person we find a definition of the concept of the symbol, phrased evidently with an eye to its application to the novel in which it occurs. Leading up to his interpretation of the song nearest to Hans Castorp's heart, "Der Lindenbaum", in Schubert's setting, he says:

"Ein geistiger, das heisst ein bedeutender Gegenstand ist eben dadurch 'bedeutend', dass er über sich hinausweist, dass er Ausdruck und Exponent eines Geistig-Allgemeineren ist, einer ganzen Gefühls- und Gesinnungswelt, welche in ihm ihr mehr oder weniger vollkommenes Sinnbild gefunden hat, —wonach sich denn der Grad seiner Bedeutung bemisst." [6]

"A conception which is of the spirit, and therefore significant, is so because it reaches beyond itself to become the expression and exponent of a larger conception, a whole world of feeling and sentiment, which, whether more or less completely, is mirrored in the first, and in this wise, accordingly, the degree of its significance is measured."

Goethe might have written this sentence without changing a word, so thoroughly does it accord with his philosophy of art. It is perfectly possible, of course, that a theme may lend itself to symbolic interpretation without any internal evidence of the author's having had any specific symbolism in mind. Heine's well-known poem about the northern fir-tree that dreams in its wintry slumber of the sun-scorched palm of the Orient, is a good example in that it may, but by no means need be taken as an expression of Zionistic longing. The case is very different, however, when it is an integral feature of the author's conscious design to make us sense, over and above the concrete action unfolding before us, and without sacrificing any of its vitality, the presence of an elusive shadow play of larger import, running parallel to it, on a higher plane. Thomas Mann does this in "Königliche Hoheit", where it is his immediate concern to develop the problems confronting a grave little prince who has to take life very seriously, whereas the accompanying shadow play reveals corresponding problems, dangers, temptations, and compensations as typical features of the literary artist's life pattern. There are moments when the characters, together with the stage on which their lives are unfolding, become transparent, as it were, allowing us to glimpse the archetypes of which they are but variations.[7]

The same is the case with the "Zauberberg". Hans Castorp, Joachim, Settembrini, Naphta, Peeperkorn, the social *milieu* of the Sanatorium generally, are intensely real in their individuality, but they stand, besides, for something larger and more inclusive. Thus the *clientèle* of Haus Berghof—this motley international group drawn from the middle and upper strata of society, all of them stamped with the mark of disease—is readily felt as a symbol representing pre-war Europe. The analysis of the prevailing mental attitude, flighty, frivolous, thrill-hungry, and insincere, becomes a searching indictment of Western civilization, and the "Zauberberg" thereby reveals itself as a *Zeitroman*, in that it strives to express the psychic temper of a whole age. As for the principal characters, they frankly function as representatives. "Du bist nicht irgend ein Mensch mit einem Namen," ("You are not, to me, just any man, with a name, like another") Hans Castorp says to Settembrini on the night of the carnival, "du bist ein Vertreter, Herr Settembrini, ein Vertreter hierorts und an meiner Seite,—das bist du" [8] ("You are a representative, Herr Settembrini, an ambassador to this place and to me").

And it is with a smile that we recall how, at their very first meeting, the simple young man from Hamburg had been grandiloquently hailed by Settembrini as "der Vertreter einer ganzen Welt der Arbeit und des praktischen Genies" [9] ("the representative of the whole world of labor and practical genius")—a rôle not exactly expressive of his natural bent, as we have occasion to find out later. Settembrini henceforth functions in Hans Castorp's thinking as a concrete symbol: "Vertreter—von Dingen und Mächten, die hörenswert waren, aber nicht allein, nicht unbedingt" [10] ("a representative—of things and forces worth hearing about, it was true, but not the only forces there were"). But this new mental slant of Hans Castorp's is not limited in its application to Settembrini; in the same context from which I have just quoted he becomes conscious of Joachim also as the impersonator of a type—the military type of existence as opposed to his own, the civilian type. And we are doubtless aware of a similar representative character applying to Clavdia Chauchat and to Naphta.

To anticipate further discussion, Settembrini stands forth as the exponent of the philosophy of Western enlightenment, the philosophy of the bourgeois-capitalist world, a blend of generous idealism and shallow utilitarianism. Precise and self-assured, master of the rhetorical phrase and the withering jibe, ardent apostle of humanity and inveterate cynic in one, Settembrini is kin to a succession of illustrious figures ranging from Voltaire to Woodrow Wilson, as every reader recognizes. Little as one might at first suspect it, the German phase of the enlightenment, too, has contributed delicious traits to his character. From time to time we catch unmistakable echoes of Goethe's Mephisto,[11] of Schiller,[12] of the young Nietzsche,[13] and of the early Thomas Mann himself[14] in Settembrini's gestures and phrases. But he comes nearest, we have good reason to believe, to being a portrait likeness of his countryman, the flamboyant Italian agitator, Guiseppe Mazzini.[15] As for his name—like the names of all of Mann's characters an integral part of his portrait, and not a mere label—it carries a suggestion of bloody radicalism[16] that Settembrini would be painfully embarrassed to avow in all but his most ardently patriotic moments; it thus contributes an indelibly humorous, if somewhat alarming accent to his humanitarian pipings.

If Settembrini is the eloquent representative of the enlightenment, there is a magnetism about Clavdia Chauchat's mute presence that serves as a focus gathering into itself all those elements of Hans Castorp's personality that assert their instinctive opposition to this way of life. In this way Clavdia becomes a symbol of the East, as opposed to the West. In Naphta, again, the spirit of protest against the bourgeois ideology and all its implications finds an articulate spokesman who is altogether a match for Settembrini. He is a much more complex type than the Italian. His personality, rooted in no steadying tradition, is a discordant blend of motley elements that have coalesced solely because of their mutual bond of hate against the bourgeois world. Naphta, a much more trenchant thinker than Settembrini, and always on the alert to expose the logical flaws concealed under the magnificent drapery of his eloquence, represents all those modern currents of thought that focus their attack upon the existing order, and he borrows his weapons alike from the Kabbala, from medieval mysticism, from the later Nietzsche, and from Karl Marx. His only positive principle is that of negation, and it is altogether in keeping with his part that he should end by blowing out his brains.

In sharpest contrast to these two intellectuals is the inarticulate Peeperkorn. It is his function to make Hans Castorp experience the phenomenon of "personality on a grand scale". Its effect, while eluding rational analysis, is overwhelming. In the great Peeperkorn's presence the two debaters shrink to diminutive stature. As for his character, it is not easy to find a just formula for this weird synthesis of the reeling Dionysus and Jesus in Gethsemane. At first blush it may seem absurd to group him with characters like Senator Thomas Buddenbrook, Lorenzo de Medici and Fra Girolamo of "Fiorenza", and Gustav Aschenbach of "Der Tod in Venedig", all of whom live a life of unrelaxed tension and self-discipline; nevertheless he is related to them. He is another, albeit a grotesque member of Thomas Mann's gallery of "heroes". An idealist, like any devotee of the ascetic life, a modern Don Quixote, he consumes himself in the service of an idea. His cult of life is a form of worship, a continuous act of self-immolation. Goaded on by a constant dread of failure, he exacts a phenomenal degree of performance from his frail physique. There are rumors afloat as to the identity of the real "model" that stands back of Peeperkorn; but the pursuit of such clues, besides forgetting the fundamental distinction between life and art, invariably leads away from the work of art instead of closer to its core. Regardless of any flesh and blood individual who may have contributed certain traits to Peeperkorn's portrait, Peeperkorn is—to reduce the matter to simplest terms—a life-size portrait of Goethe's "König in Thule".

And what of Hans Castorp himself? Gravitating as he does between Settembrini and Clavdia; steering his cautious course between the two rival educators after Clavdia's departure, he stands as a symbol of Germany, *das Land der Mitte*, politically and philosophically. Between the lines we see Thomas Mann intent on defining the rôle that Germany is called upon to play in the family of nations, holding a middle ground between the voices of the East and the West, and if we rise to a more abstract realm we read his formulation of what is the essence of the German spirit, as he conceives it. This is a feature of the "Zauberberg" which it will certainly be worth our while to probe rather thoroughly.

So the "Zauberberg" is, in addition to its other aspects, a philosophical novel. It is this in more than one sense of the word, in fact, for its deepest concern is not man's relation to society, but man's relation to the universe as a whole. The almost complete omission of the economic realm from the range of its discussion is significant. Thomas Mann even delves into the realm of metaphysics and contributes views of a profoundly startling nature on the relation of appearance and reality. We shall find that it is one of the many angles of the problem of Time which lures him into this boldest and most questionable of all his ventures.

II. ORGANIZATION

One of the themes most frequently touched upon in the "Zauberberg", with repetitions and variations, is the experience of the passage of time. In the stream of time the individual's sense of duration bears no constant relation to time as measured by the clock. Both the author and Hans Castorp remark again and again upon the fact that the experience of time as full or empty, as dragging or fleeting, is determined by laws wholly independent of physical reality.

This observation finds its most immediate illustration in the organization of the "Zauberberg". The objective time span of the novel is seven years. It also happens that the narrative is built up out of seven structural units, each consisting of a number of subdivisions, usually nine or ten. But the most casual check suffices to show that there is no question of a mechanical allotment of a chapter to each year. Chapters I and II would have to be eliminated from our calculation to start with, inasmuch as the first deals only with the arrival of Hans Castorp at Haus Berghof, while the second gives a concentrated summary of his development up to the time of his deciding upon that fateful visit. But the five remaining chapters also differ enormously as to the amounts of time covered. Chapter III gives an exhaustive account of Hans Castorp's impressions on the first full day of his sojourn at the Sanatorium. Chapter IV covers the first three weeks, the period originally allowed for the visit. Chapter V takes Hans Castorp through the seventh month of his hermetic existence, climaxed by the night of the mardi gras. Chapter VI consumes time at an even faster rate, carrying the story to the point of Joachim's death, two years and four months after Hans Castorp's arrival at Davos. Chapter VII, finally, accounts for the remaining four and a half years of the total span.

There is nothing accidental about this apportionment. It is gov-

erned by a law of perspective which reveals itself even more clearly
when the length of the individual chapters is taken into consideration.
The seven years' time is then found to be distributed in the German
text as follows:

The arrival... 26 pages
The first full day.. 90 "
The first three weeks (exclusive of first day)...................... 150 "
The first seven months (exclusive of first three weeks)............. 270 "
The succeeding term of one year and nine months................. 333 "
The remaining four and a half odd years........................ 295 "

   The reader with a mathematical turn of mind may take delight in
working out the scheme of this time perspective in the form of a
diagram. (I would insist, in fact, that a passion for accuracy must
be linked with a receptive imagination, if the reader would assimilate
the values of the "Zauberberg" in something like their entirety.)
Nevertheless, our insight into the principle of the matter would
scarcely be enhanced by such devices. The exact amounts of time
are inconsequential. What matters is that we should come to experience the first few days of Hans Castorp's exposure to the atmosphere of Haus Berghof as packed with new and strange impressions
tending to endow the swing of the pendulum with an amplitude far
in excess of the normal; and that we should then be gradually imbued
with a sense of the passage of time, that we should feel it slip by at
a progressively faster rate, coming to lose count by and by, and imperceptibly finding ourselves become dwellers, with Hans Castorp,
in a charmed circle, more and more approaching a state of pure,
changeless duration. How to make the sense of the passage of time
a vital element of the reader's experience—that was one of the tasks
Thomas Mann set himself in the "Zauberberg", and his way of
solving it attests the powers of his artistry. That there is a genuine
problem involved in raising the awareness of the passage of time
from the level of a mere conceptual fact to that of an emotionally
tinged experience, is today a matter of common knowledge to the
literary craft.[1] By way of contrast we recall Shakespeare's simple
device for bridging a gap of sixteen years in "A Winter's Tale"

by having Father Time appear in person and report on the course
of events.②

Let us see by concrete examples how the "Zauberberg" handles
these problems. To the seasoned dwellers of the mountain resort,
words relating to time assume a haziness of meaning that jolts the
time sense of the newcomer. The word "neulich" stands as a sort
of symbol of this whole complex of shifting relationships.

"Aber neulich", Joachim begins on the day after Hans Castorp's
arrival, "es ist nun, warte mal, möglicherweise acht Wochen her—"
("But the other day—let me see, wait a minute, it might be possibly
eight weeks ago—")

"Dann kannst du doch nicht neulich sagen",[3] ("Then you can
hardly say the other day", . . .) Hans Castorp shoots back alertly
in protest against the unwarranted looseness of referring to something so far back as though it had been a few days ago.

Two days later, on the third day of Hans Castorp's visit, that is,
Joachim interrupts one of Settembrini's bursts of eloquence with the
remark to his cousin: "Komisch. Etwas ganz ähnliches hast du doch
neulich auch gesagt."[4] ("Funny; you were saying something quite
like that just the other day.") Here the word *neulich* is felt by us to
be as much out of place as it was above. One does not normally use
so vague a term when it is a matter of yesterday or the day before.
This time, however, Hans is so engrossed in the train of thought set
going by Settembrini that he lets the word pass unchallenged, and
the author also glosses the point over in silence.

In the course of their first meeting Settembrini had already commented humorously on the notion of a mere three weeks' visit. The
week does not exist in our time scale, he had informed the newcomer
with mock politeness. "Unsere kleinste Zeiteinheit ist der Monat."[5]
("Our smallest unit of time is the month.") And after Hans Castorp's
three weeks of visiting are up and he has become truly an initiate
into the practices of "those up here", he quickly learns to ignore the
smaller units of time. The major rest period lasts nearly two hours,
measured by the clock, but Hans Castorp's unconscious reasoning
soon manages to reduce it to merely an hour.

"Ein Viertel über zwei Uhr—das gilt für halb drei; es gilt in Gottes Namen auch gleich für drei Uhr, da schon die Drei im Spiele ist. Die dreissig Minuten werden als Auftakt zur runden Stunde von drei bis vier Uhr verstanden und innerlich beseitigt: so macht man es unter solchen Umständen." [6]

"A quarter past two will pass for half past, will even pass for three, on the theory that it is already well on the way toward it. The thirty minutes are taken as a sort of onset to the full hour from three to four, and inwardly discounted."

After six months he has become such an adept in this practice, that he disposes of the whole month, once begun, in similar cavalier fashion:—"Den Februar zählte er nicht mehr mit, denn angebrochen war abgetan, gleichwie gewechselt so gut wie ausgegeben." [7] ("February did not count, being once begun—as money changed counts as money spent.") But even this liberal consumption of time appears niggardly in comparison to the glib proficiency he comes to demonstrate by and by in dealing with centuries and historic eras. Now it is Joachim's turn to be startled, when Hans Castorp remarks apropos of the astronomy of the Chaldeans: "Uranus ist ja erst neulich mit dem Fernrohr entdeckt worden, vor hundertzwanzig Jahren." ("Uranus was only discovered the other day, by means of the telescope—a hundred and twenty years ago.")—"Neulich?", gasps Joachim, but Hans continues unperturbed:

"Das nenne ich 'neulich', wenn du erlaubst, im Vergleich mit den dreitausend Jahren bis damals. Aber wenn ich so liege und mir die Planeten besehe, dann werden die dreitausend Jahre auch zu 'neulich', und ich denke intim an die Chaldäer, die sie auch sahen und sich ihren Vers darauf machten. . . ." [8]

"I call it the other day—with your kind permission—in comparison with the three thousand years since their time. But when I lie and look at the planets, even the three thousand years come to seem like the other day, and I begin to think quite intimately of the Chaldeans, and how in their time they gazed at the stars and put two and two together. . . ."

It is altogether in keeping with the spirit of the "Zauberberg" that we should find the author adopting his hero's sense of time even to terminology. The term "Jahre" comes to be replaced by the diminutive "Jährchen",—like so many picturesque expressions a part of Hofrat Behrens' jargon, originally—[9] and a few pages before the end, Settembrini's moral dilemma with regard to the major issues of

European politics is reported in language reminiscent of Hans Castorp's faded time sense, without so much as the lifting of an eyebrow:

"Nicht selten war sein Verhältnis zu den grossen Konstellationen der Welt zwiespältig, von Skrupeln gestört und verlegen. Neulich, zwei oder anderthalb Jährchen zurück, hatte das diplomatische Zusammenwirken seines Landes mit Österreich in Albanien sein Gespräch beunruhigt. . . ." [10]

"Not infrequently his attitude toward the existing great political systems was divided, embarrassed, disturbed by scruples. The other day, two yearlets ago, more or less, the diplomatic rapprochement between his country and Austria, their co-operation in Albania, had reflected itself in his conversation."

Now contrast this uncanny haste of time's silent whirl, first experienced as mounting in a progressive ratio, and then ceasing to trouble his consciousness altogether with what I have called the abnormal amplitude of the pendulum's swing during Hans Castorp's first day at Haus Berghof. Instead of attempting to summarize all the varied impressions that crowd in upon him, I think it more instructive to single out one group of impressions and note its development. On the first day, Hans Castorp makes the acquaintance of his table companions in the dining-room. He meets them five times, at first breakfast, at second breakfast, at dinner, at tea, and at supper. We are not directly introduced to them by the author; nor are we given a fairly complete inventory of their characteristics individually, after the manner employed in "Buddenbrooks"[11] twenty-five years earlier:—we make their acquaintance in an unsystematic and fragmentary way through the medium of Hans Castorp's own experience. At the first breakfast, Hans takes note of his companions in a cursory and provisional way. Five strangers are seated at the table, in addition to himself and Joachim, four women and one man. Only one name, that of Frau Stöhr, is noted. This female bears from the outset the definite stamp of crass vulgarity and ridiculous affectation. The others remain vaguely defined types, differentiated by a few general characteristics.[12] At the second breakfast Hans Castorp's impressions of some of his table companions become somewhat more defined by the repeated perception of characteristics already noted, and his attention is focussed in a certain degree on two new faces, an elderly Russian lady and, beside her, a pretty young girl of striking features and manner whom he hears addressed as Marusya.[13] Then, in the course of a walk down to the village, Hans Castorp and his cousin discuss the group whose table they share; Joachim mentions them individually by name and tells Hans what little he knows about them while Hans makes a few tart comments on the two women whose names he had already learned at table.[14] When the group is again assembled, this time at dinner, the first strain of novelty has departed, and we indulge with Hans Castorp in a more detailed observation of its members. In the course of the elaborate repast each one of the guests, now properly tagged with a name, makes his presence felt in some way and stamps himself more definitely upon Hans Castorp's mind.[15] Marusya, notably, has by now exhibited all those striking traits and mannerisms by which we are to know her throughout the book. As to Frau Stöhr, her talk is as voluble as it is revelatory of her plebeian soul. The fact, by the way, that her vulgar gossip is reproduced through the medium of indirect discourse is interesting to note. We—that is to say the select company composed of the author, the hero, and the reader, have not yet had our aristocratic sensibilities blunted by frequent contacts with this representative of coarse, middle-class pretentiousness. The use of indirect discourse is suggestive of an instinctive defense reaction on the part of all of us. The crudity of Frau Stöhr's outpourings is thereby passed through a filter, as it were, to soften its offensiveness.[16] But to return to our hero and the weight of impressions accumulating in his brain on the first day of his visit, we observe that by tea time his receptiveness has reached the saturation point. "Gott, ist noch immer der erste Tag?",[17] ("My God, is it still the first day?") he exclaims incredulously. Accordingly, the four o'clock tea is disposed of in a few sentences devoted chiefly to the composition of the repast. The interval between tea and supper is skipped over as "kurz und nichtig", because Hans Castorp's capacity for experiencing anything new is quite exhausted; and the supper itself marks Hans Castorp's desperate but ineffectual attempts to fight the fatigue that reduces

Marusya's laughter and Frau Stöhr's chatter to a confused din from which only an occasional scrap of meaning detaches itself to find the way to his consciousness.[18]

Enough has been said to show the importance of the psychological experience of time as a structural principle of the "Zauberberg". There is evident method in the fact that the impressions of the first day absorb nearly one thirteenth of the total narrative, whereas the twenty-five hundred odd days still to be consumed become subject to a perspective that calls for progressive foreshortening. The flow of time is not even. It does not recede like a railroad track; it resembles rather a mountain landscape viewed from a high point of vantage: nearby, the landscape is spread out in all the detail of its varying contours, but as the eye lifts the valleys are more and more lost to sight, until at the horizon nothing remains but a series of sharp peaks closely massed.

We have not done, by any means, with the part played by the time concept in the "Zauberberg". The novel is a *Zeitroman* in more than one sense, on the basis of its own claims,[19] and it will be necessary to recur to other aspects of the time problem in considering the technique of the *Leitmotiv*, and in pondering the mystical implications of the "Zauberberg's" weirdest episode. But it is of more immediate importance for us to become clearly aware of the articulation of the "Zauberberg's" impressive content, to mark the lines of cleavage that divide its bulk into definite masses, and to note the major turning-points of the action.

Without any doubt, the most conspicuous line of cleavage coincides with the end of the first volume. In three ways the night of the mardi gras rounds out the most momentous chapter of Hans Castorp's spiritual history. For one thing, it marks the consummation of his devastating passion for the slant-eyed Clavdia. The act of will involved in exposing to the test of reality the secret flame that had kept his imagination for seven months in a state of incandescence, betokened an unprecedented, a cataclysmic upheaval of his whole being. It was a frenzied gambler's gesture that staked his very existence on one card. In the second place, Hans Castorp's declaration of love,—in its rapturous worship of the physiological organism without a parallel in literature, represents also the climax of his "Sympathie mit dem Tode". During those seven months the fascination of death, familiar to Hans Castorp since early childhood, had come to be the keynote of all his interests and studies. When we meet him again in the second volume, after Clavdia's departure, the course of his life has been somehow altered. The change may be imperceptible at first, but it becomes increasingly clear that in a peculiar way the fascination of death has become subordinated to the fascination of life. The accents of his values have undergone modification. Anticipating more detailed analysis in our chapter on Disease, we may say that the lure of disease and adventurous abandon now have as a steadying counterpart a growing interest in health and a developing sense of responsibility.—In a third respect, finally, Hans Castorp terminates on that evening a chapter of his life. Up to now his attitude toward Herr Settembrini had been essentially that of a pupil to his mentor. His rôle has been receptive; his resistance, where it asserted itself, had been furtive, half-conscious, and to a large extent inarticulate. Of late, it is true, he had shown a disquieting tendency to hold his ground even in debate.[20]   On this night, however, his personality becomes suddenly integrated; he emancipates himself from Settembrini's tutelage by a dramatic act of self-assertion; he is conscious of having graduated, so to say, and the humble deference of his earlier manner yields to an air of frank equality, symbolized by the bold "Du" of his address. From this time on Hans Castorp scans Settembrini's pedagogical propositions with a detached freedom which his native courtesy succeeds but imperfectly in disguising. Settembrini is ruefully conscious of the change; he keeps up a bold front, but his occasional outbursts of irritation reveal his true emotions.

Within the scope of the first volume we find two major crises, the full significance of which is revealed by the subsequent turn of events. Twice our hero is called upon to make a cleancut choice between two courses of action,—on the evening of his first full day at Haus Berghof, when Settembrini counsels him to depart at once,[21] and again three weeks later, just before he rises from the dinner table

to keep the appointment with Hofrat Behrens which, as he fully
knows in advance, will enroll him in the roster of patients for an
indefinite stay.[22] Shall he follow the plain call of reason and duty
and spiritual safety in the broadest sense by leaving abruptly, or
shall he trust himself to the lure of perilous adventure on the remote
chance of some indefinable enrichment accruing to his being? Down
in the matrix of his self the two opposing forces fight out their tug
of war, and while the decision is apparently brought about by a passive yielding along the line of least resistance, it is in truth his innermost being that determines the choice. The chances are that
had he never left the "Flachland", and had he never been exposed
to the macabre magic of this resort, the core of his being would have
lain dormant and undiscovered throughout Hans Castorp's life. His
life would have borne the stamp of a routine existence, and his metaphysical character—to use Schopenhauer's term—would never have
become manifest. The essential attitude toward life that comes to
the fore in this decision of Hans Castorp's and asserts itself henceforth as the regulative principle of his morality, is formulated in
classic terms by Clavdia Chauchat on the night of the mardi gras.
It is like an x-ray beam rendering transparent the structural outline
of his conduct, when she says:

"Il nous semble, qu'il faudrait chercher
la morale non dans la vertu, c'est à dire
dans la raison, la discipline, les bonnes
meurs, l'honnêteté,—mais plutôt dans
le contraire, je veux dire: dans le péché,
en s'abandonnant au danger, à ce qui
est nuisible, à ce qui nous consume. Il
nous semble qu'il est plus moral de se
perdre et même de se laisser dépérir
que de se conserver." [23]

"It seems to us that one should look
for morality not in virtue, that is to
say in reason, discipline, good manners, and decency, but rather in the
opposite: in sin, that is, in abandoning oneself to danger, to what is
harmful, to what consumes us. It
seems to us that it is more moral to
lose oneself and even to abandon oneself to perdition, rather than to preserve oneself."

The attitude of adventuring into the strange, the unknown, the
dangerous, fraught with dire risk of self-destruction—this is the
morality of genius as opposed to the morality of the norm. But more
of this in its proper place.

   To these two crises we are justified, I think, in adding a third, although, unlike the first two, it involves no act of will on our hero's part but rather an act of awakening. After he has spent the first three weeks of his "novitiate" in bed, Hans Castorp is summoned to the laboratory for a thorough physical examination. There he beholds the skeleton of his own hand under the fluoroscope, and for the first time in his life he intuitively grasps the idea that some day he is going to die. This incident marks the conscious awakening of his latent sympathy with death, and all his emotionally impregnated scientific studies owe their initial impulse to that moment of intense awareness of death, involving the translation of a familiar fact into a vital experience.

Like the first, the second volume is also articulated by a series of major crises in Hans Castorp's development. The seriousness of Hans Castorp's devotion to *his* principle of morality,—the principle of losing oneself, even of abandoning oneself to perdition, is put to a rather severe test, for all the humor involved, when, in a burst of rage, Hofrat Behrens gives Hans Castorp "the gate" along with his deserter-of-a-cousin.[24] This crisis is weathered thanks to our hero's diplomacy in handling the delicate situation. In the wake of Joachim's departure, the "Flachland" sends an emissary in the person of James Tienappel to reclaim the lost sheep; but as for this abortive sally, we would not dignify it by the term of crisis, in view of its negligible effect upon Hans Castorp.[25] A very real crisis, however, is presented in the section called "Snow", where the hero, lost in the blizzard, experiences his sublimely awful visions and verbally articulate dreams of life and death. Here, in the affirmation of life, worked out as a principle transcending the dualism and the dialectics of the two pedagogical fencers, we have without question the spiritual climax of the whole novel. Hovering there between life and death, Hans Castorp is for a moment elevated to a position of clarity that marks the acme of his capacity to span the poles of cosmic experience. The vision fades almost at once, but it leaves a residual effect on his personality that time cannot obliterate. It is to this experience that he owes the resources which enable him ultimately to sublimate even his passion for Clavdia into disinterested friendship. The readjustment of this relation marks another of the outstanding crises of the volume, distributed though it is over a number of episodes, including his eminently fair reaction to his rival Peeperkorn's commanding personality, his two mutually supplementary pacts of friendship with Peeperkorn and with Clavdia, and his gesture of final renunciation at Peeperkorn's deathbed.

A crisis in Hans Castorp's development is, finally, the materialization of the deceased Joachim which brings the spiritualistic *séance* to an abrupt end. For Hans Castorp's rôle in that *séance* is quite distinct from that of the other participants in this thrill of stark emotional horror. Once more his deepest being is involved when, after a long silence, he voices his desire to see Joachim Ziemssen. Again it is an act of will reaching out in the direction of the unknown, the dangerous, and the forbidden, which manifests itself in the welling up of this desire. It is the morality of losing oneself, even of abandoning oneself to perdition, carried to the point of a "hybris" that calls down the wrath of the gods. Whereas the crowd of thrill seekers had by their joint efforts succeeded only in calling forth essentially meaningless, if staggeringly sensational phenomena, the evocation of Joachim is Hans Castorp's deed, accomplished by a tension of his disciplined will that does not shrink from spending its last reserves. The prophetic significance of Joachim's accoutrement and its implications with regard to Thomas Mann's *Weltanschauung* must be reserved for our final chapter. It is enough here to refer to it and to mention the outbreak of the World War as the physical jolt that breaks the spell of Hans Castorp's hermetic existence and transports him to the battlefield of Flanders.

III. SUBSTANCE AND EXPOSURE

Hans Castorp develops from a simple young man to a genius in the realm of experience. What are the fundamental factors that combine to effect this surprising transformation?

Genius can never be deduced from isolable, conditioning factors of heredity and environment. We are far enough removed from the outlook of an earlier positivism not to attempt any such demonstration. The tangible, outward factors that we can trace in the development of a genius may be present in a million cases without in a single instance producing anything so superior to the norm as to warrant the name of genius. Who can disentangle and weigh the myriad strands of heredity present in any individual? And as to the influence of the environment, it is one thing to expose an individual to situations of potential significance; but to predict the quality, the intensity, and the duration of the experience to which such exposure may lead, is something entirely beyond our reach. Even the most enthusiastic behaviorist must admit the piling up of imponderable elements from the moment the infant passes beyond the point of reacting to the most elemental stimuli. In following Thomas Mann's lead, then, and analyzing the factors that condition the development of Hans Castorp's genius, we do not attempt to go beyond the basic *experiences* which show up later in the tissue of his life as the elements dominating its pattern.

"Urerlebnisse" is the German term for those psychic complexes that reach into the very core of personality, as opposed to "Bildungs-erlebnisse",—experiences of more strictly intellectual scope and more derivative content. The fruitfulness of this distinction as an approach to the intuition of *Gestalt* is very happily demonstrated, for instance, by Gundolf's monumental Goethe biography, with its method of focussing first upon the nucleus of Goethe's personality, and then proceeding to build up around it, in concentric circles, as it were,

25

what it assimilated in its contacts with the outer world. But Goethe
himself, accustomed to regard the complex form of the plant and
the animal organism as developments of what he called the "Urphä-
nomen",—the archetype, has given us a classic instance of the use of
this method. I am thinking of that remarkable letter of Wilhelm
Meister's to Natalie that forms chapter eleven of book two of the
"Wanderjahre". In this letter the origin of Wilhelm's passionate
interest in surgery is traced to a fourfold root of experience back in
his childhood,—a root in which nature sense, friendship, love, and
death are inextricably blended. During his boyhood, Wilhelm found
himself transported one day out of the cramping environment of the
eighteenth century town that was his home into the utterly novel
freedom of the country landscape. It was his first outing, and this
one day sufficed to release all his latent emotional faculties and make
them burst into flower. This single day witnessed the awakening of
Wilhelm's nature sense and the awakening of his *eros* in the two distinct forms of ardent friendship and first love. But as if it had been
the design of fate to stamp this threefold complex of experience indelibly upon his mind, a fourth experience of even more poignant
intensity supervenes. At the close of the day, the country idyll
ended and the confining walls of the town about to close in on Wilhelm
again, he runs to keep a tryst agreed upon and bid farewell to his
newly found friend, when suddenly he finds his way blocked by a
procession of agitated villagers carrying stretchers, exposed upon
them the glistening naked bodies of his friend and four companions,
all of them drowned. It is as though Death, stalking its victim, had
with uncanny accuracy chosen the moment when Wilhelm's emotional awakening left him utterly defenseless, to deliver its crushing
blow. When the shock of this terribly agitating complex of experience
has subsided, it has left in Wilhelm a fixation that centres about
first-aid measures specifically, and surgery generally; and this fixation,
reinforced by highly emotional experiences of later date, finally
comes to assert itself as the interest that is to dominate his life. If
it were not for the fact that Wilhelm recounts all this in a reflective
vein, without any suggestion of his having come to unearth it in

some buried stratum of his consciousness, the contents of this letter would strike us as almost sensationally modern.   But even as it stands, it remains one of the most notable presentations of a multiple "Urerlebnis" functioning as a force that continues to exert its subtle but unrelaxed pressure long after it has ceased to trouble consciousness.

If I have allowed myself to stray into the sphere of "Wilhelm Meisters Wanderjahre" it is because a great many points of contact suggest themselves between the "Zauberberg" and Goethe's two "Meister" novels, as regards scope, temper, and even peculiarities of diction. While the "Wanderjahre" are shunned by most readers as a notoriously dull performance, because of the utter lack of tension in the handling of the very meagre plot, it may be that perhaps more than one reader who has come under the spell of the "Zauberberg" has been induced by it to return to the "Wanderjahre" and rediscover in it for himself a wealth of mature thought and profound insight that has lost none of its vitality despite the lapse of a century since its appearance. But it is time we return to Hans Castorp and *his* experiences.

We find four experiences, distributed over Hans Castorp's childhood and adolescence, that have the character of "Urerlebnisse" in the light of his later development:—Continuity, Death, Freedom, and Eros. The first two of these are analyzed in the retrospective summary that forms the content of chapter two. The latter two come to our attention only during the first phase of Hans Castorp's stay at Haus Berghof. In the case of the first two, the author functions as the interpreter of his hero's still inarticulate psyche, whereas the latter two we become aware of directly as basic elements of his experience. Each of the four is associated with a name, an object of symbolic significance, or a memorable phrase. The reader is certain to recognize the four experiences at once when I refer to them as the baptismal bowl, the Grandfather laid out in state, the advantages of disgrace, and Przibislaw Hippe.

The baptismal bowl, by virtue of its venerable age and the solemn, ceremonial, even ritualistic manner observed by the Grandfather on each occasion of its showing, impresses itself upon the receptive mind of the child as a comprehensive symbol of continuity in change. It makes him aware, at a tender age, of his being the bearer of a continuous line of tradition extending over centuries. It fills him with a spirit of religious reverence involving a sense of responsibility on his part toward the forces that have shaped him. Thus conservatism, rooted in "natural piety", is destined to become a basic ingredient of his whole attitude toward the cultural sphere of which he is a member. As we see, this experience might be rendered by a variety of other names, all intimately associated with continuity. Call it loyalty, responsibility, conservatism, traditionalism, reverence, religiosity, or even legitimacy,[①]—all these names express only different shadings of the same fundamental attitude.

The second "Urerlebnis", that of Death, is prepared for by the death of his mother and his father in close succession, but only the death of his grandfather makes it crystallize into definite form. This experience, however, unlike that associated with the bowl, is from the outset blended of two elements that face in opposite directions. On the one hand, the manifestation of death appears surrounded by an aura of religious emotion similar to the currents of feeling evoked by the bowl. All the forces of tradition come in for supreme emphasis in the stateliness and solemnity of the accompanying rites, so that death appears as the crowning moment of life, the ultimate reality, making everything that has gone before appear provisional and preparatory. But death has, in addition, another, a sinister and shocking side, the boy is quick to discover,—a side the survivors try their best to cover up by discreet silence and an abundance of tuberoses; and it is this dual nature of death, sacred and indecent at the same time, which makes it such a fascinating mystery. In the early experience of both these aspects of death we undoubtedly behold the root of what flowers into an all-embracing "Sympathie mit dem Organischen". When Hans Castorp sees the skeleton of his hand under the fluoroscope of Hofrat Behrens' laboratory, he re-experiences this same mingling of reverence with indiscreet curiosity.[2]

The third of Hans Castorp's basic experiences, expressed by the formula "die Vorteile der Schande", appears as a sort of counter-weight to the eminently respectable character of the first and, in part, the second. It dates from his school days, and it comes back to his mind as he hears Herr Albin plead that his irresponsible whims be treated indulgently in view of the fact that his is a hopeless case, comparable to that of a pupil who knows himself definitely doomed to fail of promotion and who therefore does not have to bother any more with a pretense of keeping up his lessons. This comparison had impressed Hans Castorp, for

"Er selbst war ja in Untersekunda sitzen geblieben, und er erinnerte sich wohl des etwas schimpflichen, aber humoristischen, angenehm verwahrlosten Zustandes, dessen er genossen hatte, als er im vierten Quartal das Rennen aufgegeben und 'über das Ganze' hatte lachen können. . . . Hauptsächlich schien ihm, dass die Ehre bedeutende Vorteile für sich habe, aber die Schande nicht minder, ja, dass die Vorteile der letzteren geradezu grenzenloser Art seien. Und indem er sich probeweise in Herrn Albins Zustand versetzte und sich vergegenwärtigte, wie es sein müsse, wenn man endgültig des Druckes der Ehre ledig war und auf immer die bodenlosen Vorteile der Schande genoss, erschreckte den jungen Mann ein Gefühl von wüster Süssigkeit. . . ." [3]

"He himself had stuck in the lower second and well remembered this situation, of course rather to be ashamed of and yet not without its funny side. In particular he recalled the agreeable sensation of being totally lost and abandoned, with which, in the fourth quarter, he gave up the running and was able to 'laugh at the whole business'. . . . In effect it seemed to him that, though honor might possess certain advantages, yet shame had others, and not inferior: advantages, even, that were well-nigh boundless in their scope. He tried to put himself into Herr Albin's place and see how it must feel to be finally relieved of the burden of a respectable life and made free to enjoy the infinite realms of shame; and the young man shuddered at the wild wave of sweetness which swept over him. . . ."

The " Urerlebnis " at school accounts largely for his first yielding to the seductive atmosphere of Haus Berghof and for his immediate unconscious revolt against the pedagogical disciplinarian, as revealed in the dream in which he tries to shove the organ-grinder out of the way [4]; and it helps to motivate the irresistible fascination exercised upon him by the woman who slammed doors, carried herself slouchily, and neglected her finger-nails. It expresses a yearning for escape from the regimentation of authority, from the burden of responsibility, and in doing so it attests the severity of the strain that he felt in living up to what was expected of him. But does not this yearning for release from the strain of inherited burdens also harbor a positive aspect? Is it not this, in the last analysis, which conditions his free adventuring into realms of experience where his more rigidly disciplined ancestors could never have set foot? What there is of enterprise and independence in Hans Castorp he owes to this questionable episode of his scholastic career. Without it he would never have come to embrace the morality of losing oneself, even of abandoning oneself to perdition.

The fourth and last of Hans Castorp's "Urerlebnisse", associated with the name of Przibislaw Hippe, concerns the first manifestation of his adolescent sex life. What earthly connection is there between this strange but otherwise inconsequential boyhood episode and the hammering of his heart and the nosebleed on that Monday morning walk? We have here the most strikingly Freudian feature of the "Zauberberg". According to Freud's theory, the libido of the adolescent is as likely as not to be stirred by a member of his own, as by one of the opposite sex, and all the ardent emotional friendships between youths and between girls are to be interpreted in this way. In the great majority of cases such friendships develop, flourish, and fade without the individuals' ever becoming conscious of the erotic basis of the bond. But even where, subsequently, the libido becomes defined in its aims and attaches itself to a member of the opposite sex (provided it has the good fortune to mature along "normal" lines), the earlier, tentative, and unconscious phases of its manifestation may leave their mark more or less definitely upon the mature sex life of the individual. In extreme cases a definite fixation will result from such an early attachment.[5]

In developing this theory, Freud has raised to the plane of conceptual formulation what was already vaguely sensed by earlier generations. Thus it is impossible to read that letter from Wilhelm Meister to Natalie, which we discussed above, without being aware of the pulse of libido in the origin of the friendship described there. The case is so remarkable as to warrant my quoting it in part. The example and the persuasions of his newly found friend have prevailed upon Wilhelm to undress on the bank of the stream in the open, for the first time in his life, and to wade, as far as he dares, along its gravelly bottom, while he watches the other, an expert swimmer, trust himself to the current and return at his leisure. At the point where the swimmer strikes shallow water and begins to wade back to shore, Wilhelm's account runs as follows:

"Als er sich heraushob, sich aufrichtete, im höheren Sonnenschein sich abzutrocknen, glaubt' ich meine Augen von einer dreifachen Sonne geblendet: so schön war die menschliche Gestalt, von der ich nie einen Begriff gehabt. Er schien mich mit gleicher Aufmerksamkeit zu betrachten. Schnell angekleidet standen wir uns noch immer unverhüllt gegen einander, unsere Gemüter zogen sich an, und unter den feurigsten Küssen schwuren wir eine ewige Freundschaft."

"When he rose out of the water and straightened up to dry himself in the higher sunlight, I thought my eyes were blinded as by a threefold sun: so beautiful was the human form, of which I had never had any conception. He seemed to regard me with similar attentiveness. Quickly dressed, we still seemed to face each other unclothed; our hearts heaved in mutual attraction, and amid the most ardent kisses we vowed eternal friendship."

Hans Castorp's relation to the youth with the exotic name and the eyes of exotic slant has nothing of this impulsive ardor. It is an underground affair, stealthy, secretive, and onesided to boot. It innervates his being with a steadily mounting emotional tension that does not seek release in the form of any aggressive, outward wooing but somehow provides a satisfaction of its own, in quickening his whole psychic pulse. He nurses it, he puts all the resources of his imagination at its disposal, but all the while he refrains from any move to make Hippe's social acquaintance; some instinct keeps him from exposing his jealously guarded complex to the contact of reality. But this complex evidently has its own laws of maturing. There comes a morning when he suddenly finds himself asking Hippe for the loan of a pencil, without preliminaries, on the spur of the moment, as if in acceptance of a dare that he had put to himself. And at the behest of some inner urge which he could not name, he sharpens the pencil and carefully secretes the shavings in a corner of his desk as a treasured fetish. The pencil has been returned, and Hans Castorp's bold overture has had no further consequences. But now the affair has passed the high point of its curve; the pleasurable tension imperceptibly diminishes; and a year later it is, somehow, gone. The whole episode drifts into the limbo of oblivion where it continues to slumber until that memorable day when it is resuscitated in consequence of Hans Castorp's over-exertion of his heart. As he lies on the bench, in a fainting spell, it all comes back to him, and he suddenly realizes the connection between Przibislaw Hippe and that exotic pair of eyes that has lately begun to play havoc with his emotions.

The character of Hans Castorp's infatuation with Hippe as a fixation is made strikingly clear as we observe that his consuming passion for Clavdia Chauchat is prefigured in it in every one of its essential traits. We could use almost the identical language of the last paragraph to describe the course of that passion: It also is an affair of the imagination, onesided moreover; it also is non-aggressive to the extent of deliberately avoiding any conventional social contacts with its object, while the curve of the tension rises to fantastic heights; in it also there comes a moment of crisis, induced by a startlingly abrupt act of spontaneity on Hans Castorp's part, released —we note to our amazement—by the identical symbol of the loan of a pencil; and the tangible gain of this adventure into the realm of reality is also a fetish, Clavdia's x-ray picture, treasured like the pencil shavings of old. May we trespass on speculation to the extent of wondering what would have been the further fate of Hans Castorp's passion, had not this crisis so neatly coincided with the term of Clavdia's departure? In the light of the pattern represented by the subsiding curve of his infatuation with Hippe after the pencil episode, does it seem too bold to prognosticate a similar fate to his passion for Clavdia? And if so, would it have involved a steady, if imperceptible slowing up of his rhythm, a diminution of that psychic tension which we regard as the basic condition of his development above the normal? These are questions that fill us with apprehension as to what might have been. It is our good fortune that we do not need to answer them!

We have traced the four experiences that appear as the basic elements in the pattern of Hans Castorp's personality: Continuity,

Death, Freedom, and Eros. The first of these in its entirety, and the second in one of its two aspects, serve as steadying forces, grounding his personality securely in the great cultural traditions of the race. Religious in essence, they guard him against succumbing to the danger of losing himself in a merely erratic, if brilliant radicalism. But the second in part, and the third and fourth unequivocally, contain the germs of emancipation: the experience of Death also leads to his universal "Sympathie mit dem Organischen"; the experience of the abysmal advantages of disgrace awakens his passion for free adventuring into dangerous realms; and Eros keys him up to that high state of tension which is the condition of his fabulous *Steigerung* above the range of the normal.[6]

Our analysis would be incomplete without a word about the fundamental psychic disposition which we call temperament. Temperament is the ultimate abstraction we reach in reducing all the "Urerlebnisse" to a common denominator. Hans Castorp's way of reacting to the world is essentially receptive and passive. Contemplation is more congenial to him than action. It is in keeping with his disposition that, while imbued with a tremendous respect for energetic work, it does not particularly agree with him to exert himself in this way.[7] And we are not surprised to learn that he gives evidence of no particular talents. His performance is respectable, but nothing beyond that. He drifts into a profession because it conveniently offers itself. And even the draughtsmanship of the lad of fifteen, while calling forth the admiring comment of his uncle,[8] does not warrant the inference that he had in him the makings of a great painter. It has trained his eye to habits of careful observation,—an asset indeed in assimilating the *milieu* of Haus Berghof, but it reveals no trace of creativeness. Passivity, on the other hand, does not tell the whole story. The Przibislaw Hippe episode betrays, under the cover of a placid exterior, the pulse of a consuming passion. Hans Castorp himself finds the happiest formula expressing the complexity of his temperament in the course of his memorable conversation with Clavdia, after her return, when he confesses: "Ich bin, offen gestanden, gar kein leidenschaftlicher Mensch, aber ich habe Leidenschaften,

phlegmatische Leidenschaften." [9]   ("To tell the truth, I am not a
passionate man, though I have my passions, phlegmatic ones.")

Phlegmatische Leidenschaften. . . . There is an arresting flavor
about this paradox, and I cannot resist the prompting to cast a glance
at Thomas Mann's recent "Lebensabriss" and note the way he characterizes the temper in which he worked on the huge theme of "Buddenbrooks". "Jene Geduld", he calls it, "die meine natürliche Langsamkeit mir auferlegte, ein Phlegma, das vielleicht richtiger bezähmte
Nervosität zu nennen wäre." [10]   ("That patience which my native
slowness laid upon me, a phlegm perhaps better described as restrained nervousness.")   Can this be a mere coincidence?   Or
does it not rather point the way to our reading the story of Hans
Castorp as a symbolic version, among other things, of Mann's own
spiritual autobiography?   "—Als ob ich es je mit einem andern
'Stoff' zu tun gehabt hätte als mit meinem eigenen Leben" . . .,[11] he
exclaims in another context. ("As if I had ever dealt with any other
"subject" than my own life." . . .)   Surely this earlier confession of
Thomas Mann's echoes in our ears as we follow Hans Castorp through
the mazes of his adventures in the "Zauberberg".

"Ein Stoff, der dazu taugen soll, durch äussere Einwirkungen zum
Höheren hinaufgetrieben und -gezwängt zu werden, der muss es wohl
im voraus ein bisschen in sich haben." [12]   ("Matter that is capable of
taking those ascending stages by dint of outward pressure must have
a little something in itself to start with.") It has been our aim in this
chapter to supply the commentary to this text. We have tried to
characterize the substance about to be subjected to a highly involved
experiment. Let us briefly take a glance at the factors of the new
environment to which Hans Castorp is exposed at Haus Berghof.
Let us now muster the apparatus of the "laboratory"!

The whole elaborate set-up reduces itself to a beautifully co-
ordinated system when read in terms of the primary effect which its
sundry elements contribute to produce. This is the acceleration of
Hans Castorp's physiological metabolism. The three elements involved in this process are climate, diet, and disease (fever). When
Hans Castorp finds himself lifted suddenly from the moist sea-level-

pressure area of his native Hamburg to the high, dry altitude of Davos, his heart action is instantly and permanently speeded up. The enormous, carefully balanced diet that forms an essential element of the routine of life at Haus Berghof, shames the performance of even a Hamburg stomach and keys up the activity of Hans Castorp's digestive system to full capacity. The ensuing fever contributes its share toward tuning all of his bodily functions to a level above the normal. To borrow Hans Castorp's colorful phrase descriptive of another set of organic processes, it is "ein überaus munterer Betrieb"[13] ("an exceedingly lively business").

Physiological stimulation is, of course, only the primary phase of the experiment. Its significance lies in its being translated at once into terms of psychological stimulation. And this *Steigerung*, the one we are really concerned with, involves two other factors that belong to the psychological realm as such and affect the speeding up of Hans Castorp's metabolism only indirectly and through the medium of his conscious reactions. These all-important additional factors are, of course, the challenging irritant of an aggressive pedagogy and the lure of the exotic siren.[14] As a third factor to be introduced after the experiment has been under way a long time, we should mention the appearance of a personality of grand proportions, giving a final impetus to Hans Castorp's development.

There is something whimsical about Thomas Mann's idea of exposing his hero to so highly abnormal an environment, in order to make the development of his latent genius hinge, in the last analysis, upon the coming into play of enormous physiological stimuli. Does the "Zauberberg" aim in all seriousness at something like Zola's "roman expérimental"? Does it actually hope to come any nearer to a solution of the phenomenon we call genius through the technique of the laboratory? We must spend a little time in formulating our answer to this question.

In the "Lebensabriss" referred to above, Thomas Mann tells how he came to write the "Zauberberg". In May and June 1912 the author was himself exposed to the atmosphere of a Davos sanatorium, as a visitor, for the space of three weeks, while his wife was undergoing treatment for a touch of lung trouble. In the course of this visit he collected the impressions which were to form the setting for Hans Castorp's adventures, but the word "collect", he hastens to inform us, renders very poorly the passivity of his way of experiencing things.[15] Having just come from the sombre theme of "Der Tod in Venedig", he believed he had hit upon the material for a humorous novelette in which Death was also to play a dominant rôle, by way of relief,—something after the manner of the ancients, who were wont to cap their performances of tragedy by a satyr play. But this humorous trifle turned out to have ideas of its own about the way it wanted to be developed. It grew in bulk and seriousness until it filled two volumes and ended by keeping its author chained to the task for twelve years.[16] Here, then, the way is opened to taking the whole "laboratory" idea in the spirit of half-serious, half-humorous make-believe, as something designed to keep the reader guessing, like one of those masks that keep forever altering their expression to the eye that dwells upon them.

I think, however, that we can go even so far as to trace this idea to a definite literary source. It was none other than Nietzsche whose speculation took on very similar forms, and to name Nietzsche is to name the most powerful intellectual force in Thomas Mann's development. Mann himself has acknowledged Nietzsche's influence on so many different occasions, and his work abounds to such an extent with ideas that stem from Nietzsche that the mere statement of this relationship may suffice here. When Nietzsche defines it as "das Meisterschafts-Vorrecht des freien Geistes", "auf den Versuch hin leben und sich dem Abenteuer anbieten zu dürfen," [17] ("the free spirit's prerogative of mastership: to live by experiment and offer itself to adventure") what reader of the "Zauberberg" does not immediately think of Hans Castorp! And what modern thinker has made so many startling first-hand observations on the relation of disease to genius, as Nietzsche! Even when he boasts of his health, it is as "eine Gesundheit, welche der Krankheit selbst nicht entraten mag, als eines Mittels und Angelhakens der Erkenntnis".[18] ("a soundness which does not care to dispense with disease itself as an instrument and angling-hook of knowledge.") It is to disease he acknowledges himself as owing "jene Filigrankunst des Greifens und Begreifens überhaupt, jene Finger für *nuances*, jene Psychologie des 'Um-die-Ecke-sehns'" [19] which constitutes his peculiar specialty. ("That filigree art of prehension and comprehension in general, that feeling for delicate shades of difference, that psychology of 'seeing around the corner'"). But this is not the place to follow up the arresting problem of the place of disease in a philosophy of values—it will be taken up in the next chapter—otherwise these random quotations might be multiplied indefinitely. All this leads up, however, to something Nietzsche has to say in analyzing the conditions which he holds responsible for the fostering of genius. Generalizing from his own case, Nietzsche says:

"Das Genie ist *bedingt* durch trockne Luft, durch reinen Himmel,—das heisst durch rapiden Stoffwechsel, durch die Möglichkeit, grosse, selbst ungeheure Mengen Kraft sich immer wieder zuzuführen." [20]

"Genius is conditioned by dry air, by a pure sky—that is to say, by rapid metabolism, by the constant and ever-present possibility of procuring for oneself great and even enormous quantities of strength."

In this passage from the last work that Nietzsche sent to press— the "Ecce Homo", which already abounds in symptoms of madness closing in,—in this passage, I am sure, we have the nucleus of Thomas Mann's idea of exposing his hero to dry mountain air and an enormous diet, and seeing what these will do to him. This impression is even strengthened when one takes into account Nietzsche's numerous detailed observations on the significance of diet, in the same context.

Was Thomas Mann aware in this case of following one of Nietzsche's leads? It is more than probable; and if so, this very circumstance would tend to account for the blend of seriousness and jest in the development of this idea. For what Thomas Mann absorbs of Nietzsche's thought he also transforms. Mann never takes Nietzsche seriously, in a literal sense. To quote the "Lebensabriss" again:

"Ich nahm nichts wörtlich bei ihm, ich *glaubte* ihm fast nichts, und gerade dies gab meiner Liebe zu ihm das Doppelschichtig-Passionierte, ⑳ gab ihr die Tiefe." [22]

"I took nothing literally; I *believed* him hardly at all; and this precisely it was that made my love for him a passion in two planes,—gave it in other words, its depth."

There is one word which embraces the whole sphere of this duplicity of attitude—: Irony. And of irony Thomas Mann wrote in another context, while at work on the "Zauberberg":

"Es ist nicht mehr und nicht weniger als das Problem der Ironie, dessen wir hier ansichtig werden, das ohne Vergleich tiefste und reizendste der Welt." [23]

"It is no more and no less than the problem of irony which we catch sight of here: without exception the profoundest and most fascinating in the world."

But with this idea we are already encroaching upon the fascinating theme that will absorb our attention in another chapter.

IV. DISEASE

The "Zauberberg" is the epic of disease. I have known more than one reader to take up the book and lay it down again, for fear of contracting tuberculosis through suggestion. If a hundred Anglo-Saxon readers of the "Zauberberg", selected at random, were asked to tell in one sentence what impressed them as its most extraordinary feature, a majority of them would point, I dare say, to the author's infatuation with so macabre a subject. And regardless of literary background they would be inclined to see in this predilection a reflection of the German national temperament.

The student of literature will doubtless do well to be wary of such generalizations. However, in musing on the problem, to what extent Thomas Mann's preoccupation with disease—limited by no means to the "Zauberberg"—①may be accounted for by the social factors of race, nationality, and tradition, he may be intrigued by the contrast between Thomas Mann and an equally outstanding literary figure of the Anglo-Saxon world. There is in the preface to Bernard Shaw's "Saint Joan" a sentence written as though aimed at the "Zauberberg" in anticipation of its appearance. "Crime", says Shaw, "like disease, is not interesting: it is something to be done away with by general consent, and that is all about it." ² A statement so crisp and so final in its uncompromising rationalism that it effectively shuts the door against argument.③

Whatever representative significance may attach to Shaw's flatly negative, common-sense attitude toward disease, Thomas Mann, at any rate, is far from standing alone in his own country in finding disease interesting, in endowing it with positive value, and in crediting it with the development of spiritual values that would, but for its agitating influence, have remained dormant. I have already quoted Nietzsche's testimony to this effect, but Nietzsche's point of view, in its turn, rests on an unbroken line of tradition extending back to the threshold of the nineteenth century and beyond it. To an extent it derives authority even from Goethe. Readers of "Wilhelm Meisters Lehrjahre" (1795–6) may remember that the sixth book, containing the Confessions of a Beautiful Soul, opens with a paragraph that squarely credits disease with effecting the spiritual awakening of the purported writer of these confessions:

"Bis in mein achtes Jahr war ich ein ganz gesundes Kind, weiss mich aber von dieser Zeit so. wenig zu erinnern als von dem Tage meiner Geburt. Mit dem Anfange des achten Jahres bekam ich einen Blutsturz, und in dem Augenblick war meine Seele ganz Empfindung und Gedächtnis. Die kleinsten Umstände dieses Zufalls stehen mir noch vor Augen, als hätte er sich gestern ereignet."

"Till my eighth year, I was always a healthy child; but of that period I can recollect no more than of the day when I was born. About the beginning of my eighth year, I was seized with a hemorrhage; and from that moment my soul became all feeling, all memory. The smallest circumstances of that accident are yet before my eyes, as if they had occurred but yesterday."

Ten years after the publication of that subtle piece of introspective autobiography the first brief account of the life of Novalis (d.1801) appeared, and it also attributes his extraordinary mental alertness to a severe illness that occurred in his ninth year. Whether this report[4] be based on truth or legend, Novalis himself, at any rate, found disease a fascinating topic for speculation. "Könnte Krankheit nicht ein Mittel höherer Synthesis sein?" ("Could disease not be a means of higher synthesis?"), he asks in one of his diary jottings, written about the dawn of the century, adding: "Je fürchterlicher der Schmerz, desto höher die darin verborgene Lust."[5] ("The more agonizing the pain, the higher the pleasure that lurks within it.") In another passage he writes: "Krankheit gehört zu den menschlichen Vergnügungen wie Tod."[6] ("Illness is to be numbered among human pleasures along with death.") Still again he remarks:

"Krankheiten sind gewiss ein höchst wichtiger Gegenstand der Menschheit, da ihrer so unzählige sind und jeder Mensch so viel mit ihnen zu kämpfen hat. Noch kennen wir nur sehr unvollkommen die Kunst sie zu benutzen. (To utilize them, he says, not to do away with them!) Wahrscheinlich sind sie der interessanteste Reiz und Stoff unsers Nachdenkens und unsrer Tätigkeit. . . ."[7]

"Illnesses are certainly a most highly important factor of human life, since there are such numberless varieties of them and every human being has to cope with them such a lot. To date we are very imperfectly acquainted with the art of using them. Probably they are the most interesting stimulus and object of our meditation and our activity."

And there is, finally, the following passage, significant for its blending of scientific intuition and religious mysticism:

"Alle Krankheiten gleichen der Sünde, darin, dass sie Transzendenzen sind. Unsre Krankheiten sind alle Phänomene einer erhöhten Sensation, die in höhere Kräfte übergehen will. Wie der Mensch Gott werden wollte, sündigte er. . . ." [8]

"All diseases resemble sin in the fact that they are transcendencies. All our diseases are phenomena of a heightened sensitivity that is about to be transformed into higher powers. When man wanted to become God, he sinned. . . ."

About the same time when Novalis was engrossed with disease as a theoretical problem, his most intimate friend, Friedrich Schlegel, gave expression to similar views in the second of two letters that form a chapter of his "romantic" novel "Lucinde" (1799). Schlegel tells there how a disease that reduced him to the point of death turned out to be a spiritual experience that lifted his whole being to a higher plane. Speaking of this "Krankheit", he says: "Ich fühlte, ihr geheimnisreiches Leben sei voller und tiefer als die gemeine Gesundheit der eigentlich träumenden Nachtwandler um mich her." [9] ("I felt that its mysterious life was fuller and deeper than the common health of the people about me, who struck me rather like dreaming sleep-walkers.") And this feeling reaches for him its culmination in an ecstatic anticipation of death:

"Und dann weiss ich's nun, dass der Tod sich auch schön und süss fühlen lässt. Ich begreife, wie das freie Gebildete sich in der Blüte aller Kräfte nach seiner Auflösung und Freiheit mit stiller Liebe sehnen und den Gedanken der Rückkehr freudig anschauen kann, wie eine Morgensonne der Hoffnung." [10]

"And then I now know that death, too, can be felt as beautiful and sweet. I understand how the organism, spontaneously formed, can in the fulness of all its vigor yearn for dissolution and freedom, and how it can contemplate the thought of the return with joy and attach its hopes to it as to the morning sun."

A quarter of a century later it is Heine who gives the widest currency to the association of health with grossness and stupidity, on the one hand, and of disease with distinction, refinement, and spirituality, on the other. And when Hans Castorp confesses to Settembrini that to see stupidity and illness combined in one person constitutes a dilemma for one's feelings, because one naturally assumes a stupid person to be healthy, whereas disease is expected to be found in company with intelligence and refinement,[11] he is unconsciously echoing Heine and at the same time affording an illustration of how the paradoxes of one generation tend to become the platitudes of the next. A few sentences from Heine's "Reisebilder" will make this abundantly clear: "Die Tiroler sind schön, heiter, ehrlich, brav und von unergründlicher Geistesbeschränktheit. Sie sind eine gesunde Menschenrasse, vielleicht weil sie zu dumm sind, um krank sein zu können."[12] ("The Tyrolese are handsome, cheerful, honest, doughty and of inscrutable narrowness of mind. They are a healthy race, perhaps because they are too stupid to be ill.") Or take the way in which Heine contrasts the English with the Italians:

"Und gar die blassen italienischen Gesichter, in den Augen das leidende Weiss, die Lippen krankhaft zärtlich, wie heimlich vornehm sind sie gegen die steif britischen Gesichter mit ihrer pöbelhaft roten Gesundheit. Das ganze italienische Volk ist innerlich krank, und kranke Menschen sind immer wahrhaft vornehmer als gesunde; denn nur der kranke Mensch ist ein Mensch, seine Glieder haben eine Leidensgeschichte, sie sind durchgeistet. Ich glaube sogar, durch Leidenskämpfe könnten die Tiere zu Menschen werden."[13]

"And as for the pale Italian faces, with the suffering white of their eyes and their sickly delicate lips, how silently aristocratic do they seem as compared to stiff British faces, with their vulgarly ruddy health! The whole Italian race is internally sick, and sick people are invariably more refined than the robust, for only the sick man is really a man; his limbs have a history of suffering, they are spiritualized. I believe that by suffering even animals could be made human."

Clearly, this last sentence harks back to Novalis' view that disease is essentially *Steigerung*, the elevation of the organism to a higher plane. Heine brings this same point of view to bear on his interpretation of Christianity. "Unsre Zeit—und sie beginnt am Kreuze Christi—wird als eine grosse Krankheitsperiode der Menschheit betrachtet werden"[14] ("Our age—and it begins at the cross of Christ—will come to be regarded as a great epoch of disease for humanity"), he writes a few years later. That this is not said in summary condemnation but is capable of being taken as a positive appreciation would follow from the value that we have just seen attaching to Heine's use of the terms *Krankheit* and *Gesundheit*. In this context one of Heine's undated jottings is particularly illuminating: "Im Christentume kommt der Mensch zum Selbstbewusstsein des Geistes

durch den Schmerz—Krankheit vergeistigt, selbst die Tiere."[15] ("In
Christianity man attains to self-consciousness of the spirit through
pain.—Illness spiritualizes, even animals.") As every student of
Heine knows, this is not the whole Heine: his mercurial temperament
kept him effectively from championing any one cause consistently.
We find him at other times raising the battle-cry of health and affixing
the epithet *krank* to everything against which he enters the lists,
as when he feels it incumbent upon himself to defend the Flesh
against the encroachments of the Spirit. But in this see-saw of
shifting values the descriptive tags remain essentially the same.
The Christianity that Heine attacks as a disease of the human race
is that same Christianity that makes for progressive spiritualization.
What the human race needs for the time being, Heine's thought
runs, is more Flesh and less Spirit,—the word Spirit being sufficiently indefinite in its connotation to stand for other-worldliness,
asceticism, or intellectualism, as the occasion may demand. The
epithet *krank* somehow remains associated with the whole realm of
Geist, including, it is interesting to note, also the creative impulse of
the artist. Thus Heine's "Schöpfungslieder"—that superbly witty
little aesthetic treatise in disguise—sees all the problems of the
creative artist anticipated in the original act of the world's creation,
among them the artist's ever-present temptation to plagiarize himself, and reduces the creative impulse itself to the formula:

"Krankheit ist wohl der letzte Grund
Des ganzen Schöpferdrangs gewesen;
Erschaffend konnte ich genesen,
Erschaffend wurde ich gesund." [16]

"Disease may well have been the
ground
In full for that creative urge;
Creation was my body's purge,
Creating I've grown sane and
sound."

If I have dwelt somewhat longer on Heine, it is not because he
is particularly original or profound in his play with the terms *Gesundheit* and *Krankheit*, but rather because every German read and
quoted him throughout the nineteenth century. Ever since the days
of Novalis it had been common to find disease interesting and to
regard it as a vehicle of spiritual growth. One does not have to go
far among Heine's contemporaries to find similar ideas expressed

by writers of the most varying shades. Grillparzer's poem, "Der Genesene" (1820) contains these significant lines:

"Krankheit, du bist Gottes Gabe,	"Illness, thou art a gift of God,
Er soll drum gepriesen sein." [17]	Let him be praised for thee."

Friedrich Hebbel is another who repeatedly testifies to the heightened activity of all his mental faculties during periods of illness. On March 8, 1843 he writes to his common-law wife, Elise Lensing: "Mir geht es, wie du weisst, immer so, dass mein inneres Leben in krankhaften Zuständen nicht abnimmt, sondern sich steigert." ("As you know, it always happens to me that during states of illness my inner life is intensified rather than diminished.") And again in a letter to Elise of October 25 of the same year, he records the observation, "dass ich in Krankheiten, die bei den Meisten alle Geistes-Functionen aufheben, mit einer fast noch grösseren Lebhaftigkeit, wie in gesunden Zuständen, Ideen entwickle und darstelle". ("Diseases that in the case of most people reduce all spiritual functions to a stand-still affect me in such a way as to make me evolve and formulate ideas with an almost greater intensity than is my wont when I am well.") I am by no means sure whether Hebbel is telling the truth here; his imagination often played his sense of fact false; he may well have written these passages under the influence of romantic theories as to the effect illness ought to produce upon literary genius. However, whether Hebbel imagined it or truly experienced it makes no difference:—the legend derives support from his testimony in either case. I am using the word "legend" here to denote a prevailing mental slant that is absorbed by the individual and passed on uncritically. Such legends arise when opinions that have a strong emotional ingredient and elude the check of accurate testing are given wide currency. The premises upon which a legend rests may be arbitrarily selected and highly distorted elements of fact. They may be such an array of garbled half-truths as to make the effect of a pure fabrication upon one unfamiliar with their social background. The legend itself, however, whatever its relation to fact, is always a significant factor to be reckoned with. By tracing its genesis and development, by charting the momentum of its growth, by delimiting the social group or stratum in which it is current, we may derive the most valuable insight into the spiritual temper of a social group, a nation, or an age. Legends in this sense are the views that prevail in a nation with regard to its own national character and that of its neighbors.

Enough has been said to show that Thomas Mann's preoccupation with disease as a literary theme, in the "Zauberberg", has for its background a well-established legend, closely associated with the German Romantic Movement and running through the whole of the nineteenth century. There is in Germany a body of opinion sponsored, transmitted, augmented, and popularized by many of the most prominent literary figures of the last century to the effect that disease is more than something to be done away with; that it is a fascinating phenomenon and, possibly, a vehicle of evolution; and that it may be one of the distinguishing marks of genius. Familiarity with this legend is part of the literary background of the average cultured German, and Thomas Mann tacitly works on this assumption in developing his theme. Hans Castorp, predisposed by temperament and environment to avoid trenchant thinking, to absorb ideas in a vegetative way rather than by active analysis and criticism, is a perfectly naïve exponent of the legend when he first arrives at Davos, and it takes the bracing contact with the alien mentality of Settembrini to make him rub his eyes and wake up to the fact that there is a point of view wholly at odds with his own, and that it is incumbent upon him to scrutinize the web of his beliefs in the light of reason. Reluctantly he sets about this task. Unskilled as he is in mental gymnastics, he does more listening than talking for a long time, bent upon spying out weaknesses in the humanist's position, and exulting secretly whenever he catches the champion of logic in a contradiction. But Hans Castorp does not confine himself to reasoning. He calls into play his faculty of observation. He pays close attention to a host of empirical data presented by the patients at the Sanatorium, than which there could be no more favorable field for the inductive study of his problem. And reluctantly he has to concede in case after case that there is precious little evidence

of any ennobling or spiritualizing influence of disease to be noticed
among these folk; that even disregarding the paradoxical aspect of
Frau Stöhr's offending presence, these patients are a giddy, frivolous,
squirrel-brained lot, thrill-hunters and sensualists without the inhibitions that tend ordinarily to hold the appetites of the healthy
in check. Hans Castorp secretly hopes that this picture of things
applies only to the lighter cases, to those able to flit about the dining-
room and the sun-parlors. But he meets with one disillusionment
after another when he begins playing the good Samaritan to all the
"moribundi". Case after case presents the same story of frivolity, of
vanity, of distraction and coquetry, so far as the women are concerned, and of an absurd clinging to the banal business interests of
the world about to be left behind, in case of the men.[18] In not a
single case does he find that special *élan*, that spiritual elevation, that
transcending serenity of soul which his imagination was wont to
associate with the phenomena of disease and dying. All the empirical data are severely negative. Does he concede, then, that they
prove the case against him? Is he ready to admit that his whole
reverent approach to disease was atavistic and based on romantic
tradition? Is he convinced that disease spells deterioration, physical,
mental, and moral, and not some indefinable precious value? Convinced, in part; but not wholly persuaded. Observation and logic
have, indeed, sobered him. Critical analysis has operated in Hans
Castorp's mind as a powerful ferment during these first months at
Davos. He would no longer be caught stammering something about
the spectacle of disease coupled with stupidity presenting a dilemma
for one's feelings. But Hans Castorp has also had experience of a
different sort to weight the other side of the scales. He has been
experiencing the effects of disease on his own person. He has been
awakened, stimulated, raised to a plane of intellectual and emotional
intensity compared with which his former life in the "Flachland"
appears as a vegetative existence. This awakening is partly the work
of disease; and neither the empirical evidence of case study nor the
generous rhetoric of the humanist can budge Hans Castorp's intuitive consciousness of the fact of his own transformation. More-

over, there is a transcendental aspect to disease which is out of reach
of the attacks levelled by empirical data: The concept of disease is
amalgamated in Hans Castorp's mind with that of death; and death,
we know, is one of those "Urerlebnisse" out of which the structural
tissue of his personality is woven. He experienced death as an ambiva-
lent phenomenon, having besides its indecent a sacred aspect. And
just as all reasoning falls short of penetrating to the core of Hans
Castorp's experience of death, similarly disease, bound up as it is with
that complex, is tinged with that same aura of reverence and sanctity.

Whatever else disease is to Hans Castorp, it is interesting, it is
fascinating. Disease takes him out of the beaten path of respectable
mediocrity. Disease breaks for him the fetters of traditional thinking
and acting. Disease unlocks the door to life, revealing a thousand
unexplored paths luring to uncharted, unstandardized experiences in
the realms of emotion and intellect. Disease is synonymous with
the atmosphere of adventure in the widest sense. Hans Castorp's
surrendering to disease has the same symbolic significance as Faust's
concluding his pact with the devil. By his decision to place himself
under the law of disease (for as a decision, a metaphysical decision
Thomas Mann would have us view it), Hans Castorp renounces
security in every sense of the word; he cuts himself off from the safe
and the known to face untried situations and unknown perils,—perils
that threaten not merely his body but the integrity of his whole
mental-moral personality. By embracing the law of disease, Hans
Castorp puts himself beyond the pale of the bourgeois law of mental-
moral behavior—of the law that hedges the individual about with
norms and restrictions and standards for his safety, the law that
provides a set of tested rules calculated to lead to comfort and success
within a conventionally delimited sphere of aims and pursuits. All
this he throws overboard in exchange for the right to ask he knows
not what questions as to the Why, the Whence, and the Whither,
to try he knows not what new avenues of experience. He cuts loose
from all that is tried, sanctioned, and familiar, in obedience to an urge
that, while bidding him renounce the world, may well lead him to lose
his soul into the bargain. For in embarking on so radical an adven-

ture, the odds are a thousand to one that his personality, caught up in the whirl of unknown forces, will be reduced to a mass of wreckage.

If the miracle does come to pass, if Hans Castorp does save his soul, despite what may be the fate of his body in the shell-torn field, it is because of the spark of genius that proved to be latent in our hero. Long before he has reached the end of his career Hans Castorp has come to realize (as has Thomas Mann with him) that except for an infinitesimal number of favored individuals, the lure of disease as an avenue to life leads to utter destruction. As a matter of fact, even Hans Castorp would have been doomed, had it not been for a counterweight to the lure of adventure so securely fixed in the core of his personality as to safeguard his equilibrium even in the face of the acutest dangers. We have come across this counterweight in his "Urerlebnis" of reverence, of loyalty, of continuity, of responsibility to the past. This "Urerlebnis" had established in Hans Castorp the mental pattern of relating the immediate to the remote, the present to the past, the individual to the continuity represented by the race, and this pattern effectively prevents him from losing himself in the mere quest of new sensations; for it is by correlating his new sensations to his psychic core that he transforms them into experience in the real sense of the word. It is his sense of continuity that turns his "leben" into "erleben". "Leben um des Lebens willen" (Life for the sake of living) is the formula to which the impressionist (in our case: Clavdia Chauchat) subscribes. Hans Castorp is not an impressionist, philosophically speaking, for his formula reads: "Leben um des Erlebnisses willen" [19] (Life for the sake of experience).

Hans Castorp's surrender to disease is the immediate symbol of that impulse which bids him explore uncharted realms. His sense of continuity is the counterweight that prevents an aimless and destructive scattering of his energies. These two forces, the one centrifugal, the other centripetal, jointly govern his life. It is in the nature of things that the first of these should be more in evidence in the first half of the narrative. If we watch closely we observe that volume one of the "Zauberberg" registers the increasing momentum of Hans Castorp's abandonment to the unknown, while the second volume shows the applying of a curb, gently, almost imperceptibly at times, but none the less steadily. Volume one shows our hero's orbit in the constellation of disease; volume two shows the curve swinging around in the direction of health. Volumes one and two stand in the relation of passion to control, abandonment to restraint, adventure to responsibility. In volume one Hans Castorp is the heir-apparent sowing his wild oats; in volume two he sobers down to consider the problems of "government". For "regieren" (govern) is that symbolic code word which he uses to designate his activity of correlation, as he sits by the waterfall among the columbines and speculates on the Homo Dei and his place in the cosmos.[20] The word "regieren" occurs some twenty times, as one of the most insistent *Leitmotivs* of volume two. But "regieren" entails responsibility, a sobering up after the intoxicating abandon. Volume one made irresponsibility imperative, —there was always that disciplinarian Settembrini to jerk the tether; but the night of the mardi gras had marked the rupture of that pedagogue-pupil relationship, Hans Castorp was now entirely on his own, and the problem of self-discipline therewith became a factor. Now it is a far cry from the days when Hans Castorp had lumped together "Gesundheit" and "Dummheit", and "Krankheit" and "Vornehmheit" respectively, as synonyms. The change of attitude is fully revealed in an exchange of remarks between Hans and Joachim, a few weeks after the mardi gras, when they have just finished listening for the first time to Settembrini's and Naphta's verbal fencing. "Ach Mensch", says Joachim to Hans, "du wirst ja immer klüger hier oben. . . . Und dabei sind wir doch hier, um gesünder, und nicht um gescheuter zu werden, . . ." ("Oh, you, with your learning! Getting wiser all the time. . . . But we didn't come up here to acquire wisdom. We came to acquire health, to get healthier until we are entirely well . . .") To which Hans Castorp replies summing up the divergence of their points of view,

"Ja, so kannst du sagen als Landsknecht und rein formale Existenz, die du bist. Bei mir ist es was andres, ich bin Zivilist, ich bin gewissermassen verantwortlich. . . . Du sagst zwar,

"Yes, you can say that because you are a soldier, and your existence is purely formal. But it's different with me, I am a civilian, and more or less responsible. . . . You say we

wir sollen hier nicht klüger werden, sondern gesünder. Aber das muss sich vereinigen lassen, Mann, und wenn du das nicht glaubst, dann treibst du Weltentzweiung, und so was zu treiben, ist immer ein grosser Fehler, will ich dir mal bemerken." [21]

did not come up here to get wiser, but healthier, and that is true. But there must be a way of reconciling the two; and if you don't think so, why then you are dividing the world up into two hostile camps, which, I may tell you, is a grievous error, most reprehensible."

What Hans Castorp aims at is clearly a synthesis of the characteristic values of disease and health, in the same way as his approach to life comes to be more and more a synthesis of the ethos of adventure and that of responsibility.

So far our concern with disease has turned on the question of its value. We cannot leave the subject, however, without touching upon the discussion of its nature,—a topic that figures very prominently among the problems of the "Zauberberg". How is disease to be interpreted? Is its primary significance physiological or psychological? Is it caused by disturbing factors that enter the chemico-physical organism from without and are then reflected in symptoms of consciousness, or is the process the reverse of this, supposing that either alternative goes to the heart of the matter? In asking these questions we find ourselves face to face with one of the fundamental questions of philosophy; for it is, of course, none other than the age-old mind-body problem that confronts us here in somewhat specialized form. From time immemorial philosophers have debated whether it is the body that determines the mind or the mind that determines the body. Fortunately for me, I am not concerned here with trying to solve the mind-body problem as such, but only with reviewing briefly the questions raised in connection with it in the "Zauberberg".

A very general observation on Thomas Mann's way of dealing with problems in the "Zauberberg" suggests itself here. Thomas Mann brings the dialectic method to bear upon the general phenomena that he tries to interpret. He weighs one side of a problem against the other with a view to striking a balance between them. We have just seen him employ the antithesis of disease and health in this fashion, and we may expect to meet other instances of this method before we have finished with our study. In the case of the present problem his procedure is the same. Here the dialectic process is dramatized in the characters of the two physicians, Behrens and Krokowski. ⌈The therapy of Behrens, the surgeon, presupposes the primacy of the physiological symptom, whereas Krokowski, the psycho-analyst, regards the organic symptom as secondary and ascribes all disease to the devious workings of the libido. The premises of the one are materialistic (chemico-physical), while those of the other are idealistic (psychological). The one stresses material disturbances that affect the organism willy-nilly, whereas the other makes any disturbance contingent upon a willingness of the organism to harbor the enemy; accordingly, the therapeutic efforts of the one are concerned with the body, while the other seeks to influence the psyche directly. The available data, unfortunately, will support opposite conclusions. Hans Castorp's own case illustrates this beautifully. Directly upon his arrival his heart begins to beat faster, and he is in a state of constant excitement without there being anything to motivate his excitement. He puts his hands to his heart with the gesture of a person in love [22]; he experiences violent emotions as to form, but without their customary content.[23] When he hears the door of the dining-room slammed behind his back for the third time, he whispers, with a vehemence all out of proportion to the incident, "Ich muss es wissen" [24] ("I must find out"), before he turns to see who is responsible for the disturbance. In due time Hans discovers that he is in love, and now all is well, so to say; for now the erratic beating of his heart has a good and sufficient reason: the body no longer performs "on its own hook", the connection between body and soul has been re-established.

"Eine rechtfertigende Gemütsbewegung liess sich der exaltierten Körpertätigkeit zwanglos unterlegen. Hans Castorp brauchte nur an Frau Chauchat zu denken—und er dachte an sie —, so besass er zum Herzklopfen das zugehörige Gefühl." [25]

"He could say, without stretching the truth, that such a connection now existed, or was easily induced: he was aware that he felt an emotion to correspond with the action of his heart. He needed only to think of Madame Chauchat—and he did think of her—and lo, he felt within himself the emotion proper to the heartbeats."

This certainly looks like a vindication of the James-Lange theory of
the emotions, and would satisfy any psychological behaviorist. It
does not satisfy Hans Castorp, however, who promptly establishes a
psychological connection between his passion for Clavdia and his
adolescent infatuation with his exotic school-mate Przibislaw Hippe,
and who, in a moment of tense ecstasy, goes so far as to utter the
conviction that what lured him from Hamburg to Davos was none
other than the power of his love for Clavdia.[26]   But leaving such
fanciful perspectives out of account, what reader is there who has
not at least a strong suspicion that Hans Castorp's cold during the
third week of his stay at Davos was directly induced by his will,
however subconsciously, not to be separated from the object of his
passion? To explain his fever as a case of shamming would not help
things in any way, for his symptoms were demonstrably objective,
like those of any other patient. If one were to argue, on the other
hand, that the physiological stimulation induced by the Davos atmosphere was the primary factor, and that it was bound to translate
itself into emotional terms in one way or another, hence his falling
in love, whereupon the hook-up with associated memories (the
Przibislaw episode) is effected in due course,—there would be no way
of disproving such a point of view, even though it is reasonably clear
that the author himself would not subscribe to it. It is just as well,
perhaps, not to complicate the picture any further by bringing up
an exactly analogous situation and asking precisely *what* was the
relation between the adolescent's infatuation with Hippe and the
old, calcinated spot on Hans Castorp's lung discovered by Behrens,—
for related they are, without any question. Whatever view we incline
to, Hans Castorp's is a special case, it will be conceded, and no binding
conclusions can be drawn from it with regard to all disease generally
or even the specific disease of tuberculosis. Incidentally, Hans sub-
mits to both kinds of therapy—the dietetics and the routine prescribed by Behrens and, for a time, a series of special injections; and
he also has psycho-analytic conferences with Krokowski; but we
fail to see that either method has any visible effect upon the state of
his health.

Joachim's case is another illustration of the problem, and the conclusions to be deduced from it are equally ambiguous. Body and soul seem to be decidedly at odds in his case. Seeing the doggedness of his determination to conquer the dread disease by the most punctilious observance of all the rules, we should be guilty of disloyalty towards him if we were to question the sincerity of his will to get well. Every minute of his daily routine is planned with a view to his making himself fit for military service. That his organism fails to respond to so steadfast a will spells tragedy for him. If his quiet zeal in performing his duty wins our sympathy, the gallantry of his final attempt to force the issue elicits our admiration. Despite his heroic struggle he is doomed. The meaning of this outcome in terms of our problem would seem to be, first, that an organic lesion was the primary factor in Joachim's failure; and secondly, that the power of the will over the body has its limits. The matter is not so simple, for all that. While the first of our conclusions seems unassailable in the absence of more complete data, the second may be subjected to further analysis. Was Joachim's will to get well backed by his whole psyche?—that is the question. Or did his heroic way of holding out against certain feminine charms—charms to which part of his self passionately longed to respond—contribute to his undoing, according to the principle of: Heads I win, tails you lose? Was not Joachim all the time a house divided against itself? And did not those elements of his psyche that were ruthlessly overridden by the ruling faction plot a cunning revenge? But instead of trying to develop the implications of these questions ourselves, let us participate in Hans Castorp's musings after he gets the telegram announcing Joachim's return:

"Hm, hm, es liegt eine hübsche Portion Gemeinheit darin, höhnische Gemeinheit, es ist ein gegen-idealistisches Faktum. Der Körper triumphiert, er will es anders als die Seele, und setzt sich durch, zur Blamage der Hochfliegenden, die lehren, er sei der Seele untertan. Es scheint, sie wissen nicht,

"H'm, it's certainly a skin game, it's playing it low down on poor Joachim, —hardly in line with the contentions of idealism. The body triumphs, it wants something different from the soul, and puts it through—a slap in the face of all those lofty-minded people who teach that the body is subordinate to the soul. Seems to me

was sie sagen, denn wenn sie recht
hätten, so würfe das ein zweifelhaftes
Licht auf die Seele, in einem Fall wie
diesem. *Sapienti sat,* ich weiss, wie
ich's meine. Denn die Frage, die ich
aufstelle, ist eben, wie weit es verfehlt
ist, sie gegeneinander zu stellen, wie
weit sie vielmehr unter einer Decke
stecken und eine abgekartete Partie
spielen,—das fällt den Hochfliegenden
zu ihrem Glück nicht ein. Guter
Joachim, wer wollte dir und deinem
Biereifer zu nahe treten: Du meinst
es ehrlich—aber was ist Ehrlichkeit,
frage ich, wenn Körper und Seele mal
unter einer Decke stecken? Sollte es
möglich sein, dass du gewisse erfri-
schende Düfte, eine hohe Brust und
ein grundloses Gelächter nicht hast
vergessen können, die am Tische der
Stöhr deiner warten? . . ." [27]

they don't know what they are
talking about, because if they were
right, a case like this would put the
soul in a pretty equivocal light.
Sapienti sat. I know what I mean.
The question I raise is how far they
are right when they set the two
over against each other; and whether
they aren't rather in collusion, playing the same game. That's something that never occurs to the lofty-
minded gentry. Not that I am for a
moment saying anything against
you, Joachim, and your doggedness.
You are the soul of honor—but what
is honor, is what I want to know,
when body and soul play the same
game? Is it possible you have not
been able to forget a certain re-
freshing perfume, a tendency to gig-
gle, a swelling bosom, all waiting for
you at Frau Stöhr's table? . . ."

These musings of Hans Castorp's sound plausible indeed. Psychology has taught us to regard the unity of the self as the expression of
a very complex situation. The self is very much like a state in which
a number of parties compete for mastery. There is a government,
and there is an opposition that may be composed of mutually hostile
elements banded together to procure the defeat of the existing régime.
Although the governing faction determines the policies, the opposition, while overruled, is not thereby nullified. It remains a vital
force, exerting pressure through propaganda, which may be powerful
enough to vitiate the policies of the governing party and to paralyze
the effectiveness of the executive. It is the same way with the self.
There is a conflict of impulses, and some of them are bound to be
overruled by others; but the overruled impulses are as real a part of
the psyche as those that triumph. And even after a given conflict
has been settled by an act of will, all is not serene. The trouble is
that the overruled impulses continue to exert pressure upon the self,
and if their struggle to turn the tables by legitimate means is un-
availing they make themselves felt in other ways. To apply this
view to Joachim's case, may we not attribute his failure to sabotage?

Krokowski would undoubtedly do so. According to his philosophy all organic disease is caused by the libido in one way or another. And where does Thomas Mann stand? For all his ironic objectivity, it is evident that he leans more to Krokowski's view than to that of Behrens, and this notwithstanding the fact that we warm to Behrens' immensely likeable personality, while something furtive and slimy attaches to all of Krokowski's works; in fact, I would point to precisely that circumstance in support of my view. Artistic balance requires just such a distribution of accents. This situation has a striking analogy in the pair of pedagogical disputants: Settembrini is lovable, while Naphta grates on our nerves; yet—or rather, for that reason—Settembrini is the rhetorical organ-grinder, whereas Naphta exposes the live nerve of the problem almost every time. Personalities are one thing and ideas another. We may be convinced that there is something dubious and unsavory about Krokowski's interest in disease; we may suspect that his lectures, ostensibly introduced in order to dispel morbid curiosity in his curative methods, are calculated rather to add one more intensely piquant aphrodisiac to the already overcharged erotic atmosphere of the Sanatorium; we may feel that the surreptitious gratification of Krokowski's own libido is the chief end to be served by his rôle of father confessor:—all this may be conceded, and yet he may be closer to an understanding of the relation obtaining between mind and body than a good physiologist and fine surgeon who is a capital fellow besides.[28]

Settembrini loathes Krokowski. But his own point of view at times comes close to that of the psycho-analyst. On one occasion he impulsively refers to disease as "eine Form der Liederlichkeit".[29] I say impulsively; for when Hans Castorp tries to pin him down and make him own up to the larger implications of so sweeping a statement, he dodges the issue and launches a tirade on the nefariousness of paradox. The reason for his evasion is obvious: Krokowski too would cheerfully subscribe to the dictum that disease is a form of immorality, but he would do so with an ambiguous smile neutralizing the accent of moral condemnation inherent in the word immorality; for Krokowski's interest in practical morality is nil;

whereas Settembrini is interested in psycho-analysis only to the extent to which it can be made to serve the cause of practical morality. That dictum about disease being not merely a result but a form of immorality sinks into Hans Castorp's mind more deeply than its sponsor intended. He tries to apply it to Clavdia's case, and he finds it fits [30]—much to Settembrini's chagrin, if he could have known it, because our hero's passion suffers no diminution in consequence of this insight.

"Krankheit . . . eine Form der Liederlichkeit." There is no question but that Thomas Mann too subscribes to this formula adopted by his hero. Let me mention some specific illustrations of this that come to mind. Readers of "Königliche Hoheit" will recall that the American heiress, Imma Spoelmann, has a very queer lady companion, Gräfin Löwenjoul by name, who has fits of abstraction during which she talks arrant nonsense and insists on being addressed as Frau Meier.[31] There is no doubt but that her insanity has the function of an escape from responsibility, and that it is voluntaristic in essence. She herself refers to it as "the boon". The same interpretation suggests itself with regard to the epileptic fit of Pópow, minutely described in the "Zauberberg". In his lectures Krokowski had characterized epilepsy as the equivalent of love and an orgasm of the brain, and the scene to which we are treated has all the earmarks of such a performance, so that we tacitly subscribe to Krokowski's version.[32] Mann himself, moreover, speaks of epilepsy in very similar terms in a brief essay, dated 1920, where we read with regard to Dostoevsky, among other things, that he was "ein Epileptiker, und man ist heute auf dem Punkte, diese mystische Krankheit für eine Form der Unzucht zu erklären"[33] (. . . "an epileptic, and the tendency today is to interpret this mystical disease as a form of sexual gratification"). In his "Lebensabriss", finally, Thomas Mann recounts an episode of his own life, showing how the desire to escape from an intolerable situation translated itself into physical symptoms sufficiently grave to effect his release. Like every pre-war German found physically fit, he had to report for military training. He submitted to the inevitable at the time when "Buddenbrooks" was in the hands of the publisher, whose decision on the bulky manuscript was awaited with considerable anxiety. But he soon found the yelling of the drill-sergeant, the waste of time, and the insistence on machine-like spot-lessness ("eiserne Schmuckheit") repugnant beyond endurance.

"Erst einige Wochen lebte ich im Dunstkreis der Kaserne, als meine Entschlossenheit, mich zu befreien, bereits einen tödlichen und, wie sich erwies, unwiderstehlichen Charakter angenommen hatte." [34]

"Only a few weeks had I lived in the barracks atmosphere when my determination to free myself had already assumed a deadly and—as the course of events proved—an irresistible character."

This is Thomas Mann's own way of accounting for the inflammation of the tendons of the ankle which he incurred in learning the goose-step and which eventually brought about his discharge. Perhaps only a drill-sergeant would refer to this affliction as a form of immorality, but on the basis of his own account Thomas Mann would concede his right to call it just that. While differing with the drill-sergeant on the ethical aspects of the case, he would agree that his physical infirmity reflected an ineradicable perversity of his nature.

"Krankheit . . . eine Form der Liederlichkeit." Let us ponder the meaning of that phrase a little longer. The emphasis rests, no doubt, upon the word "form". Thomas Mann carefully refrains from saying that disease is a result of immorality, and just as carefully that immorality is a result of disease. Specific cases of disease and immorality would doubtless warrant such a description, but Thomas Mann is concerned with the specific fact as an illustration of a general problem. The general problem is the same if we replace the terms disease and immorality by the more general terms, organic symptom and a state of mind. What is the relation of these two factors in the human economy, Thomas Mann asks himself; and he despairs of expressing their relation in terms of any cause and effect series. The dilemma that results from the attempt to approach the problem through the categories of cause and effect is neatly expressed in the following musings:

"Der Materialist, Sohn einer Philosophie der blossen Robustheit, wird es sich niemals nehmen lassen, das

"The materialist, son of a philosophy of sheer animal vigor, can never be dissuaded from explaining spirit as

Geistige als ein phosphoreszierendes Produkt des Materiellen zu erklären. Der Idealist dagegen, ausgehend vom Prinzip der schöpferischen Hysterie, wird geneigt und sehr bald entschlossen sein, die Frage des Primats in vollständig umgekehrtem Sinn zu beantworten. Alles in allem liegt hier nichts Geringeres als die alte Streitfrage vor, was eher gewesen sei: Das Huhn oder das Ei,—diese Streitfrage, die eben durch die doppelte Tatsache eine so ausserordentliche Verwirrung erfährt, dass kein Ei denkbar ist, das nicht vom einem Huhn gelegt worden wäre, und kein Huhn, das nicht sollte aus einem vorausgesetzten Ei gekrochen sein." [35]

a mere phosphorescent product of matter; whereas the idealist, proceeding from the principle of creative hysteria, is inclined, and very readily resolved, to answer the question of primacy in the exactly opposite sense. Take it all in all, there is here nothing less than the old strife over which was first, the chicken or the egg—a strife which assumes its extraordinary complexity from the fact that no egg is thinkable except one laid by a hen, and no hen that has not crept out of a previously postulated egg."

Starting from the assumption that the organic and the psychic are fundamentally different in kind, one can argue until doomsday without bridging the gap between them or demonstrating how phenomena belonging to the one series can translate themselves into terms of the other. One is confronted with the same impasse that blocked Hans Castorp in his attempts to understand how any transition from inorganic matter to organic life could be made logically thinkable.

We are ready to understand, then, that Thomas Mann's use of the word "form" with regard to disease has a special meaning. It is one of the ways he takes to express the conviction that mind and body, spirit and matter, are two manifestations of an underlying reality that encompasses them both. The equation that unites them will forever elude intellectual formulation. Whether, as materialistic monists, we take matter as our starting point, or whether, as idealistic monists, we try to conceive everything in terms of spirit, neither approach will ever succeed in solving the riddles of the universe that have their locus in man, the Homo Dei. So we leave this part of our discussion without having arrived at a positive answer. Nor is the answer negative for that matter; for in so far as it is an answer at all, it "passeth the understanding", as our final chapter will endeavor to show.

V. THE IRONIC TEMPER

"Ich habe oft empfunden, dass Nie- tzsches Philosophie einem grossen Dichter auf ganz ähnliche Weise zum Glücksfall und Glücksfund hätte wer- den können, wie die Schopenhauers dem Tristan-Schöpfer: nämlich zur Quelle einer höchsten, erotisch-ver- schlagensten, zwischen Leben und Geist spielenden Ironie." [1]

"I have often felt that Nietzsche's philosophy might have turned out to be as happy a trove and accident for some great poet as was Schopen- hauer's to the creator of Tristan: it might have become the source of a supreme irony, playing between life and the spirit and embracing them both with an infinitely subtle love."

This reflection, found in Thomas Mann's volume of war-time essays and couched in the grammatical form of the past contrary-to-fact conditional, is followed by the statement: "Nietzsche hat seinen Künstler nicht, oder noch nicht, wie Schopenhauer, gefunden" ("Un- like Schopenhauer, Nietzsche has not—or not yet—found his artist"). How now, we are prompted to ask; what about Thomas Mann's own artistic production? And our eye lights upon a passage in which Mann designates the quintessence of his own experience with Nie- tzsche as the cultivation of the attitude of irony. In the preface to that same volume—a "musical" preface, written after the completion of the opus and summarizing all its themes in overture fashion—we read:

"Es sind in geistig-dichterischer Hin- sicht zwei brüderliche Möglichkeiten, die das Erlebnis Nietzsches zeitigt. Die eine ist jener Ruchlosigkeits-und Renaissance-Ästhetizismus. . . . Die andere heisst Ironie—und ich spreche damit von meinem Fall." [2]

"As regards his effect upon the spirit of the creative artist, the experience of Nietzsche may release two dis- tinct brotherly attitudes. The one is that cult of ruthlessness and Renaissance aestheticism. . . . The other is called irony—and with that I am speaking of my own case."

Is it modesty then, is it resignation, that makes him speak of the translation of the Nietzschean temper into art as a might-have-been or as a not-yet? Modesty, doubtless, in part; but resignation? Re- member that this "or not yet" was written several years after the

"Zauberberg" had already begun to germinate. What if Thomas Mann had come to feel even then, with nine more years of gestation ahead, that this new plasm promised to mature into something so startling, so vast, and so unprecedented as to dwarf his whole previous production in comparison—something which would show for the first time to what heights in the realm of art the application of the Nietzschean temper was capable of leading? Supposing this to be the case,—what a surge of feelings plays about those three little words "or not yet"! Hope, doubt, confidence, restrained exultation become perceptible to the imaginative ear as overtones accompanying that most inconspicuous and non-committal of reservations. In all seriousness, what other, lesser interpretation will those words bear? For what is the "Zauberberg" but the superlative flowering of that tentatively envisaged dream of a supreme irony, playing between life and the spirit and embracing them both with an infinitely subtle love! [3]

Without question, this passage heralds the spiritual temper that was to find expression in the "Zauberberg". What is this temper, which constitutes the very essence of the "Zauberberg's" flavor, its peculiar ethos, the principle of its inner form, or what we might boldly call the soul of its style?

Irony, as Thomas Mann uses the word, and as it applies pre-eminently to the "Zauberberg", claims only a distant kinship with the rhetorical device that goes under this name, as described in textbooks on the art of writing. The common variety of irony is a weapon, cold, glittering, sharp as a razor, a showy weapon in the hands of a dexterous verbal fencer, such as Herr Settembrini, who delights in its use, and he defines it by implication when he warns Hans Castorp against the poisonous variety of the same species, to be carefully distinguished from his own, the ornamental variety:

"Hüten Sie sich vor der hier gedeihenden Ironie, Ingenieur! Hüten Sie sich überhaupt vor dieser geistigen Haltung! Wo sie nicht ein gerades und klassisches Mittel der Redekunst ist, dem gesunden Sinn keinen Augen-

"Guard yourself, Engineer, from the sort of irony that thrives up here; guard yourself altogether from this mental attitude! Where irony is not a direct and classic device of oratory, not for a moment equivocal to a

blick missverständlich, da wird sie zur Liederlichkeit, zum Hindernis der Zivilisation, zur unsauberen Liebelei mit dem Stillstand, dem Ungeist, dem Laster." [4]

healthy mind, it makes for depravity, it becomes a drawback to civilization, an unclean traffic with the forces of reaction, vice, and materialism."

Hans Castorp is neither particularly edified by this lecture, nor can he get excited over the variety of irony that his mentor approves of. "Ahem", he muses to himself,

"er spricht von der Ironie ganz ähnlich wie von der Musik, es fehlt nur, dass er sie 'politisch verdächtig' nennt, nämlich von dem Moment an, wo sie aufhört, ein 'gerades und klassisches Lehrmittel' zu sein. Aber eine Ironie, die 'keinen Augenblick missverständlich' ist,—was wäre denn das für eine Ironie, frage ich in Gottes Namen, wenn ich schon mitreden soll? Eine Trockenheit und Schulmeisterei wäre sie!"

"he talks about irony just as he does about music, he'll soon be telling us that it is 'politically suspect'— that is, from the moment it ceases to be a 'direct and classic device of oratory'. But irony that is 'not for a moment equivocal'—what kind of irony would that be, I should like to ask, if I may make so bold as to put in my oar? It would be a piece of dried-up pedantry!"

Whereupon the author in his turn comments on Hans Castorp's musings in terms of an "unmistakable" irony that cruelly parodies Herr Settembrini's pedagogical efforts: "So undankbar ist Jugend, die sich bildet. Sie lässt sich beschenken, um dann das Geschenk zu bemäkeln" [5] ("Thus ungrateful is immature youth! It takes all that is offered, and bites the hand that feeds it").

The last two sentences quoted are an example of the common, the Settembrini variety of irony, with the added humorous flavor of frank parody. The passage taken as a whole, however, illustrates an irony of a subtler sort. As we listen to Settembrini's eloquent warning and to Hans Castorp's instinctive opposition, our inner ear catches faint echoes of a war-time controversy in which the "Zivilisationsliterat" and Thomas Mann figure as the principals. Thomas Mann's qualified defense of German militarism during the war, against the furious onslaughts of ententophile radicalism at home, was the outgrowth of an "ironic" attitude that, refusing to be stampeded into seeing things only as black or white, often sought refuge in reducing apparently simple issues to a tangle of contradictions,—an attitude that involved, moreover, the avowed awareness of a clinging trace of irresponsible artistic play even when he was fighting in deadliest earnest in defense of the very roots of his spiritual existence.[6] This predisposition to play the part of devil's advocate exposed him to the charge of having succumbed to the dangers of the ironic attitude, as leading "zur Liederlichkeit, . . . zur unsauberen Liebelei mit dem Stillstand, dem Ungeist, dem Laster" ("to depravity . . . to unclean traffic with the forces of reaction, vice, and materialism"); it made him, in those days when passions were at white heat, the target of attacks that branded his whole artistic essence as parasitism—"Schmarotzertum".[7] Accordingly, Thomas Mann's impressive volume of war-time essays turns out to be as much a work of self-defense as it is a defense of his country.

Thus, in the reader who has lived through the war and remembers Thomas Mann's memorable stand, Settembrini's little discourse on irony stirs a train of associations of the most extended scope. While Settembrini lectures so glibly on the nature and the dangers of irony and Hans Castorp registers his silent opposition to the implications of this doctrine, the whole complex of war-time controversy looms in the background and impregnates the scene with an added meaning over and above what is apparent on the surface. This background does not tend to displace or blot out the concrete principals of our scene,—they lose none of the sharpness of their contours; they are rather the gainers in richness and vitality, in the same way that a melody gains by the support of orchestration. And a sense of elation transmits itself from author to reader, a tingling of intellectual pleasure, whenever this double focus makes itself felt. This sense of elation, released by the play of the spirit in spanning two realms at once, the immediate and the remote, forms the characteristic accompaniment of the ironic temper.

The common variety of irony is a way of suggesting what one means by saying its opposite. The ironic temper of Thomas Mann consists in his always conveying more than he appears to be saying. The ironic temper has an intellectual flavor. It never fuses completely with the object on which it is focussed: the mind never surrenders control of the situation to the emotions. For the ironic temper the concrete situation never has the character of finality: it is but the meeting-ground, so to speak, of relations that extend forward and backward, into space and into time, into the self and into the cosmos; of energies that link the individual with the universal. The word "Beziehung",—relation, has always had a peculiarly impressive ring for him, Thomas Mann tells us in his "Lebensabriss".[8] The ironic temper involves consciousness, detachment, freedom. It spurns all commitments of an absolute character. It makes no pronouncement on values without limiting the scope of its validity by a reservation, expressed or implied. While it would include in its range the most passionate intensity of experience, it refuses to yield the clarity of its vision for any price. Serious to the point of austerity, conscientious to that of pedantry, as it may be, it never abandons its essential character of play. It has about it an air of lightness, an agility and intellectual elasticity. Just because it would never stop short of the absolute in its adventurous quest, it cannot invest anything finite with absolute seriousness, neither any phenomenon of the outer world nor any of the author's own psychological attitudes, no matter how many the curtains that the author parts in his exploration of the gallery of chambers constituting the inner self. Thus the ironic temper is seen to work both ways: its questioning smile embraces impartially the author and his subject alike.

It was in Nietzsche that Thomas Mann encountered the ironic temper as the vital essence organizing the contradictory elements of his genius into a unity of a higher sort. But we can go all the way back to German Romanticism (as we did in considering disease) and find the same attitude there as the most characteristic symptom of the new spiritual awakening. If there is one word that could serve as the abbreviated symbol of the new life pulsing in that small band of free spirits, that word is irony. To the fullest extent this applies to the intellectual leader of the group, Friedrich Schlegel. Irony is Friedrich Schlegel's all-inclusive term for the ethos of spiritual adventure. "Ironie ist klares Bewusstsein der ewigen Agilität des unendlich vollen Chaos", he writes in the "Athenaeum"[9] ("Irony is clear consciousness of the eternal restless movement of the infinitely abounding chaos"). Irony is the most protean term of Schlegel's cryptic terminology. He defines it and redefines it in numerous aphorisms.[10] The presence of the ironic temper in a work of philosophy or literature is for Schlegel the superlative criterion of excellence. And his own writings, the essays, the aphorisms, and the much maligned hybrid of a novel "Lucinde" represent his efforts to communicate by example the spirit of the doctrine.⑪ Friedrich Schlegel was a great critic but no artist. Thus, while his essays brilliantly illustrate the ironic temper—making due allowance for his overstraining of the point in the excessive zeal of the apostle—his "Lucinde" turned out in the main to be an extreme caricature of the idea. But the bizarre distortion that the idea underwent in some of Schlegel's own practice and that of disciples like Brentano, does not detract from his distinction of being the first to sense and formulate that ironic temper which was destined to find its most perfect expression in Nietzsche and Thomas Mann. Schlegel's name will live as that of an initiator, even though his later development serves as a melancholy reminder of Heine's pessimistic pronouncement: "Der Initiator stirbt—oder wird abtrünnig" [12] ("The initiator dies—or turns traitor").

Friedrich Schlegel, it may be remembered, found one contemporary piece of literature to embody the spirit of irony to a supreme degree:—"Wilhelm Meisters Lehrjahre". And Schlegel's essay, "Über Goethes Meister" [13]—the best review in the German language a critic of Gundolf's rank terms it—[14] represents in the main an appreciative elucidation of this spirit. Reading "Wilhelm Meister" today, we are apt to find the spirit of irony in this novel latent rather than manifestly present. Weighing our own impression as against that of Schlegel's essay, we are likely to feel that he read about as much into Goethe's novel as he read out of it. But, Schlegel would counter, is not this exactly what I had in mind in calling for a "divinatory" art of criticism?[15] Aside from this, however, the way Schlegel's review anticipates the temper of the "Zauberberg" is nothing short of amazing. It is not "Wilhelm Meister" that he is characterizing, it is the "Zauberberg"!, I exclaim to myself over and over again in coming upon some arresting formulation in that essay. It is divinatory criticism indeed!

A few examples. I realize that, brought in at this point of our chapter, they must be far from convincing except, perhaps, to the reader who finds in these pages essentially a confirmation of his own independent observations. I bring them up in the order of their occurrence in Schlegel's essay.

Schlegel speaks of Wilhelm's "grenzenlose Bildsamkeit" ("his infinite plasticity"). He praises "die leise und vielseitige Empfänglichkeit, welche seinem Geiste einen so hohen Zauber gibt" ("the subtle and versatile impressionability which imparts to his mind such a high degree of charm"). The same might be said of Hans Castorp.

Later portions of "Wilhelm Meister" present themselves to Schlegel as "a musical repetition" of earlier ones. The movement of the narrative is felt as "magisches Schweben zwischen Vorwärts und Rückwärts" ("a magical hovering between forward and backward"). This holds at least equally true for the "Zauberberg".

In "Wilhelm Meister" Goethe was concerned not only with producing a work of art, but also with incorporating within it a whole theory of art.

"Es war die Absicht des Dichters, eine nicht unvollständige Kunstlehre aufzustellen. . . . Bei allen Zwecken ist doch auch alles Poesie, reine hohe Poesie."

"It was the intention of the poet to present a not incomplete theory of art. . . . In spite of all (theoretical) aims, everything is at the same time poetry, pure, high poetry."

What could more aptly characterize the theorizing, for instance, about the time problem in its relation to narrative art, in the "Zauberberg"? This blending of theory with practice is, of course, one of the most characteristic aspects of the ironic temper.

With regard to irony specifically in "Wilhelm Meister" we read:

"Man lasse sich also dadurch, dass der Dichter die Personen und die Begebenheiten so leicht und launig zu nehmen, den Helden fast nie ohne Ironie zu erwähnen, und auf sein Meisterwerk selbst von der Höhe seines Geistes herabzulächeln scheint, nicht täuschen, als sei es ihm nicht der heiligste Ernst."

"The fact that the poet seems to take the characters and the events so lightly and humorously, that he scarcely ever mentions the hero without irony, and that he seems to smile down upon his own masterpiece from the height of his spirit, must not deceive us, as though he were not in holiest earnest about it."

And again:

"Nur dem der vorlesen kann und sie vollkommen versteht, muss es überlassen bleiben, die Ironie, die über dem ganzen Werke schwebt, . . . denen die den Sinn dafür haben, ganz fühlbar zu machen. Dieser sich selbst belächelnde Schein von Würde und Bedeutsamkeit in dem periodischen Stil . . ."

"Only for him who understands the art of reading aloud and has caught the ironic flavor to perfection, must it be reserved to communicate fully the irony that hovers over the whole work to those who have the capacity to grasp it. This semblance of dignity and significance in the periodic style, smiling at itself all the time. . ."

The illusion that Schlegel is talking about the "Zauberberg" is complete in this passage.

"Dieses schlechthin neue und einzige Buch, welches man nur aus sich selbst verstehen lernen kann" ("this absolutely new and unique book, for the understanding of which there is no key but the book itself"), is one of Schlegel's tributes to "Wilhelm Meister". I quote the passage because it not only praises but characterizes as well. In showing how the "Zauberberg" is linked with the great Romantic tradition I would certainly not be misunderstood as denying its uniqueness.

Let us turn now from these more general aspects of the ironic temper to some of its concrete manifestations in the "Zauberberg". By our roundabout way of approach we have avoided the danger of seeming to spread out an assortment of unrelated features; for as we now take them up, one by one, they will automatically have the character of branches springing from a common root.

There is the great realistic tradition in the field of prose fiction. Its way of presenting characters and events is straightforward, unambiguous, and objective. The author remains invisible. His rôle tends to become reduced to that of an impersonal recording voice,— the name of Flaubert will occur to everyone in this connection. His omniscience with regard to the sphere of action encompassed by his theme is an axiomatic assumption which it does not occur to the reader to question.[16] The action tends to interpret itself. Where the author supplements it by comment and analysis, his interpretation is absolute and final. In case the author chooses, occasionally, to step out upon the platform, as it were, and address the reader directly, he does so in more or less conscious violation of laws that safeguard the realistic novel as a literary form.

Only the superficial eye can charge the "Zauberberg" with such a violation. For while the "Zauberberg" derives from the realistic tradition in some of its surface aspects (and would be unthinkable without it), it stems in its essence from the tradition of German Romanticism. In accordance with the dialectic method which is in evidence throughout the "Zauberberg", we suspect that the author's genius envisaged a synthesis of the characteristic values of realism and romanticism. In many particulars the "Zauberberg" departs consciously, steadfastly, and consistently from the canons of the realistic novel. The whole "Zauberberg" obviously presents not reality but a very bold *Steigerung* of reality. One need only think of the fabulous verbal memory of all the principal characters! The author himself here plays a rôle totally at variance with that of the author in the realistic novel. Far from being impersonal and invisible, he is highly personal and, in fact, omnivisible. Already in his "Vorsatz", renderable both as "preface" and as "intention", he makes a playful plea for our indulgence on behalf of the story about to be told. He promises that it will be interesting, and he warns that it will be long. He takes pains from the outset to enlist the reader's sympathies with his hero by stressing his simple, ingenuous nature from the moment of his first introduction. He persists later in calling him "ein einfacher junger Mann", and "eine schlichte Seele", quietly putting a damper upon the rising tide of the reader's skepticism, as he watches Hans Castorp's awakening. Events here do not explain themselves, the author explains them. He takes us literally into his confidence. Cautiously, circumspectly, with scrupulous care he has us accompany him in his search for the exact word, the exact phrase that will render the emotional coefficient of his hero's reactions to his novel environment. He reflects in the first person upon the spiritual temper of the age into which his hero is born.[17] He distributes value accents among all the phenomena that he touches, negatively as well as positively; for when he refuses to commit himself, when he formulates a thing tentatively and provisionally, hedging his comment about with reservations, his language is always precise and explicit. He puts himself to the greatest pains to communicate his own attitudes. He will record even his own gestures, the play of his own features, the ring of his own voice, as he tells something of particular moment,—like an actor letting us see him put on his make-up before he acts his part. Sometimes we are invited to watch as he arranges the setting for a scene of importance and adjusts the lighting effects before raising the curtain. In effecting an imperceptible transition from a general survey to a specific scene he will call the change of perspective to our attention in a parenthetical remark. All this has the effect of showing the author's mind keyed to a pitch of awareness that exercises a conscious control over the most infinitesimal details of the vast pattern—the "Romanteppich Maja"— that he is weaving; [18] and it has the additional effect of stimulating the reader to a similar degree of wide-awake alertness in following his lead.

A striking example of this visible omnipresence of the author in his work is Thomas Mann's way of bringing home to us Hans Castorp's realization that he is in love with Clavdia Chauchat. Since they both eat in the common dining-hall, each meal brings Hans Castorp into a special physical proximity with the slant-eyed siren. His feelings on those occasions are analyzed as follows:

"Hans Castorp konnte sich, wenn er von einer gemeinsamen Mahlzeit aufstand, ganz unmittelbar auf die nächste freuen,—sofern nämlich 'sich freuen' das richtige Wort war für die Art von Erwartung, mit der er dem neuen Zusammensein mit der kranken Frau Clawdia Chauchat entgegensah, und nicht ein zu leichtes, vergnügtes, einfältiges und gewöhnliches. Möglicherweise ist der Leser geneigt, nur solche Ausdrücke, nämlich vergnügte und gewöhnliche, in bezug auf Hans Castorps Person und sein Innenleben als passend und zulässig zu erachten; aber wir erinnern daran, dass er sich als ein junger Mann von Vernunft und

"Hans Castorp, when he rose from one meal, could straightway by anticipation begin to rejoice in the next—if, indeed, rejoicing is not too facile, too pleasant and unequivocal a word for the sentiments with which he looked forward to another meeting with the afflicted fair one. The reader, on the other hand, may very likely find such expressions the only ones suitable to describe Hans Castorp's personality or emotions. But we suggest that a young man with a well-regulated conscience and sense of fitness could not, whatever else he did, simply 'rejoice in' Frau

Gewissen auf den Anblick und die Nähe Frau Chauchats nicht einfach 'freuen' konnte und, da wir es wissen müssen, stellen wir fest, dass er dies Wort, wenn man es ihm angeboten hätte, achselzuckend verworfen haben würde."[19]

Chauchat's proximity. In fact, we—who must surely know—are willing to assert that he himself would have repudiated with a shrug any such expression if it had been suggested to him."

. . . "da wir es wissen müssen" ("we—who must know"). We make a mental note of this phrase in passing, to return to it later. Obviously, there is a world of difference between the realist's implied axiom of omniscience and this avowed and explicit claim of its prerogatives. But to continue our quotation:

"Ja, er wurde hochnäsig gegen gewisse Ausdrucksmittel,—das ist eine Einzelheit, die angemerkt zu werden verdient" ("It is a small detail, yet worthy of mention, that he was growing to have a contempt for certain ways of expressing himself"). Thus, catching himself humming a banal love ditty, he checks himself with the exclamation:

"Lächerlich! . . . An solchem innigen Liedchen mochte irgend ein junger Mann Genüge und Gefallen finden, der 'sein Herz', wie man zu sagen pflegt, erlaubter-, friedlicher-, und aussichtsreicherweise irgendeinem gesunden Gänschen dort unten im Flachlande 'geschenkt' hatte und sich nun seinen erlaubten, aussichtsreichen, vernünftigen und im Grunde vergnügten Empfindungen überliess. Für ihn und sein Verhältnis zu Madame Chauchat—das Wort 'Verhältnis' kommt auf seine Rechnung, wir lehnen die Verantwortung dafür ab—schickte sich ein solches Gedichtchen entschieden nicht. . . ."[19]

"Idiotic! . . . It was the sort of thing to satisfy a young man who had 'given his heart', as we say, given it wholly, legitimately, and with quite definite intentions, to some healthy little goose in the flatland and thus might be justified in abandoning himself to his orthodox and gratifying sensations, with all the consequences they entailed. But for him and for his relations with Madame Chauchat (we are not responsible for the word relations; it was the word Hans Castorp used, not we), such a ditty was decidedly out of place."

A number of words and phrases in the passage quoted are set in quotation marks,—enhancing one's awareness of the fact that the quotation bristles with invisible quotation marks!

To the same general context belongs the following passage:

"Unmöglich, dass Madame Chauchat von den Fäden, die sich von einem gewissen Tische zu ihr spannen, nicht irgend etwas hätte bemerken

"Impossible that Madame Chauchat should know nothing of the threads that were weaving between her and a certain table. Indeed, Hans Cas-

sollen; und dass sie etwas, ja möglichst viel davon bemerke, lag zügelloserweise durchaus in Hans Castorps Absichten. Wir nennen das zügellos, weil er sich über die Vernunftwidrigkeit seines Falles völlig im klaren war. Aber um wen es steht, wie es um ihn stand oder zu stehen begann, der will, dass man drüben von seinem Zustande Kenntnis habe, auch wenn kein Sinn und Verstand bei der Sache ist. So ist der Mensch." [20]

torp definitely, wilfully purposed that she should know something, or even a good deal. We say wilfully because his eyes were open, he was aware that reason and good sense were against it. But when a man is in Hans Castorp's state—or the state he was beginning to be in—he longs, above all, to have her of whom he dreams aware that he dreams, let reason and common sense say what they like to the contrary. Thus are we made."

A grave, judicial, and conscious formulation of the moral epithet that applies to Hans Castorp's conduct. Followed by an equally grave and judicial generalization. And yet the whole passage vibrates in the light of high comedy! What invisible geni is responsible for this effect? It is, of course, the utter absence of any trace of moral indignation. The perfect "Gelassenheit"—nonchalance—with which an avowedly moral judgment is phrased, and the contradiction in terms that this involves, gives to this passage, like so many others, its delicious ironic ring.

When the three weeks are almost up and the logic of events seems to make Hans Castorp's departure imminent, there is something gently teasing about the author's way of rationalizing Hans Castorp's desire to prolong his stay:

"Hans Castorp fühlte herzliches Mitleid mit seinem Vetter, dem die Trauer über den nahe bevorstehenden Verlust des menschlichen Gesellschafters in den Augen zu lesen war,—fühlte in der Tat das stärkste Mitleid mit ihm, wenn er bedachte, dass der Arme nun immerfort ohne ihn hierbleiben sollte, während er selbst wieder im Flachland lebte und im Dienste der völkerverbindenden Verkehrstechnik tätig war: ein geradezu brennendes Mitleid, schmerzhaft für die Brust in gewissen Augenblicken und, kurz, so lebhaft, dass er zuweilen ernstlich daran zweifelte, ob er es über sich gewinnen und Joachim allein würde hier oben lassen können. So sehr also brannte ihn manchmal das Mitleid, und dies war denn wohl auch der Grund, weshalb er

"Hans Castorp grieved for his cousin, reading in his eyes his pain at the approaching parting. He felt the strongest possible sympathy at the thought of the poor chap's having to stay on up here when he himself was down in the flat-land, helping bring the nations together through the development of commerce and communications. His own regret was at times so lively as to burn in his breast and cause him to doubt whether he would have the heart, when the time came, to leave Joachim alone; and this vicarious suffer-

selbst, von sich aus, weniger und weniger von seiner Abreise sprach: Joachim war es, der hin und wieder das Gespräch darauf brachte; Hans Castorp, wie wir sagten, schien aus natürlichem Takt und Feingefühl bis zum letzten Augenblick nicht daran denken zu wollen." [21]

ing was probably the reason why he himself referred less and less to his impending departure. It was Joachim who came back to it; for Hans Castorp, moved by native tact and delicacy, seemed to wish to forget it up to the last moment."

Nobody is deceived as to the weight of the reasons alleged. There is no ambiguity about this irony. Yet there is nothing chilling about it; on the contrary, the dominating note in this irony is the author's affectionate sympathy with Hans Castorp, as he suffers under the strain of impulses that would make him deviate from the path of duty and reason. It is this quality of warmth, of sympathy, which Thomas Mann has in mind in characterizing his irony as "erotisch-verschlagen".

The same warm glow is felt to irradiate Thomas Mann's irony as he reports on the erotic daydreams with which Hans Castorp beguiles the hours during the three weeks that he has to spend in bed:

"An ihren Mund, ihre Wangenknochen, ihre Augen, deren Farbe, Form, Stellung ihm in die Seele schnitt, ihren schlaffen Rücken, ihre Kopfhaltung, den Halswirbel im Nackenausschnitt ihrer Bluse, ihre von dünnster Gaze verklärten Arme hatte er gedacht während der einzelnen Stunden des zerkleinerten Tages,—und wenn wir verschwiegen, dass dies das Mittel gewesen, wodurch ihm die Stunden so mühelos vergingen, so geschah es, weil wir sympathisch teilnehmen an der Gewissensunruhe, die sich in das erschreckende Glück dieser Bilder und Gesichte mischte." [22]

"In each hour of his diminished day he had thought of her: her mouth, her cheek bones, her eyes, whose color, shape, and position bit into his very soul; her drooping back, the posture of her head, her cervical vertebra above the rounding of her blouse, her arms enhanced by their thin gauze covering. Possessed of these thoughts, his hours had sped on soundless feet; if we have concealed the fact, we did so out of sympathy for the turmoil of his conscience, which mingled with the terrifying joy his visions imparted."

Here we see make-believe carried to the point of the author's confessing to collusion with his hero.

Comment of the gravest seriousness and the most profound import is playfully cloaked under extreme modesty in a passage like the following:

"Wie jedermann, nehmen wir das Recht in Anspruch, uns bei der hier laufenden Erzählung unsere privaten

"We have as much right as the next person to our private thoughts about the story we are relating; and we

Gedanken zu machen, und wir äussern die Mutmassung, dass Hans Castorp die für seinen Aufenthalt bei Denen hier oben ursprünglich angesetzte Frist nicht einmal bis zu dem gegenwärtig erreichten Punkt überschritten hätte, wenn seiner schlichten Seele aus den Tiefen der Zeit über Sinn und Zweck des Lebensdienstes eine irgendwie befriedigende Auskunft zuteil geworden wäre." [23]

would here hazard the surmise that young Hans Castorp would never have overstepped so far the limits originally fixed for his stay if to his simple soul there might have been vouchsafed, out of the depth of his time, any reasonably satisfying explanation of the meaning and purpose of man's life."

Another instance combines a number of very characteristic features of Thomas Mann's method. Speaking of Hans Castorp's tendency to betray his infatuation to the inquisitive eyes about him, he says:

"Ein Blinder hätte bemerken müssen, wie es um ihn stand: er selbst tat nichts, um es geheimzuhalten, eine gewisse Hochherzigkeit und noble Einfalt hinderte ihn einfach, aus seinem Herzen eine Mördergrube zu machen, worin er sich immerhin—und vorteilhaft, wenn man will,—von dem dünnhaarigen Verliebten aus Mannheim und seinem schleichenden Wesen unterschied. Wir erinnern und wiederholen, dass dem Zustande, in dem er sich befand, in der Regel ein Drang und Zwang, sich zu offenbaren, eingeboren ist, ein Trieb zum Bekenntnis und Geständnis, eine blinde Eingenommenheit von sich selbst und eine Sucht, die Welt mit sich zu erfüllen,—desto befremdlicher für uns Nüchterne, je weniger Sinn, Vernunft und Hoffnung offenbar bei der Sache ist." [24]

"A blind man must have seen how it stood with the youth; he himself did nothing to conceal his state, being prevented by a certain native and lofty simplicity. He inclined rather to wear his heart upon his sleeve, in contrast—if you like, favorable contrast—to the devotee from Mannheim, with his thin hair and furtive mien. But in general we would emphasize the fact that people in Hans Castorp's state regularly feel a craving for self-revelation, an impulse to confess themselves, a blind preoccupation with self, and a sense to possess the world of their own emotions, which is the more offensive to us sober onlookers, the less sense, reasonableness, or hope there lies in the whole affair."

Here we have psychological analysis of a moral orientation, bestowing reserved approval, as it does, upon one phase of the hero's otherwise questionable development. This analysis leads from the particular to the general, and it affects that tone of sober detachment, that "Sachlichkeit" which is one of the devices by which the author accentuates the intense bond of sympathy that unites him with his hero.

There are passages where Thomas Mann's irony becomes, literally, the theme of its own play. ("Ironie der Ironie", Friedrich Schlegel called this.) Dwelling upon the peculiarly tense erotic atmosphere that pervaded Haus Berghof, he says:

"Hans Castorp hatte nämlich den eigentümlichen Eindruck, dass auf einer Grundangelegenheit, welcher überall in der Welt eine hinlängliche, in Ernst und Scherz sich äussernde Wichtigkeit zugebilligt wird, hierorts denn doch ein Ton-, Wert- und Bedeutungszeichen lag, so schwer und vor Schwere so neu, dass es die Sache selbst in einem völlig neuen und, wenn nicht schrecklichen, so doch in seiner Neuheit erschreckenden Lichte erscheinen liess. Indem wir dies aussagen, verändern wir unsere Mienen und bemerken, dass, wenn wir von den fraglichen Beziehungen bisher in einem leichten und spasshaften Ton gesprochen haben sollten, es aus denselben geheimen Gründen geschehen wäre, aus denen es so oft geschieht, ohne dass für die Leichtigkeit oder Spasshaftigkeit der Sache damit irgendetwas bewiesen wäre; und in der Sphäre, wo wir uns befinden, wäre das in der Tat noch weniger der Fall als anderwärts." [25]

"Hans Castorp, on this subject, received a singular impression: it was that a certain fundamental fact of life, which is conceded the world over to be of great importance, and is the fertile theme of constant allusion, both in jest and earnest, that this fundamental fact of life bore up here an entirely altered emphasis. It was weighty with a new weight; it had an accent, a value, and a significance which were utterly novel— and which set the fact itself in a light to make it look much more alarming than it had been before. In saying this, we readjust our features before remarking that thus far, whenever we have referred to the relations in question at Haus Berghof, we have done so in what may have seemed a light and jesting tone; this without prejudice as to the levity, or otherwise, of these relations as such, and solely for the usual obscure reasons which prompt other people to adopt the same,—reasons which apply with peculiar force, moreover, to our present sphere."

This passage incidentally contains one of the allusions to the play of the author's own features.

I have mentioned Thomas Mann's practice of calling explicit attention to transitions,—his way of showing not merely a scene but also the hand responsible for its arrangement. Here is a case in point:

"Wir schildern Alltägliches; aber das Alltägliche wird sonderbar, wenn es auf sonderbarer Grundlage gedeiht. Es gab Spannungen und wohltätige Lösungen zwischen ihnen,—oder wenn nicht zwischen ihnen (denn wie weit Madame Chauchat davon berührt wurde, wollen wir dahingestellt sein lassen), so doch für Hans Castorps

"All this is sheerest commonplace; but the commonplace becomes remarkable when it springs from remarkable soil. There were periods of strain and periods when the tension between them beneficently relaxed— though perhaps the tension existed less between them than it did in Hans Castorp's fevered imagina-

Phantasie und Gefühl. Nach dem Mittagessen pflegte in diesen schönen Tagen ein grösserer Teil der Kurgesellschaft sich auf die dem Speisesaal vorgelagerte Veranda hinaus zu begeben. . . . Um denn mit einem oder dem anderen Beispiel auf jene 'Spannungen und Lösungen' zurückzukommen, so mochte bei einer solchen Gelegenheit Hans Castorp auf einem lackierten Gartenstuhl und in gesprächiger Unterhaltung mit Joachim . . . an der Hauswand sitzen, während vor ihm Frau Chauchat mit ihren Tischgenossen eine Zigarette rauchend an der Brüstung stand. Er sprach für sie, damit sie ihn höre. Sie wandte ihm den Rücken zu. . . . *Man sieht, wir haben jetzt einen bestimmten Fall im Auge.*" [26] (Italics mine.)

tion, for how far Madame Chauchat was affected we can only guess. In these days of fine weather the majority of the guests would betake themselves to the veranda, after the midday meal. . . . But to return, by way of example, to some of those strains and stresses to which Hans Castorp's state was prone. Our young man might be sitting on a painted garden chair, with his back against the wall, talking to his cousin, whom he had forced, against his will, to come outside, while in front of him, by the balustrade, Frau Chauchat stood smoking with her table-mates. He talked for her benefit; she turned her back. . . . It is evident, we now have a particular incident in mind."

Another characteristic example is the way Thomas Mann effects the transition from the first to the second of two scenes built along strictly parallel lines,—the two tête-à-têtes in the first of which Hans Castorp and Clavdia pledge themselves to friendship on Mynheer Peeperkorn's behalf, while in the second Hans Castorp and the great Peeperkorn enter into a similar compact for Clavdia's benefit:

"Während also die Lippen Hans Castorps und Frau Chauchats sich im russischen Kusse finden, verdunkeln wir unser kleines Theater zum Szenenwechsel. Denn nun handelt es sich um die zweite der beiden Unterredungen, deren Mitteilung wir zusicherten, und nach Wiederherstellung der Beleuchtung, der trüben Beleuchtung eines zur Neige gehenden Frühlingstages, zur Zeit der Schneeschmelze, erblicken wir unseren Helden in schon gewohnter Lebenslage am Bette des grossen Peeperkorn. . . ." [27]

"So while these youthful lips meet in their Russian kiss, let us darken our little stage and change the scene. For now, instead of the dimness of the hall we have the rather pensive light of a declining spring day in the season of melting snows; and our hero is seated in his wonted place at the bedside of Mynheer Peeperkorn, in friendly and respectful converse with that great man."

This is the technique of a writer who plays with his theme in sovereign fashion and incidentally makes sport of the reader. He does not tell us everything he knows by any means. He uses his discretion with regard to what he tells and when and how he tells it. On occasion he springs surprises sudden enough to bowl one over.

Who does not sit up incredulously in reading for the first time Hans Castorp's amazing declaration of love—in French, pages of French? For we smilingly recall Hans Castorp's sense of achievement on the first day, when, after plenty of time to prepare himself, he had managed to offer his condolences to Madame Tous les Deux in the form of one simple French sentence free from grammatical errors.[28] We are more than likely to have forgotten, however, that he had actually had the presence of mind, a couple of months after his arrival, to respond to Madame Chauchat's "pardon" with a cavalier "pas de quoi", when she had brushed against him in the crowd gathered before the window where the mail was distributed.[29] And we had certainly not attributed any particular significance to the fact that the scientific volumes over which he pored in his reclining-chair included some in the French language.[30] Indeed we should probably be wrong in attaching too much weight to those incidentals now. Even so, the *Steigerung* that he experienced on the night of the mardi gras cannot be held wholly responsible for that sufficiently clear and highly technical vocabulary which he employs on that occasion. His mastery of the foreign idiom appears as a miracle true enough, but even as a miracle it is not outside the pale of psychological law.

In passing, we stop to observe that the great dialogue of passion between Hans Castorp and Clavdia is carried on in French, whereas their great philosophical dialogue that appears as its counterpart in the second volume takes place in German.[31] That this linguistic balance is not the result of accident goes without saying.

The author certainly used his discretion, to the keen disappointment of all Frau Stöhrs, in lowering the curtain where he did, before the night of the mardi gras was very far advanced, and in raising it again only after Clavdia Chauchat had already departed from Haus Berghof. He does not choose to reveal in any detail what happened on that night. In recording much later that Hans Castorp yielded to the beseechings of the wretched Wehsal and gave him particulars about the physical consummation of his passion, he merely teases such readers as may be on the lookout for a display of erotic fireworks.

"Dennoch haben wir Gründe, ihn (den Leser) und uns davon aus-
zuschliessen"[32] ("Nevertheless we have reasons for not making the
reader a party to these intimacies"). In such summary fashion
Thomas Mann disposes of that subject. As a matter of fact, while
hints of a fairly positive nature are liberally strewn through the opening pages of the second volume, the reader has to travel a considerable
way before his conjectures as to the events of the night are raised to
the point of certainty. To illustrate: The opening pages of volume
two reproduce Hans Castorp's latest speculations on time and eternity, on the finiteness and the infinity of space. Ever since his arrival
up here he had shown a tendency to muse on such problems, but
this tendency had lately taken an intensified turn, so the author informs us with studied casualness, "durch eine schlimme, aber ge-
waltige Lust, die er seitdem gebüsst"[33] ("through a wicked but powerful desire, since gratified"). A little later we hear that Hans had
actually returned Clavdia's pencil to her on the evening in question
and had received a souvenir in return which he now carried in his
pocket.[34] That Clavdia had made good her announced intention to
depart, despite whatever may have happened in the interval, is announced in the next sentence, in the form of a subordinate clause,
followed by this gem of ironic utterance:

"Dass diese Abreise vorläufiger Art, nur eine Abreise für diesmal sein solle, dass Frau Chauchat wiederzukehr-en beabsichtigte,—unbestimmt wann, aber dass sie einmal wiederkommen wolle oder auch müsse, des besass Hans Castorp Versicherungen, direkte und mündliche, die nicht in dem mit-geteilten fremdsprachigen Dialog ge-fallen waren, sondern folglich in die unsererseits wortlose Zwischenzeit, während welcher wir den zeitgebund-enen Fluss unserer Erzählung unter-brochen und nur sie, die reine Zeit, haben walten lassen."[35]

"That her absence would be only temporary, that she intended to re-turn, that she would or must return, at some date yet unspecified, of this Hans Castorp possessed direct and verbal assurances, given, not during that reported conversation in the French tongue, but in a later inter-val, wordless to our ears, during which we have elected to intermit the flow of our story along the stream of time, and let time flow on pure and free of any content whatever."

Then follows the account of the circumstances of Clavdia's departure,
notable in this context through the consistent use of the pluperfect
tense, which imparts an air of remoteness to the whole performance.

We have to read on for another two pages before we find something
like a definite confirmation of our surmises,—though we may be at
a loss by now whether to take the author's remarks in a literal or a
metaphorical sense.[36] A little further on we are told that the curve
of Hans Castorp's fever chart had risen permanently since the night
in question, "in steiler Zacke, die er mit einem Gefühl von Festlich-
keit eingezeichnet"[37] ("a steep rise that he traced on his chart with a
festive thrill"). His conversation with Hofrat Behrens, in the course
of his receiving a hypodermic injection, is characterized by hedging,
intriguing the reader's curiosity still further, without satisfying it.
But from that same conversation the reader, at any rate, draws
certain inferences as to Behrens' own amorous relations with Clavdia,[38] even if Hans Castorp fails, by so much as the flicker of an eye-
lash, to betray any sign of Behrens' innuendo having scored in his
consciousness. "Niedlich, was?" ("Cute, eh?"), is Behrens' tell-tale
rejoinder to Hans Castorp's admission: "Gesprächsweise sind wir
uns näher gekommen"[39] ("We came a little closer to each other in
conversation"). Our curiosity is teased once more when Settembrini
fires the point-blank question: "Nun, Ingenieur, wie hat der Granat-
apfel gemundet?"[40] ("Well, Engineer, how did you enjoy the pome-
granate?") and Hans Castorp takes cover under a pretense of slow-
wittedness such as might have been in keeping with his somnolent
mental faculties on the night of his arrival. But somewhat later,
when Settembrini and his doughty new antagonist Naphta debate
the relative merits of work and contemplation—of the treadmill and
the downy couch, in the symbolic terminology of the middle ages,
Hans Castorp's contribution to the discussion is an altogether delicious revelation of the complex of passionate experience that lingers
ever just below the threshold of his consciousness:

"Wenn ich mir's überlege und soll die
Wahrheit sagen, so hat das Bett, ich
meine damit den Liegestuhl, verstehen
Sie wohl, mich in zehn Monaten mehr
gefördert und mich auf mehr Gedanken gebracht, als die Mühle im Flachlande all die Jahre her, das ist nicht zu
leugnen."[41]

"The more I think of it, the surer I
am that the couch—by which I mean
my deck-chair, of course—has advanced me more and given me more
food for thought in these ten months
than the mill down in the flat-land
in all the years before."

Finally, after all this teasing, the author removes the last veil of ambiguity as he describes the souvenir that Hans received from Clavdia,—

"das gläserne Angebinde . . . das transparente Bild des Menschenleibes, Rippenwerk, Herzfigur, Zwerchfell-bogen und Lungengebläse, dazu das Schlüssel- und Oberarmgebein umge-ben dies alles von blass-dunstiger Hülle, dem Fleische, von dem Hans Castorp in der Faschingswoche ver-nunftwidrigerweise gekostet hatte." [42]

"the glass keepsake . . . the trans-parent image of the human form, the bony framework of the ribs, the out-line of the heart, the arch of the diaphragm, the bellows that were the lungs; together with the shoulder and upper-arm bones, all shrouded in a dim and vaporous envelope of flesh—that flesh which once, in Carnival week, Hans Castorp had so madly tasted."

While Clavdia is absent in body from the first half of the second volume, she is ever present in spirit.[43] In introducing her physical presence once more, Thomas Mann again resorts to the same sov-ereign teasing play that keys up the reader's suspense in anticipation of events. The first hint of her impending return is conveyed when Joachim's mother, who had accompanied her boy back to the San-atorium, mentions their having met in a Munich restaurant a lady, a former fellow-patient, who wanted to be remembered to Hans Castorp.[44] After Joachim's death, Clavdia's return is suddenly sprung upon us in this amazing fashion:

"Wie lange Joachim eigentlich hier oben mit ihm gelebt, bis zu seiner wilden Abreise oder im ganzen ge-nommen; wann, kalendermässig, diese erste trotzige Abreise stattgefunden, wie lange er weggewesen, wann wieder eingetroffen und wie lange Hans Castorp selber schon hier gewesen, als er wieder eingetroffen und dann aus der Zeit gegangen war; wie lange, um Joachim beiseite zu lassen, Frau Chauchat ungegenwärtig gewesen, seit wann, etwa der Jahreszahl nach, sie wieder da war (denn sie war wieder da), und wieviel Erdenzeit Hans Castorp im 'Berghof' damals verbracht gehabt hatte, als sie zurückgekehrt war: bei allen diesen Fragen . . . hätte Hans Castorp . . . entschieden nicht recht Bescheid gewusst." [45]

"How long Joachim had lived here with his cousin, up to the time of his illegitimate leave, or taken all in all; what had been the date of his defiant departure, how long he had been gone, when he had come back; how long Hans Castorp himself had been up here when his cousin returned and then bade time farewell; how long—dismissing Joachim from our calcula-tions—Frau Chauchat had been ab-sent; how long ago, in what year let us say, she had come back (for she was back); how much mortal time Hans Castorp himself had spent in Haus Berghof by the time she returned: to all these questions . . . Hans Castorp could not have given any very specific answers."

In all this the pluperfect is the reigning tense. Then Clavdia drops out of the picture for another page and a half, to be reintroduced with the following teasing aside, again couched in the pluperfect:

"Als Frau Chauchat wiedergekehrt war (anders, als Hans Castorp es sich hatte träumen lassen—aber davon an seinem Orte), hatte wieder einmal Adventszeit geherrscht . . ." [46]

"When Frau Chauchat had returned —under circumstances very different from those Hans Castorp had imagined, but of that in its place— when she had returned it had once again been the Advent season . . ."

For another eight pages we hear nothing further about her. Meanwhile the opening of a new section has turned our interests into other channels, and we have been following for a page and a half the whimsically involved and roundabout introduction of Mynheer Peeperkorn. Finally, with that same studied air of presenting something incidental and of secondary importance, the teasingly guarded secret is let out of the bag:—

"Mynheer Peeperkorn traf mit demselben Abendzuge in Station 'Dorf' ein, wie Madame Chauchat, und fuhr mit ihr in demselben Schlitten nach Haus Berghof, woselbst er mit ihr zusammen im Restaurant das Abendessen einnahm. Es war eine mehr als gleichzeitige, es war eine gemeinsame Ankunft . . ." [47]

"Mynheer Peeperkorn arrived at the Dorf station by the same evening train as Frau Chauchat. They drove up in the same sleigh to House Berghof, and supped together in the restaurant. Their arrival was more than simultaneous, it was joint."

There is one ironic touch incidental to Clavdia's return, too good to be overlooked. When Joachim's mother tells about meeting in Munich the exotic lady who had charged them with conveying her regards to him, she mentions that the lady had spoken of her plan to spend the autumn in Spain. Hans Castorp is too much master of himself by now to betray his agitation overtly. He covers it up by talking, taking Spain as his cue and soliloquizing about the severely disciplined austerity of the Spanish temperament as it is engraved upon his imagination through Schiller's "Don Carlos". "Das Türenwerfen werde ihr dort wohl vergehen" ("She'd probably get over slamming doors there"), his speculation runs, as he tries to fit Clavdia into this Spanish setting.[48] Little does he dream then in how cruel a way this conjecture is to be verified! When Clavdia re-enters the dining-hall for the first time after her return and Hans awaits the sharp report of the door in breathless tension, the event fails to come off; for entering behind her, Mynheer Peeperkorn had quietly closed the door.[49]

All the elements of Thomas Mann's technique join hands in the light-footed dance of high comedy. Those endless minutiae of painstakingly accurate observation, for instance,—ends in themselves in the novel of naturalistic realism—are present in the "Zauberberg" only in a spirit of play. They are, first of all, the virtuoso's exhibition of his skill in the playing of his literary instrument,—a skill that has become second nature to him by now; and he smiles to himself at the thought that part of his public is so enraptured by his performance as to forget to listen to his music. We catch this smile, coupled with a warning wink, on occasion, as when Thomas Mann leisurely arranges the setting for that long awaited first conversation between Hans Castorp and Clavdia upon her return from Moscow, Spain, and God knows where. Without any hint as to what an exciting scene is in the making, Hans Castorp on that evening is shown sitting "in der Nähe des offenen Durchganges zum Klavierzimmer, den Rücken der Portiere zugewandt, mit einer Zeitung auf dem Stuhl, der dort eben gestanden hatte, einem plüschbezogenen Renaissancestuhl, wenn man ihn sehen will, mit hoher, gerader Rückenlehne und ohne Armlehnen" [50] ("near the open door to the music-room, with his back to the portières, on a chair that happened to be standing there, a plush-covered chair in Renaissance style, if one cares to see it, with a high straight back, and no arms"). *Wenn man ihn sehen will* . . . ?—but why should one bother to visualize that particular chair? And with the puzzling echo of that deliberately gratuitous contingency ringing in our ear, we become a party to Hans Castorp's sullen mood of bitter disappointment, and we see him about to quit the drawing-room in disgusted boredom and lay down his paper on "diesen zufälligen und unbequemen Stuhl" (again that chair!) when the sound of Clavdia's voice, addressing him from behind, transforms the situation. Well, we need only follow the ensuing scene to realize that that particular chair figures as one of the expressive elements of the situation. Has it ever occurred to us that all the chairs mentioned in the "Zauberberg" are expressive; that some of the psychic content of man's life is subtly infused into these mechanical artefacts? What a variety of chairs and associated expressive functions come to mind! There is the reclining-chair in which one is ensconced in snug comfort, the body reduced to the proportions of a mummy,—a significant analogy![51] There is the "Triumphstuhl" in which Clavdia listens, in a posture of relaxation, to Hans Castorp's declaration of love;[52] whereas the mercurial Marusya quite fittingly fidgets in her rocking-chair on the one occasion when Joachim opens his heart, just before he lies down never to rise again.[53] And as for the Spartan caned chairs in Herr Settembrini's den,—"die Physiognomie der Stühle gewann etwas politisch Wühlerisches in den Augen der jungen Leute" ("the chairs straightway began in their eyes to betray affinity with political agitation"), and Joachim hastens to rise apprehensively from the one on which he had been sitting when he hears that they are an heirloom dating back to the redoubtable grandfather Guiseppe.[54]

Related to the way the chairs in the "Zauberberg" have of reflecting personality is Thomas Mann's practice, generally speaking, of endowing articles of manufacture with a life of their own,—both individual objects and classes—and of making us feel an affection for them and an intimacy with them that we are wont to extend only to what is alive. This is a translation of the "Naturbeseelung" of the Romanticists into peculiarly modern terms and reflects the fact that we live in a machine age. That the Baptismal Bowl has absorbed some of the life of the many generations that have veneratingly held it in trust will cause no surprise,—Rilke has taught us to feel how everything old is saturated with the flavor of the life it has served—but who ever felt how a cigar could breathe before meeting Maria Mancini! And in varying degrees we feel the same pulse of life about the thermometer, the pencil, the x-ray machine, the x-ray picture, the watch, and the phonograph disk.[55]

There are other things that show as fundamentally Thomas Mann's departure from the tradition of realism.

A while ago we were struck by the expression: "da wir es wissen müssen" ("we—who must know"),—a phrase calculated to jar, if not to destroy the reader's implicit faith in the author's omniscience with regard to the inner workings of his hero's emotions. Why endanger the sacredness of this fundamental poetic license by turning the skeptical light of reason upon it? But there is evident design in the raising of this problem, for it is done repeatedly,—most boldly, perhaps, in telling of the encroachment of the demon of stupor upon Hans Castorp:

"Man wird urteilen, der Erzähler trage dick und romantisch auf, indem er den Namen des Stumpfsinns mit dem des Dämonischen in Verbindung bringe und ihm die Wirkung mystischen Grauens zuschreibe. Und dennoch fabeln wir nicht, sondern halten uns genau an unseres schlichten Helden persönliches Erlebnis, dessen Kenntnis uns auf eine Weise, die sich freilich der Untersuchung entzieht, gegeben ist, und das schlechthin den Beweis liefert, dass Stumpfsinn unter Umständen solchen Charakter gewinnen und solche Gefühle einflössen kann." [56]

"The reader will accuse the writer of laying it on pretty thick when he associates two such ideas as these, and ascribes to mere staleness a mystical and supernatural character. But we are not indulging in flights of fancy. We are adhering strictly to the personal experience of our simple-minded hero, which in some way defying exact definition it has been given us to know, and which indicates that when all the uses of this world unitedly become flat, stale, and unprofitable, they are actually possessed by a demonic quality capable of giving rise to the feelings we have described."

Whatever the earlier passage may have been, this is not a mere intellectual caper, to keep the reader on the alert,—this is a direct challenge. Under the mask of ironic play, it suggests a bond of kinship between author and hero that warrants no other term than identity. If anywhere, it is here that Thomas Mann looks us straight in the eye and confesses that Hans Castorp's story is his own story, that, *mutatis mutandis*, the "Zauberberg" is the symbolic record of his own spiritual development. More of this later. We need here merely record the conjecture that, in dwelling on "der grosse Stumpfsinn" in this fashion, Thomas Mann is for a moment lifting the curtain from one of the intimate phases of his own emotional experience of the World War.

Another instance of the identification of the author with his hero is altogether too charming to be passed over unrecorded. There comes a moment when Thomas Mann steps down from the conductor's platform, as it were, and, with a bow, hands the baton to his protégé. It will be recalled, perhaps, that we get the first succinct and comprehensive sketch of that weird phenomenon Peeperkorn not from Thomas Mann, but from Hans Castorp in person. It is not for nothing that he has trained his senses and his mind for so many years under the auspices of a hermetic pedagogy. From the start he showed himself an adept at snatching up and then developing the neat formulations of his mentors: now is his chance to give a wholly original demonstration of his ability to sense and size up a significant phenomenon independently. With Hofrat Behrens as his audience, Hans Castorp makes a striking thumb-nail sketch of the newcomer, accurate and balanced, employing Thomas Mann's own favorite method of "polarization" in defining Peeperkorn as "robust und auch wieder spärlich" [57] ("robust and at the same time sparse"). After Hans Castorp has thus performed, he hands the baton back to Thomas Mann, who continues: "Es ist ihm überlassen geblieben, von der Figur des neuen, unerwarteten Gastes ein ungefähres Bild zu zeichnen, und er hat seine Sache nicht schlecht gemacht,—wir hätten sie auch nicht wesentlich besser machen können" ("We have left it to him to describe the unlooked-for guest, and he has not come off badly—we could scarcely add anything essential to the picture"). Then, after dwelling on the favorable point of vantage from which Hans Castorp had been privileged to observe the newcomer, Thomas Mann proceeds to elaborate the sketch by a series of operations:— by noting further striking traits of Peeperkorn's features, by supplementing his appearance by the play of his gestures and that of the complicated pattern of lines on his forehead,[58] by sampling the manner of his talking, and by the device of a great deal of repetition in the interest of emphasis and further precision. Altogether the scene will be remembered as one of the most memorable exhibitions of Thomas Mann's craftsmanship.

Another highly significant aspect of Thomas Mann's irony faces us in the discussion of free-masonry and its underlying symbolism,—

a topic that again shows the "Zauberberg" as related to the sphere of "Wilhelm Meister's Lehrjahre" and its "Society of the Tower ". Modern free-masonry, the kind to which Settembrini owes allegiance, is a trivial affair, according to Naphta, who deluges it with his sarcasm:

"Man unterhält sich dort jetzt wieder über Natur, Tugend, Mässigung und Vaterland. Ich nehme an: auch über das Geschäft. Mit einem Wort, es ist die bourgeoise Misere in Klubgestalt . . ." [59]

"In it they once more discuss nature, virtue, moderation, the fatherland; business too, I suppose. In a word, it is a god-forsaken bourgeoisiedom, in the form of a club."

But there was a period in the history of the order when it stood for higher things, Naphta informs Hans Castorp.

"Die strikte Observanz war gleichbedeutend mit einer Vertiefung und Erweiterung der Überlieferungen des Ordens, mit einer Zurückverlegung seiner historischen Ursprünge in die Geheimniswelt, die sogenannte Finsternis des Mittelalters. Die Hochmeistergrade der Logen waren Eingeweihte der *physica mystica*, Träger magischen Naturwissens, in der Hauptsache grosse Alchimisten." [60]

"The Strict Observance meant the broadening and deepening of the traditions of the order, it meant referring its historical origin back to the cabalistic world, the so-called darkness of the Middle Ages. The higher degrees of Free-masonry were initiates of the *physica mystica*, the representatives of a magic natural science, they were in the main great alchemists."

Now alchemy, in addition to its grosser and more popular associations, Naphta elucidates, represents essentially the principle of

"Läuterung, Stoffverwandlung und Stoffveredlung, Transsubstantiation, und zwar zum Höheren, Steigerung also,—der *lapis philosophorum*, das mann-weibliche Produkt aus Sulfur und Merkur, die *res bina*, die zweigeschlechtige *prima materia* war nichts weiter, nichts Geringeres als das Prinzip der Steigerung, der Hinauftreibung durch äussere Einwirkungen,—magische Pädagogik, wenn Sie wollen." [61]

" . . . purification, refinement, metamorphosis, transsubstantiation, into a higher state, of course; the *lapis philosophorum*, the male-female product of sulphur and mercury, the *res bina*, the double-sexed *prima materia*, was no more, and no less, than the principle of levitation, of the upward impulse due to the working of influences from without. Magical pedagogy, if you like."

At the sound of the words "Transsubstantiation ", "Steigerung ", "magische Pädagogik ", we prick up our ears. By some strange coincidence those same words also describe somehow the processes that we see at work transforming the stuff of our hero's inner self. But to listen further to Naphta's lecture:

"Ein Symbol alchimistischer Transsubstantiation . . . war vor allem die Gruft . . . die Stätte der Verwesung. Sie ist der Inbegriff aller Hermetik . . . Die Gruft, das Grab war immer das hauptsächliche Sinnbild der Bundesweihe." [62]

"The primary symbol of alchemic transmutation . . . was *par excellence* the sepulchre . . . the place of corruption. It comprehends all hermetics . . . The grave, the sepulchre, has always been the emblem of initiation into the society."

The tomb constituted the central feature of the rites of initiation. To be admitted to them, the neophyte has to be

"wissbegierig und furchtlos. Der Lehrling, der zum Wissen Einlass begehrende Grünling, hat unter ihren Schaudern seine Unerschrockenheit zu bewähren, der Ordensbrauch will, dass er probeweise in sie hinabgeführt wird, und in ihr verweilen muss, um dann an unbekannter Bruderhand daraus hervorzugehen. Daher die verworrenen Gänge und finsteren Gewölbe, durch die der Novize zu wandern hatte, das schwarze Tuch, womit selbst der Bundessaal der strikten Observanz ausgeschlagen war, der Kultus des Sarges, der bei dem Einweihungs- und Versammlungszeremoniell eine so wichtige Rolle spielte. Der Weg der Mysterien und der Läuterung war von Gefahren umlagert, er führte durch Todesbangen, durch das Reich der Verwesung, und der Lehrling, der Neophyt, ist die nach den Wundern des Lebens begierige, nach Erweckung zu dämonischer Erlebnisfähigkeit verlangende Jugend, geführt von Vermummten, die nur Schatten des Geheimnisses sind." [63]

". . . athirst for knowledge and of dauntless courage. The neophyte coveting admission to the mysteries must always preserve undaunted courage in the face of their terrors; it is the purpose of the Order that he should be tested in them, led down into and made to linger among them, and later fetched up from them by the hand of an unknown Brother. Hence the winding passages, the dark vaults, through which the novice is made to wander, the black cloth with which the Hall of the Strict Observance was hung, the cult of the sarcophagus, which played so important a rôle in the ceremonial of meetings and initiations. The path of mysteries and purification was encompassed by dangers, it led through the pangs of death, through the kingdom of dissolution; and the learner, the neophyte, is youth itself, thirsting after the miracles of life, clamoring to be quickened to a demonic capacity of experience, and led by shrouded forms which are the shadowing-forth of the mystery."

Is it necessary to comment explicitly on the "transparency" of this passage? Is not that last sentence, in particular, the magic key that unlocks for us the Magic Mountain, revealing the esoteric meaning, the innermost principle of design of the "Zauberberg"? Is not the "Zauberberg" in just this way the long drawn-out process of Hans Castorp's initiation into life, through the agencies of death and decomposition? Has there ever been a book that has shed such a magic light over its own pages?

Self-consciousness playing with its own content, reflecting it in a series of mirrors that make it sparkle on a succession of planes simultaneously,—that is the essence of Thomas Mann's ironic temper. Conscious in the highest degree of every substantial and formal feature of the artistic production taking shape under his hands, Thomas Mann would kindle a similar awareness in the reader. Thus his great book becomes a blend of theory and practice. In following out the immanent laws that obtain in the domain of his art, he formulates these laws at the same time and speculates upon them. He does what Schlegel praises Goethe for doing in "Wilhelm Meister" and what Schlegel postulates as a quality of all "Transzendentalpoesie", in the 238th *Fragment* of the "Athenaeum": he achieves a conscious synthesis of creation and its criticism.[64]

In this connection we think of certain sidelights on aesthetic theory which we owe to Hofrat Behrens' attempts in the field of portrait painting that prompted him to remark one afternoon:

"Es ist eben gut und kann nicht schaden, wenn man auch unter der Epidermis ein bischen Bescheid weiss und mitmalen kann, was nicht zu sehen ist,—mit anderen Worten: wenn man zur Natur noch in einem anderen Verhältnis steht als bloss dem lyrischen, wollen wir mal sagen; wenn man zum Beispiel im Nebenamt Arzt ist, Physiolog, Anatom und von den Dessous auch noch so seine stillen Kenntnisse hat,— das kann von Vorteil sein, sagen Sie, was Sie wollen, es gibt entschieden ein Prä." [65]

"If a man knows a bit of what goes on under the epidermis, that does no harm either. In other words, if he can paint a little below the surface, and stands in another relation to nature than just the lyrical, so to say. An artist who is a doctor, physiologist, and anatomist on the side, and has his own little way of thinking about the under side of things—it all comes in handy too, it gives you the inside track."

As he expatiates in this vein and elucidates the enrichment that accrues to artistic expression if the artist approaches the engrossing problem of man from one or more auxiliary angles, we are aware, of course, that Behrens is doing more than airing the views of some inconsequential dilettante: he is giving expression to Thomas Mann's own practice. We are fully aware of this even if we do not happen to know that Thomas Mann himself sponsors the same line of thought in all but identical language in a passage of his essay, "Goethe und Tolstoi", [66] written as an intermezzo to the work on the "Zauberberg". And what wider vistas are not opened up by those casual remarks of Behrens'! They awaken a multitude of dormant interests in Hans Castorp, and in consequence of them three separate lines of approach come to converge in his sympathy with organic nature generally and the human body in particular: the lyrical, the medical, and the mechanical.[67] Hans Castorp's progressively expanding sympathy suggests by implication a theory of art which we are entitled to formulate as follows: It is the ideal aim of art and the highest conceivable goal of its aspirations to embrace the totality of man's multiple relations with the universe in a vital synthesis. Every such attempt is bound to fall short of full attainment. But it is something to see that the "Zauberberg" has its compass set in the direction of this goal.

The element of theory in its turn must be impregnated with an imaginative flavor, Schlegel had demanded in his "Wilhelm Meister" essay from which we quoted above. Such elements of theory we find in the "Zauberberg", above all, in some of the author's musings on the problem of time in its relation to narrative art. A typical example occurs at the end of the first three weeks of Hans Castorp's visit at Haus Berghof, at the moment when the physical examination to which he submitted has resulted in putting a new complexion upon the extension of his stay.

"Hier steht eine Erscheinung bevor, über die der Erzähler sich selbst zu wundern gut tut, damit nicht der Leser auf eigene Hand sich allzusehr darüber wundere. Während nämlich unser Rechenschaftsbericht über die ersten drei Wochen von Hans Castorps Aufenthalt bei denen hier oben . . . Räume und Zeitmengen verschlungen hat, deren Ausdehnung unseren eigenen halb eingestandenen Erwartungen nur zu sehr entspricht,—wird die Bewältigung der nächsten drei Wochen seines Besuches an diesem Orte kaum

"And now we are confronted by a phenomenon upon which the author himself may well comment, lest the reader do so in his stead. Our account of the first three weeks of Hans Castorp's stay with those up here . . . has consumed in the telling an amount of time and space only too well confirming the author's half-confessed expectations; while our narrative of his next three weeks will scarcely cost as many lines, or even words and minutes, as the earlier

so viele Zeilen, ja Worte und Augen-
blicke erfordern, als jener Seiten, Bo-
gen, Stunden und Tagewerke gekostet
hat: im Nu, das sehen wir kommen,
werden diese drei Wochen hinter uns
gebracht und beigesetzt sein.

Dies also könnte wundernehmen;
und doch ist es in der Ordnung und
entspricht den Gesetzen des Erzählens
und Zuhörens. Denn in der Ordnung
ist es und diesen Gesetzen entspricht
es, dass uns die Zeit genau so lang oder
kurz wird, für unser Erlebnis sich
genau ebenso breit macht oder zusam-
menschrumpft, wie dem auf so uner-
wartete Art vom Schicksal mit Be-
schlag belegten Helden unserer Geschichte, dem jungen Hans Castorp;
und es mag nützlich sein, den Leser in
Ansehung des Zeitgeheimnisses auf
noch ganz andere Wunder und Phänomene, als das hier auffallende, vorzube-
reiten, die uns in seiner Gesellschaft
zustossen werden." [68]

three did pages, quires, hours, and
working-days. We apprehend that
these next three weeks will be over
and done with in the twinkling of an
eye.

Which is perhaps surprising; yet
quite in order, and conformable to
the laws that govern the telling of
stories and the listening to them. For
it is in accordance with these laws
that time seem to us just as long, or
just as short, that it expand or con-
tract precisely in the way, and to the
extent, that it did for young Hans
Castorp, our hero, upon whom fate
has so unexpectedly laid an arresting
hand. It may even be well at this
point to prepare the reader for still
other surprises, still other phenomena, bearing on the mysterious element of time, which will confront us
in our hero's company."

The immediate problem of conveying to the reader the experience
of the passage of time has already been discussed. For some of the
other marvels and phenomena promised here we turn to the "Strand-
spaziergang" at the opening of chapter seven,—that truly lyrical intermezzo, standing between the death of Joachim and the arrival of
Peeperkorn. Besides taking us too far afield, it would serve no useful
purpose to recapitulate in dry prose Thomas Mann's analysis of the
dual rôle of time in narrative art,—its "musical" reality on the one
hand, and its perspective character on the other; we must refrain
likewise from lingering over his ingenious way of injecting the problem
of disease into the time concept.[69] There occurs an observation in
this context, however, that turns such a penetrating beam of light
upon the inner organization of the "Zauberberg" that it is absolutely
essential to dwell upon it, the more so as the author utters it under
his breath, as it were, and the reader may fail to catch its true significance:

"Die Zeit ist das Element der Erzählung wie sie das Element des Lebens
ist,—unlösbar damit verbunden, wie
mit den Körpern im Raum. Sie ist

"Time is the medium of narration, as
it is the medium of life. Both are inextricably bound up with it, as inextricably as are bodies in space.

auch das Element der Musik, als welche die Zeit misst und gliedert, sie kurzweilig und kostbar auf einmal macht: verwandt hierin, wie gesagt, der Erzählung, die ebenfalls (und anders als das auf einmal leuchtend gegenwärtige und nur als Körper an die Zeit gebundene Werk der bildenden Kunst) nur als ein Nacheinander, nicht anders denn als ein Ablaufendes sich zu geben weiss, und *selbst, wenn sie versuchen sollte, in jedem Augenblick ganz da zu sein,* der Zeit zu ihrer Erscheinung bedarf." [70] (Italics mine.)

Similarly, time is the medium of music; music divides, measures, articulates time; music can while time away and enhance its preciousness, both at once. Thus music and narration are alike, in that they can only present themselves as a flowing, as a succession in time, as one thing after another; and both differ from the plastic arts, which are complete in the present, and unrelated to time save as all bodies are, whereas narration—like music—even if it should try to be all there at any given moment, would need time to do it in."

Even if it should try to be all there at any given moment . . . Whatever this concessive modification of those more general observations applying to narrative art as a whole may mean, it is evidently a beam of light trained upon the "Zauberberg" specifically. In what way *can* a piece of narration attempt to be "all there" at every moment of its unfolding? In a metaphoric way Thomas Mann elucidates this cryptic remark a few pages later, when, having allowed himself to stray, apparently, from the contemplation of the pulse of time to the related rhythm of the sea, he raises his voice to the pitch of direct invocation:

"O Meer, wir sitzen erzählend fern von dir, wir wenden dir unsere Gedanken, unsre Liebe zu, ausdrücklich und laut anrufungsweise sollst du in unserer Erzählung gegenwärtig sein, wie du es im stillen immer warst und bist und sein wirst." [71]

"O sea, far from thee we sit and spin our tale; we turn toward thee our thoughts, our love, loud and expressly we call on thee, that thou mayst be present in the tale we spin, as in secret thou ever wast and shalt be!"

Just as the eternal rhythm of the sea, the vastest sensuous symbol of the pulse of time, has played with uninterrupted beat upon the author's inner ear, so the philosophic experience of time, merging into the experience of eternity, pervades every page of the "Zauberberg".

But there is another, a definitely concrete and tangible way in which the "Zauberberg" aims at the ideal of being "all there" all the time. Our most convenient approach to this is by noting Thomas

Mann's employment, on a scale never previously attempted in fiction, of the *Leitmotiv*, as used in music.

The use of the *Leitmotiv* has been a characteristic device of Thomas Mann's art from the very beginning. In the early *Novellen* and in "Buddenbrooks" every reader is struck by the frequent recurrence of descriptive phrases and snatches of dialogue that are of a peculiar, luminous intensity. They are largely responsible for the full-bodied sensuous presence of Thomas Mann's characters. Without doubt Thomas Mann owes this method in a large degree to the example of Dickens and, in a measure, to Fritz Reuter. The "Zauberberg", too, uses this same device in abundant measure. Thus the name of Settembrini immediately calls to mind a pair of checked trousers; Frau Stöhr cannot talk without retracting her upper lip from her rabbit's teeth; and Hofrat Behrens always appears with his head characteristically poised, and with his blue cheeks and bloodshot eyes.

But in the "Zauberberg" the *Leitmotiv* is charged with a second, a much subtler function. In his "Lebensabriss" Thomas Mann himself touches upon this matter, stressing the fact that this transformation of the Leitmotiv already makes itself felt in "Tonio Kröger". Referring to the latter, he says:

"Hier wohl zum erstenmal wusste ich die Musik stil- und formbildend in meine Produktion hineinwirken zu lassen. Die epische Prosakomposition war hier zum erstenmal als ein geistiges Themengewebe, als musikalischer Beziehungskomplex verstanden, wie es später, in grösserem Massstabe, beim 'Zauberberg' geschah. . . . Vor allem war darin das sprachliche 'Leitmotiv' nicht mehr, wie noch in 'Buddenbrooks', bloss physiognomisch-naturalistisch gehandhabt, sondern hatte eine ideelle Gefühlstransparenz gewonnen, die es entmechanisierte und ins Musikalische hob." [72]

"Here for the first time I grasped the idea of epic prose composition as a thought-texture woven of different themes, as a complex of musical relations—and later, in the 'Zauberberg', I made use of it to an even greater extent. . . . In particular, the linguistic 'leitmotiv' was not handled, as in 'Buddenbrooks', purely on an external and naturalistic basis, but was transferred to the more lucent realm of the idea and the emotions and therewith lifted from the mechanical into the musical sphere."

The Leitmotiv in this second sense is also a word or phrase of a peculiarly suggestive ring that tends to impress itself on the memory at once, and often this impression is reinforced by the word or phrase being repeated a second, third, or fourth time very soon after its first occurrence. But while coined originally to express a specific situation, it has an inherent tendency to expand the radius of its meaning. It is surrounded by an aura of suggestion. It is a focal point from which lines extend in a multitude of directions, linking a great variety of elements in a complex network of relations. When Hans Castorp is struck for the first time by the word "hermetisch", he says: "Es ist ein richtiges Zauberwort mit unbestimmt weitläufigen Assoziationen" [73] ("It is a regular magic word with vaguely ramified associations"). This casts an interesting light on the title; for structurally the "Zauber-berg" is a cumulation of such "Zauberworte". Each time such a Leitmotiv is sounded, all its associated content stirs in the reader's mind and plays about the immediate theme like a series of overtones. Thus, at every successive point of the narrative, increasingly large and complex portions of the themes already developed are carried along in concentrated form, by means of these "code" words, so that our experience in reading the "Zauberberg" is much more like a cumulative addition than a mere succession of elements. The interpenetration of themes forms so close a web that the whole of the "Zauberberg" tends to be present at every moment of the flow of its narrative. Taken literally, this is, of course, an overstatement, as freely conceded by Thomas Mann:

"Dass nicht alles auf einmal da ist, bleibt als Bedingung des Lebens und der Erzählung zu achten, und man wird sich doch wohl gegen die gottgegebenen Formen menschlicher Erkenntnis nicht auflehnen wollen!" [74]

"Let us not forget the condition of life as of narration: that we can never see the whole picture at once—unless we propose to throw overboard all the God-conditioned forms of human knowledge."

But taken as a tendency, it uniquely characterizes the principle of the "Zauberberg's" inner form. I doubt whether any other book in the world's literature is so perfectly integrated. Certainly, no other novel has ever aspired, in any way comparable to that of the "Zauberberg", to be "all there" at any given moment. It may be objected that there is something pedantic about carrying the principle of form to such lengths. There is something in this; I suppose the Gothic cathedrals, too, were pedantic in their articulation. But Hans Castorp himself might be quoted in support of this charge. "Form ist ete-pe-tete" [75] ("Form is folderol"), he disdainfully puts it on one occasion, and: "La forme, c'est la pédanterie elle-même!" [76] ("Form is the essence of pedantry"), on another. It is all very well to quote Hans Castorp to this effect, provided one remembers that these two impatient ejaculations reveal Hans Castorp as yielding himself in headlong abandon to the lure of Death, and provided one remembers that this disdain of form involves the disdain of life itself, as defined in the same context: "Leben ist, dass im Wechsel der Materie die Form erhalten bleibt" [77] ("Life is that which preserves the form through change of substance"). If that defines life, it also defines the "Zauberberg".

Examples of this interpenetration of themes suggest themselves by the score. We see this most easily by observing how Hans Castorp's passion for Clavdia—ready at every instant to emerge into his consciousness—is shot through with a variety of associated themes. Thus, when Hans Castorp says to Settembrini by way of commenting on Naphta: "Er ist auf seine Art auch so was wie ein Sorgenkind des Lebens, ein *joli jésuite* mit einem *petite tache humide*" [78] ("He is in his way also something of a problem child of life, a *joli jésuite* with a *petite tache humide*"), the formulation of this French phrase instantly recalls to mind the superciliously indulgent smile and the caressing touch of Clavdia and the timbre of that slightly husky voice that had addressed him as "*petit bourgeois, joli bourgeois . . .*" on the night of the mardi gras. [79] As for the phrase about the "Sorgenkind des Lebens", originally one of Settembrini's formulations of Hans Castorp's problematic existence, [80] it had also been woven into the tissue of that French dialogue, [81] not in Settembrini's sense, exactly, but rather in a more extended sense, to characterize the German temperament generally. All these themes,—Hans Castorp's problematic existence, the Clavdia complex, the problematic character of the German temperament—all these come into play as overtones when Hans Castorp, on the occasion of his near-fatal adventuring into the realm of eternal snow muses upon "der Mensch, und . . . sein Stand und Staat" as the "Sorgenkind des Lebens" [82] ("man and his status in the universe, as Life's problem child") in the widest sense. To cite another example, also associated with the evening of the mardi gras,—there is Hans Castorp's contribution to the debate of his two mentors on time and eternity. "Fortschritt sei nur in der Zeit" ("Only in time was there progress"), is the tenor of his remarks; "in der Ewigkeit sei keiner und auch keine Politik und Eloquenz. Dort lege man, sozusagen, in Gott den Kopf zurück und schliesse die Augen" [83] ("in eternity there was none, nor any politics or eloquence either. There, so to speak, one laid one's head back in God, and closed one's eyes"). For us the image of this posture merges with that of Hofrat Behrens, as he performs his stunt of drawing a little pig, with eyes closed, while Hans Castorp strides over to Clavdia and asks her for the loan of her pencil:

"Er zeichnete mit geschlossenen Augen, im Stehen, über den Tisch gebückt, dabei aber zurückgelegten Kopfes, damit alle sehen konnten, dass er die Augen geschlossen hielt." [84]

"Bent over the table with his eyes closed and his head thrown back in evidence of good faith, he was sketching with his mighty hand a figure on the back of a visiting-card, the outline of a pig."

In the course of that evening this act already comes to figure as a symbol of eternity in the great French dialogue.[85] To mention another example of the interweaving of themes from another, though related context,—when Peeperkorn lectures Hans Castorp on the virtues of quinine, on the bark of the cinchona tree, and on the ingeniously complex structure of bark tissue generally—"von der Epidermis bis zum Cambium,—sie hätten es in sich, sagte Peeperkorn" [86] ("from the epidermis to the cambium—they had it in them, said Peeperkorn") who does not recall the avid attention with which Hans Castorp had sometime followed Hofrat Behrens' discourse on the structure of the human skin and all its ingenious contrivances for awakening an emotional response? [87] As a final example, let us note how even such apparently unrelated spheres as music and Maria Mancini come to vibrate in unison, through the medium of a third agency. On his first day with Joachim, Hans Castorp winds up a long speech in praise of tobacco with the remark:

"Selbst die Polarforscher statten sich reichlich mit Rauchvorrat aus für ihre Strapazen, und das hat mich immer sympathisch berührt, wenn ich es las. Denn es kann einem sehr schlecht gehen,—nehmen wir mal an, es ginge mir miserabel; aber so lange ich noch meine Zigarre hätte, hielte ich's aus, das weiss ich, sie brächte mich drüber weg." [88]

"Even polar expeditions fit themselves out with supplies of tobacco to help them carry on. I've always felt a thrill of sympathy when I read that. You can be very miserable: I might be in a perfectly wretched fix, for instance; but I could always stand it if I had my smoke."

(Delicious—this platonic interest in strenuous adventure, against the background of Hans Castorp's love of creature comforts! A typical *petit bourgeois* combination of attitudes!) On the evening of Christmas day a special treat awaits the residents at Haus Berghof in the form of a song recital. Fortunately for Hans Castorp, "die Schmaläugige und der Pädagog" do not stay through the performance, so that he can yield himself to the music without any distractions, and the flavor of his mood is rendered by the author's remark: "Er fand es gut, dass in der ganzen Welt und noch unter den besondersten Umständen Musik gemacht wurde, wahrscheinlich sogar auf Polarexpeditionen" [89] ("He found it a satisfying thing that in the whole world and even under the most peculiar circumstances people made music, on polar expeditions too, in all probability"). Here it is the apparently irrelevant allusion to polar expeditions that subtly bridges the spheres of tobacco and music, suggesting that they have the same pleasantly narcotic effect upon Hans Castorp's mental faculties, and perhaps reminding us, in addition, of Settembrini's terse dictum, on another occasion: "Bier, Tabak und Musik. Da haben wir Ihr Vaterland!" [90] ("Beer, tobacco, and music. Behold the Fatherland!") Hans Castorp's interest in polar expeditions seems to be subtly integrated with the sphere of his passion, moreover, when he makes friends with Anton Karlowitsch Ferge, to hear him tell about Russia, "von der dortigen Menschenart, ihrer nördlichen und darum in seinen Augen desto abenteuerlicheren Exotik" [91] ("of the race of people there and their exotic manners—all the more thrilling in his sight because it was northern").

The unique artistic aim of the "Zauberberg", to be all there all the time, can, in the nature of things, be felt only more or less vaguely at the first reading. It grows upon us, as we read it a second time with the memory of our first experience freshly in mind. Only then, of course, can the interpenetration of themes be appreciated as pointing forward, as well as backward. Only then, for instance, shall we be conscious of the play of ironic overtones about Hans Castorp's remark: "—nehmen wir mal an, es ginge mir miserabel" ("I might be in a perfectly wretched fix, for instance"), when our anticipating memory recalls its final vision of Hans Castorp, forging ahead, as one of three thousand comrades, in the face of bursting shrapnel, through the mire of the Belgian battlefield. And the same vision will superimpose itself upon the imagery of Naphta's discourse on the initiatory rites of free-masonry, where the neophyte is made to experience the mysterious terrors of the tomb, "um dann an un-bekannter Bruderhand daraus hervorzugehen" ("in order to be led forth at last at the hand of an unknown brother").

Thus the ironic temper of the "Zauberberg" sparkles in a multi-tude of facets. In all its phases it exhibits the spirit of sovereign play in which the author treats his theme, himself, and his reader. Despite the vastness of the pattern, conscious control is manifest down to the most infinitesimal details of its composition; and a spirit of elation, composed of intellectual detachment blended with warmth,[92] hovers over all. The ironic temper is humor in its most sublime form, a highly intellectual humor, avoiding both the gross and the sentimental extremes.

VI. WHAT IS GERMAN?

The "Zauberberg" is a symbolic novel. All the phenomena and events recorded have a multiple valence. They move on several planes. The characters that live in the "Zauberberg's" pages are more vivid, more intensely lighted, more concretely tangible to the aesthetic imagination than the people we see and touch in real life, but the very sharpness of their contours makes the shadows they cast stand out that much more boldly. "Alles Vergängliche ist nur ein Gleichnis" ("Everything transient is only a parable"), the mystic chorus proclaims at the end of "Faust"; and this, Goethe's final verdict on the significance of life's passing show is but the reaffirmation of an age-old point of view, now deliberately ignored or forgotten, now rediscovered and re-experienced in turn, as in the life of an individual and in that of an age the hunger for life alternates with the search for meaning. As already remarked, there is a divide between "Buddenbrooks" and the "Zauberberg". These two works, separated by a quarter of a century, are peaks that bear the legend of the author's spiritual travels in the intervening span, and at the same time they reflect the shift in the temper of literary Germany during a period of which Thomas Mann will probably figure for posterity as the greatest, certainly the most articulate representative. (That the difference is one of degree rather than of kind, however, so far as Thomas Mann is concerned; that the latter phase was already latent in his earliest work, should be equally remembered. How impressively those same Goethean lines about the parabolic value of everything transient are repeatedly employed even in "Buddenbrooks" [1] to illuminate the drive of Senator Thomas, whose personality, singular blend of austerity and ambition, bears so close a resemblance to the mature Thomas Mann!)

"Ich spreche . . . in einem weiteren und geistigeren Sinn, für den ich nachgerade Verständnis bei Ihnen sollte voraussetzen dürfen" [2] ("I am speaking in a broader, more intellectual sense, your comprehension of which I felt I might presume upon, by now "). The words are Settembrini's, addressed to our hero by way of remonstrance. They are at the same time an admonition on the part of Thomas Mann to the reader, whose ear at this point may be presumed to have learned to distinguish the serious overtones that accompany the infinitely diverting narrative. Everything about the "Zauberberg" is symbolic, including its title which, though occurring in the text only once, very near the end, has about it that characteristic iridescence that stimulates the imagination to link it with a wide range of associations and brings to mind all that body of legend and fairy-tale that tells of persons being lured or spirited away into mountains and held there, by the spell of magic. The first volume alludes to this sphere in the form of the "Rattenfänger" legend, when Dr. Krokowski leaves the lecture hall after one of his psycho-analytic talks and we see his spell-bound listeners trooping after him like the children fascinated by the strains of the pied piper.[3] And a number of times the related theme of the "Vogelfänger" from the "Zauberflöte" is touched, Settembrini being the first to sound this note when he clothes his warning against the ensnaring lure of the place in a quotation from the "Magic Flute ".[4] The imagery associated with that warning promptly reappears in the stuff of Hans Castorp's dreams the following night;[5] later it again turns up in his reveries.[6] And near the end of volume one Hofrat Behrens, in his quaint jargon, deliciously impersonates the clownish magician lording it over his menagerie of captive birds.[7] As for Hans Castorp's own status, he wakes up and rubs his eyes at the end of the story like the "Siebenschläfer" of German legend [8] which has its counterpart in our tale of Rip Van Winkle. Too obvious to require any specific allusions is the parallelism between Hans Castorp's relation to Clavdia and the spell Venus cast over Tannhäuser in her mountain grotto. The symbolism of the magic mountain takes a different turn, again, in its being the place of Hans Castorp's hermetic education, where he is sealed up, as it were, shut off from contacts with the outside world, the "Flachland", in order that his simple nature may be distilled and redistilled; on the last page we are reminded that it was a hermetic story to which we have listened. And another sphere of associations surrounds the title as we come to feel that "die Grottendecke des Sündenberges",[9] the grotto of iniquity from which Hans at last emerges, covers all the shams and trifles, the vain pursuits, the hedonistic frivolity of pre-war civilization. As we read the twelve hundred pages of the book, its title always in the background of our consciousness, and as we finally come upon this title in the text, it is as though we had been waiting all the time for the word "Zauberberg" to be uttered and as if all the associations that we had heretofore been vaguely aware of crystallized in our consciousness at its sound.

The "Zauberberg" is a symbolic record of Thomas Mann's spiritual autobiography. In all essentials Hans Castorp is Thomas Mann.[10] Author and hero are identical in their way of experiencing the world, in their morality, in their emotional pattern. Hans Castorp's ethos of experiment, of adventuring into forbidden realms—the realm of "sin" as opposed to that of "virtue"—is the peculiar ethos of the artist, as developed on many occasions by Thomas Mann. There is, undeniably, the difference between the young man, groping his way under the strain of forces that pull in opposite directions, and the mature author who chronicles the young man's spiritual adventures with that ironic blend of sympathy and detachment which I have tried to characterize in the last chapter. But thanks to the fiction of the alchemy of the hermetic pedagogy Hans Castorp matures at a supernaturally rapid rate, and we have already glimpsed Thomas Mann, at critical moments, making Hans Castorp party to feelings, experiences, speculations of a most intimately personal and auto-biographical character. To one familiar with Thomas Mann's development such things come to mind as that sublimely terrible snow storm, during which Hans Castorp's physical existence and his spiritual essence alike are neatly poised between Life and Death, before his loyalty to Life tips the scales. Or one thinks of Hans Castorp's succumbing to the spell of "der grosse Stumpfsinn", the great stupor; or of his preternaturally discerning analysis of his favorite song, "der Lindenbaum" and the implications involved in his attachment to it;[11] or of his experiences in the realm of the occult. In all these matters Hans Castorp is privileged to anticipate experiences that fell to the lot of Thomas Mann later—during the long years of the War and the most trying phase of the reconstruction period. Spiritually speaking, the young man of thirty who breaks the seven years' spell of the magic mountain to follow the summons of the call to the colors, has the features of the Thomas Mann who finished his novel at the age of fifty.

Thomas Mann's personality being what it is, however, this involves a symbolism infinitely more far-reaching than the stylized portrayal of an individual author. Thomas Mann has long come to regard himself as a "representative" in a very special sense. As I have already mentioned, this appraisal of himself was expressed, long before the War, under the symbol of a little prince who is predestined both by his high station and by his temperament to take his responsibilities very seriously.[12] The very childhood of Klaus Heinrich is passed in the shadow of duties of government. And we now recall that "regieren" became Hans Castorp's favorite code word embracing all the content of his musings on man as the Homo Dei, from the time he first experienced a special sense of responsibility as the correlate of his specially privileged spiritual adventurings.[13] But it was only during the War that Thomas Mann's endowment and qualifications for the rôle of representative and spokesman acquired the force of a destined mission,—to use language that truly expresses the compulsion to which he felt himself subject. It was during the War that Mann came to regard himself as singled out to plead the case of spiritual Germany before God and man. He came to regard himself as the incarnation of the German conscience. His book on the War contains the memorable words:

"Sollte dies Buch, das ein Dokument sein und als solches übrig bleiben möchte, wenn die Wasser sich verliefen, dereinst die Schmähung widerlegen helfen, es habe Deutschland in diesen Tagen an Gewissen gefehlt . . ., so ist es nicht umsonst geschrieben." [14]

" This book would like to figure as a document and remain as such after the waters of the flood have subsided. If it should succeed some day in helping to refute the slur that Germany was lacking in conscience during these days . . . then it has not been written in vain."

In view of these facts it seems to follow of necessity that the simple young man who reflects Thomas Mann's own way of coming to grips with life, should in a measure represent that outlook on life and that pattern of responding to stimuli in the widest sense which is peculiarly German or which, at any rate, Thomas Mann regards as peculiarly German. In following this lead we shall find, as a matter of fact, that Hans Castorp is designed in the most thoroughgoing way to stand forth as the embodiment of spiritual Germany.

It may be advisable to pause and define what we mean by the term: spiritual Germany. That nations, like individuals, have not only a definite physiognomy but also a definite character is almost universally taken for granted. In practice we all think of the German, the Englishman, the Frenchman, the American as sufficiently distinct types. The rub comes when we try to put our discernment of differences on a scientific basis. The methods of exact science are obviously unable to cope with a problem of this kind. Only the pseudo-science that flourishes in periods of popular hysteria can claim to speak here with any authority. As for approaching the problem by comparative measurements and tabulations of the mental habits and moral characteristics of whole populations, it is enough to face the idea to realize its absurdity. There would be no agreement on essential criteria in the first place, and even if there were, nobody would attach any significance to the results obtained from statistical charts. The study of character is, of course, not a science but an art. And just as different observers will see the character of a given individual in different lights and vary in their appraisal, similarly there can be no scientific agreement on national character. The portrayal of national character calls into play the special aptitudes of the artist and the philosopher, and also their ethos, their sincerity, as differentiated from the scientist and his specialized sense of responsibility. Character portrayal is expression; and like all forms of expression, it expresses first and foremost—if incidentally—the personality of the portrayer, whereas the character of the object portrayed will always tally with the portrait in only a partial and limited way. The portrait can never get wholly away from subjective intuition.

It is highly desirable, then, to become clear as to what limited meaning can legitimately attach to the term: national character. For one thing, national character is nothing rigid or permanent. Being attached to life, it is in a state of flux; and each of the important units composing Western civilization has shown a succession of distinct physiognomies during different epochs, as recorded by the intuitive genius of qualified observers from among their own midst.[15] No one realized this more keenly than Nietzsche, who did not dream, iconoclast though he was, of discarding the concept of national character, but thought only of redefining it. In his words:

"Das, worin man die nationalen Unterschiede findet, ist viel mehr, als man bis jetzt eingesehen hat, nur der Unterschied verschiedener *Culturstufen* und zum geringsten Theile etwas Bleibendes (und auch diess nicht in einem strengen Sinne). Desshalb ist alles Argumentieren aus dem National-Charakter so wenig verpflichtend für Den, welcher an der *Umschaffung* der Überzeugungen, das heisst an der Cultur arbeitet. Erwägt man zum Beispiel, was Alles schon deutsch *gewesen ist*, so wird man die theoretische Frage: 'was *ist* deutsch?' sofort durch die Gegenfrage verbessern: 'was ist *jetzt* deutsch?'—und jeder *gute* Deutsche wird sie praktisch, gerade durch Überwindung seiner deutschen Eigenschaften, lösen. Wenn nämlich ein Volk vorwärts geht und wächst, so sprengt es jedesmal den Gürtel, der ihm bis dahin sein *nationales* Ansehen gab . . ." [16]

"National differences consist, far more than has hitherto been observed, only in the differences of various grades of culture, and are only to a very small extent permanent (nor even that in a strict sense). For this reason all arguments based on national character are so little binding on one who aims at the alteration of convictions—in other words, at culture. If, for instance, we consider all that has already been German, we shall improve upon the hypothetical question, 'What is German?' by the counter-question, 'What is *now* German?' and every good German will answer it practically, by overcoming his German characteristics. For when a nation advances and grows, it bursts the girdle previously given to it by its national outlook."

Nations are not eternal. In their physical constitution the product of a motley blending of races, they derive what we call their character from the play of historical forces that accompanied their rise and development, from their evolving traditions and cultural institutions, from their internal and external rivalries, from the contours of their borders, from the soil and its products, in the widest sense, of the countries that they inhabit. Some of these elements show more stability than others, but to the long range view the permanence of them all is a relative matter. An additional factor that has played an increasingly important rôle during the last century and a half particularly, is the growing self-consciousness of nationalities, the will to regard themselves as distinct in type from their neighbors, the conviction of each that it has a unique contribution to make to humanity, and the conscious effort to interpret the play of the historical forces to which they were exposed as the external manifestation of an immanent logic of their development. This involves an editing of national history, a selection of fact and a distribution of emphasis as regards the phases of its past that a nation chooses to remember,—all of which again makes for a sense of difference, even though, to take the long range point of view again, all Western nations show these tendencies in common and reveal an identity of pulse in their development as well as a consciousness of difference.

People often think of national character as a residue that is left in an individual of a given nationality after stripping him of everything that communal habits of life, cultural institutions, language, and historical education have contributed to his make-up, as if it were a matter of "race" or blood. That is pure myth; it is, on the contrary, these social appurtenances of which our hypothetical individual has been stripped, in which his national character resides. The term national character, properly used, is nothing other than a concentrated symbol for those features of a national community's past development and environment that are felt as still alive and recognizably active in that community at a given moment. As such it is an abstraction and at the same time a reality of a higher order.

Another side of the matter which needs to be scrutinized is this: In generalizing upon a nation's character, what part of the nation is in the focus of one's attention? Is it the masses or the classes? Is it the country folk, the city proletariat, the middle class—privileged in the matter of means and education—or is it a nation's men of genius that one has in mind? Depending upon the focus, the estimate will vary enormously. An outsider, moreover, is bound to focus differently from a member of the group. In time of war this divergence is so apparent that it is unnecessary to amplify, even discounting the element of wilful distortion involved in all directed propaganda. Yet the severest strictures may at times emanate from an insider. The Germans have had no more merciless a critic than Nietzsche, who directed his most telling broadsides against the intellectual habits of the educated classes, disciplinarian and moralist that he was. It was also Nietzsche, however, who realized that a nation's character is but imperfectly expressed by the record of its actual conduct and accomplishment. Equally revealing are its dreams, its aspirations, its strivings, the standards it sets itself:—in one word, its ideals. The goal set is as characteristic as its pursuance, the reach as significant as the grasp. This holds true for individuals and nations alike. In the inimitable language of his Zarathustra:

"Leben könnte kein Volk, das nicht erst schätzte; will es sich aber erhalten, so darf es nicht schätzen, wie der Nachbar schätzt . . .

Eine Tafel der Güter hängt über jedem Volke. Siehe, es ist seiner Überwindungen Tafel; siehe, es ist die Stimme seines Willens zur Macht.

Löblich ist, was ihm schwer gilt; was unerlässlich und schwer, heisst gut; und was aus der höchsten Noth noch befreit, das Seltene, Schwerste,—das preist es heilig."

" No people could live that did not, in the first place, value. If it would maintain itself it must not value as its neighbor doth . . .

A table of values hangeth over each people. Behold, it is the table of its overcomings; behold, it is the voice of its will to power.

That is laudable which is reckoned hard; what is indispensable and hard is named good; and that which freeth from the extremest need, the rare, the hardest,—that is praised as holy."

And, without mentioning nationalities by name, Nietzsche sketches with a few bold fresco strokes the salient ideal of the Greek, the Persian, the Jew, and then continues:

"'Treue üben und um der Treue willen Ehre und Blut auch an böse und gefährliche Sachen setzen': also sich lehrend bezwang sich ein anderes Volk, und also sich bezwingend wurde es schwanger und schwer von grossen Hoffnungen." [17]

"'To keep faith and, for the sake of faith, risk honor and blood in evil and dangerous affairs'—thus teaching itself another people conquered itself, and thus conquering became pregnant and heavy with great hopes."

The reference is to Germany,—even to a Germany seen through Romantic eyes, and it shows how Nietzsche could at the same time castigate his country mercilessly and feel himself linked to it by a bond of common striving.

It would be an interesting task to develop in broad outlines the major trends of the German's analysis of his own national character from the second half of the eighteenth through the nineteenth and into the twentieth century. From the time of Herder down, we should find in the main that the fundamental lines of his spiritual self-portrait are conditioned both by a sense of difference and by a will to differentiate himself from his western neighbor.[18] And we should find that the interpretations of the German spirit fall into two distinct classes, depending upon the perspective chosen. If only Germany and France are in the focus, we find Germany portrayed as the opposite of France; if, on the other hand, the point of view embraces all of Europe and the Orient within its field, with the spotlight centered upon Germany, we should find assigned to the German spirit the rôle of mediator between the civilization of the Latin countries and the philosophy of life of the Orient. On the basis of the more restricted point of view, France and Germany are very apt to be viewed by the German as standing to each other in the relation of "Sein" to "Werden", of being to becoming,—a relation stressed at the time of the national awakening by Novalis, Görres, Fichte, Kleist, and echoed by all their lesser followers in an attempt to make a virtue out of necessity,—a heroic attempt, in truth, for a very positive virtue springs from this rivalry. In a somewhat different way, the enormously vivid, if facile, play in which Heine, a generation later, indulges with the concepts German and French is the application of his axiomatic—if not always conscious—assumption that German and French must correspond to each other as precise complementary opposites, embracing between them all the basic values of humanity. But even where the wider point of view is attempted, as in Adam Müller's thesis of the Germans as "das Volk der Mitte", as the people destined to mediate between West and East, there is an acute consciousness of difference between the French and the German genius. In Adam Müller's philosophizing, incidentally, supreme importance attaches to the concept of "Vermittlung"—mediation— and hence to the nation in which this principle is, as it were, incarnate. It would be interesting to follow up the concrete applications of all this ideology, but such a study would, of course, far exceed the scope of this essay. Yet it was necessary at least to touch upon these prin-

ciples of perspective, as it goes without saying that all of Thomas
Mann's musings about the nature and the mission of the German
genius are conditioned by this long tradition of national philosophizing and derive support from it at every point. We cannot afford to
forget at any moment that every attempt to formulate national
character involves perspective, and that this holds true in a very
special sense when a nation's character is symbolically portrayed in
a concrete individual, like Hans Castorp; and perspective, by its
very nature, involves foreshortening, idealization, and the elimina-
tion of subordinate features. As regards the case we are about to
consider in detail, it should be remarked that this necessity of foreshortening has led to interesting results: While Hans Castorp figures
as the representative of the German spirit in the broadest sense, his
cousin Joachim Ziemssen typifies in an outstanding way a special
peculiarity of the German ethos,—its "military" side, in the symbolic code of the "Zauberberg", as contrasted to the "civilian" ethos
of Hans Castorp himself; and this contrast is fundamental, provided
we do not forget that, in a higher sense, Hans Castorp's civilian ethos
comes to embrace within it the military ethos as one of its essential
components. Moreover, as if to remind us that there is a very real
difference between the spirit of Germany and Germany in the flesh,
Hans Castorp and his cousin are made to rub shoulders every day
with that incarnation of middle-class vulgarity, Frau Stöhr, herself
a sufficiently common phenomenon of German actuality.

But how did Hans Castorp come to take shape in his author's
mind as a representative of things German?

When the War broke out, its immediate effect upon Thomas Mann
was the total paralysis of his artistic work. He felt an inner compulsion to concern himself solely with the spiritual issues raised by the
War, to search his own soul to discover whither his own inmost
sympathies tended, and to justify them by a long and arduous process
of rationalization. Three years were spent in the writing of his bulky
volume on the War, the "Betrachtungen eines Unpolitischen". Instinctively Thomas Mann sided with his country. The cause of
Germany was his own cause, and he identified himself wholeheartedly

with Germany's embattled armies. That does not mean, however,
that he was ever a one hundred per cent patriot, or that he ever saw
the intellectual and moral issue of the War as a case of white versus
black, good versus evil, God versus the Devil. On the contrary, for
Thomas Mann the most fundamental distinction between the German
spirit and that of Western Liberalism lay in the fact that, while to
the mentality of the West the issue seemed to resolve itself into a
choice between black and white, the German simply could not see
it in terms of such a cleancut antithesis. In his War Book Thomas
Mann is from the outset quite clear upon one point, namely, that
a rational defense of spiritual Germany is a vastly more difficult
undertaking than any such exposition of the ideology of the Western
Allies.[19] This for two reasons: first, because Germany, spiritually
considered, is not a disciplined phalanx, but rather a house divided
against itself, both as regards its intellectual standard bearers taken
as a group and as regards the individual German personality. In
Thomas Mann's formulation: "Seelischer Kampfplatz für europäische
Gegensätze zu sein: das ist deutsch" [20] ("To be a spiritual battle-
ground for European issues—that is German"). The German genius,
according to Mann, does not subscribe to the formula "either-or",
but rather to the formula "the one as well as the other". Not an
out-and-out choice between opposites, but rather the inclusion of
opposites, and the attempt to reconcile them as best one may, is
characteristically German. (The perspective, we already see, is
essentially the same as Adam Müller's.)[21] In the second place,
however, granting a provisional antithesis between the German and
the Western spirit, and pushing this antithesis to its most extreme
limit, as is bound to happen in time of war, we find perched as riders
on the opposite ends of the see-saw, rationalism and irrationalism
known by their more familiar labels as "Civilization" and "Kultur"
respectively. Now, in the very nature of things, the attempt to
speak in defense of the irrationalistic extreme suffers from an in-
surmountable handicap:—To employ language, argument, logic in
defense of the irrational—is not that sheer folly? If the defender
of irrationalism can be baited, tricked, cajoled into using reason as

his weapon, what conceivable outcome can there be to the contest except his defeat? Is he not yielding himself as beaten from the outset? This is the question Thomas Mann ponders in the initial pages of his War Book, and with Dostoevsky to lean upon for support, he characterizes Germany as "das unliterarische Land", as the country that is mute and inarticulate in the face of the world's challenge,[22] and he comes back to this point time and again.[23] Germany, however, while lacking the power of articulate speech, has its own vehicle of expression, and that is "music"—music in quotation marks; for music, in the code language of the "Betrachtungen"—like the "Zauberberg" it is written in code and full of pitfalls for the reader who takes it literally!—music stands for the language of the emotions, for poetry in the broadest sense, as it already does to E. T. A. Hoffmann a century earlier. But can music be used as a weapon, can it bite and sever? Therein lies the absurdity of the undertaking of spiritual Germany to stand up in defense against the articulate aggression of Western thought!

Thomas Mann's philosophizing about Germany in his War Book moves on two distinct planes. Theoretically, he does not subscribe to that simple view of things that makes of German Kultur and Western Civilization two out-and-out opposites. He endeavors rather to see Germany as representing a medial position between Western (French) rationalism on the one hand and Eastern (Russian) mysticism on the other,—a position between a philosophy keyed to action and one keyed to contemplation. Leaning on the Romanticist Adam Müller and more directly on Nietzsche,[24] he interprets Germany as "das Volk der Mitte". "Ist nicht deutsches Wesen die Mitte, das Mittlere und Vermittelnde und der Deutsche der mittlere Mensch im grossen Stile?"[25] (". . . the people of the middle. Is it not essentially German to occupy a middle ground and to mediate? Does not the German typify the mean on a large scale?"), he asks. And he pictures it as Germany's mission in the concert of nations to act the part of moderator and stabilizer rather than that of ruler. He speaks of Germany's function as that of a European ferment.[26] Particularly as the War progresses, it seems more and more doubtful to him that a nation so torn by internal discord as the German should be qualified to hold the reins of government and speak the deciding word in the clamor of national rivalries.[27] This is Thomas Mann's theoretical position. In practice, however, his War Book all but loses sight of the Eastern pole of his philosophical antithesis. This was bound to be the case at a time when the East had joined forces with the West, and when Russia's voice, in so far as it was articulate, had chosen to swell the chorus of Western Liberalism. In practice Thomas Mann finds himself forced to the stand of playing off Germany's point of view against that of France as if they were out-and-out opposites. It is inherent in the nature of all argument to overstrain vital antagonisms, to turn and twist every problem until its complexities yield a distinct cleavage of hostile abstractions, to be pitted against each other as mutually exclusive alternatives. In Thomas Mann's case this tendency was enhanced by the fact that he saw the French thesis aggressively impersonated in his own brother Heinrich Mann, thereby adding an intensely bitter personal touch to the rivalry of conflicting principles. And it made the feud no less poignant that Thomas Mann realized to what an enormous extent the tendencies combated by him as characteristically Western and French formed part of the web of his own personality, and that every stroke directed against his brother cut deeply into his own vital tissues. Time and again Thomas Mann ponders this paradox, as when he says:

"(Der Zivilisationsliterat) will und betreibt eine Entwicklung,—die ich für notwendig, das heisst: für unvermeidlich halte; an der auch ich meiner Natur nach unwillkürlich in gewissem Grade teilhabe; der zuzujauchzen ich aber gleichwohl keinen Grund sehe. Er fördert mit Peitsche und Sporn einen Fortschritt,—der mir, nicht selten wenigstens, als unaufhaltsam und schicksalsgegeben erscheint, und den an meinem bescheidenen Teile zu fördern, mein eigenes Schicksal ist; dem ich aber trotzdem aus dunklen Gründen eine gewisse konservative Opposition bereite." [28]

"The ententophile intellectual desires and promotes a development—that I regard as necessary, that is, as unescapable; a development to which, by my nature, I also involuntarily contribute to a certain degree; for all that, however, I see no reason to hail it with cheers. With whip and spur he promotes a progress—which seems to me, not infrequently at any rate, irresistible and fated; as my fate would have it I am doing my own modest share to the same end; yet for obscure reasons I am at the same time standing in a certain conservative opposition to it."

This does not keep him, however, from confessing to the feeling—

"das Gefühl, das mich zu Anfang des Krieges bis in den Grund meines Wesens beherrschte, dass ich nicht hätte leben—ohne im geringsten ein Held und todesmutig zu sein, buchstäblich nicht weiter hätte leben mögen, wenn Deutschland vom Westen geschlagen, gedemütigt, im Glauben an sich selbst gebrochen worden wäre, so dass es sich 'schicken' und die Vernunft, die *ratio* der Feinde hätte annehmen müssen."[29]

"the feeling that at the beginning of the War possessed me to the core of my being that, without in the least being a hero or eager to face death, I should literally not have cared to go on living, if Germany had been beaten by the West, humiliated, broken in its faith in itself, and forced to 'be good' and accept the philosophy of reason of the enemy."

a confession for which it would be only too easy to find a thousand duplicates in both embattled camps.

For three years Thomas Mann mulled over the intellectual issues raised by the War, for three years he analyzed, dissected, and argued, twisting the concepts "Zivilisation" and "Kultur" so that they glittered in a bewildering variety of facets. He felt the compulsion to do so if he were to keep on living, and his enormous mastery of dialectics supplied enough zest to make the task endurable. All that time, however, he was aware of an inner voice protesting against all this intellectualistic argument, against the procedure of turning "vital" dissonances into logical abstractions that glared at each other across an unbridgeable chasm. It was the voice of the creative artist pleading his case against the dialectician, and this voice rises above the din of the argument in many passages of the War Book, but most clearly and steadily in the following memorable passage that takes its cue from the title of one of Thomas Mann's early War essays, not incorporated in the "Betrachtungen eines Unpolitischen":

"Es gibt unkörperhafte, flächige, einäugig-einseitige Geistesprodukte, die dennoch—und zwar wohl gar schon in ihrem Titel—das Gepräge des 'Ästhetizismus' tragen. 'Gedanken im Kriege' zum Beispiel,—das wäre ein solcher Titel.[30] Es wäre eine Einschränkung, der Ausdruck einer Bedingtheit dieser Gedanken, einer *reservatio mentalis*, um mich jesuitisch

"There are two-dimensional, flat-surfaced, one-eyed and one-sided intellectual productions that nevertheless—perhaps in their very title—bear the stamp of 'aestheticism'. 'Thoughts in Wartime', for example, would be such a title. Such a title would indicate that these thoughts are valid in a limited way only. It would involve a mental reservation, to use that Jesuit

auszudrücken, der Vorbehalt jemandes, der weiss, dass Kriegsgedanken notwendig anders aussehen, als Gedanken im Frieden, der überdies weiss, dass durchaus *alles* bloss Gesagte bedingt und angreifbar ist, so absolut und apodiktisch es auch im Augenblick empfunden werden und sich gebärden möge, und unangreifbar einzig und allein die Gestalt; dass die köstliche Überlegenheit der Kunst über das bloss Intellektuelle in ihrer lebendigen Vieldeutigkeit, ihrer tiefen Unverbindlichkeit, ihrer geistigen *Freiheit* besteht. . . . Man muss durchaus verstehen, dass jemand, der nicht gewohnt ist, direkt und auf eigene Verantwortung zu reden, sondern gewohnt, die Menschen, die Dinge reden zu lassen,— dass jemand, der *Kunst* zu machen gewohnt ist, das Geistige, das Intellektuelle *niemals ganz ernst nimmt*, da seine Sache vielmehr von jeher war, es als Material und Spielzeug zu behandeln, Standpunkte zu vertreten, Dialektik zu treiben, den, der gerade spricht, immer recht haben zu lassen. . . . Der intellektuelle Gedanke im Kunstwerk wird nicht verstanden, wenn man ihn als Zweck seiner selbst versteht; er ist nicht literarisch zu werten,—was selbst raffinierte Kritiker zuweilen vergessen oder nicht wissen; er ist zweckhaft in Hinsicht auf die Komposition, er will und bejaht sich selbst nur in Hinsicht auf diese, er kann banal sein, absolut und literarisch genommen, aber geistreich innerhalb der Komposition.'' [31]

phrase, a tacit admission that thoughts in wartime necessarily look different from peace-time thoughts; it would involve the realization, moreover, that all mere pronouncements are relative and vulnerable, regardless of the pretensions to absoluteness and finality with which they may be felt and uttered, and that only the shapes of aesthetic creation are impervious to the ravages of time. The precious superiority of the product of art over that of mere intellect consists in its protean vitality, its non-committal independence, its spiritual freedom. . . . It is by all means necessary to understand that a person who is not accustomed to speak directly and on his own responsibility, but accustomed rather to let men and things speak with their own voice—that a person who is accustomed to make *art*, in other words, never takes intellectual matters absolutely seriously, since it has always been his wont to use them as material for aesthetic play, to experiment with points of view, to practise dialectics, to be always identified with that character who happens to be speaking at that moment. To take an intellectual idea proffered in a work of art, as an end in itself, is to misunderstand it; it is not to be judged on its intellectual merits,—a fact that even subtle critics are at times prone to forget; it is contrived with an eye to the compositional scheme; it claims validity solely within this scheme. Taken absolutely and on its own merits, it may be banal; while taken in its setting it may impress one as brilliant.''

This is the personal confession of an artist, and aside from being a confession it is a truly classic formulation of the ideal relation of content to form in the literary work of art. It explains why Thomas Mann, having fought his long word duel and the din of strife still in his ear, was under compulsion to take those discordant voices a second time and fashion them into "music", to take those dissonances and let them develop in a vital medium affording the basis for an inclusive harmony. On whatever lines the "Zauberberg" may originally have been planned, it explains why Thomas Mann now had to expose his impressionable young hero to the political eloquence of the Western rationalist on the one hand, and to the silent, wholly unliterary but ineffably seductive lure of the East on the other, resulting in an inner tension that made for growth. It explains why this same young man, no longer altogether guileless and inexperienced, is later subjected to the crossfire of two highly articulate pedagogues, our Western friend having found his match in the ex-Jew Jesuit whose logic, compounded of medieval conservatism and modern ultra-radicalism, is full of dangerous pitfalls for the unwary. It explains why, after having benefited from this crossfire, after having learned to judge with reservations and to differentiate the positive elements of value in the position of each from their exaggerated pretensions, our young hero is finally confronted with the phenomenon of personality in the weird figure of the Dutch coffee king, as a dynamic and magnetic entity, an indefinable—a mystical force, in the presence of which the ardor of the debaters wilts and their words, usually catapulted with unerring aim, fall as though dead to the ground. And it explains, among other things, why the tension between Settembrini and Naphta, having reached an intolerable pitch, finds its release in the physical challenge when Naphta is stung beyond endurance by having his way of arguing branded as an act of infamy.[32] That same epithet "Infamie", hurled at Thomas Mann by his brother Heinrich, had made the author of the "Betrachtungen" turn livid with controlled rage, and the tensest pages of the War Book are concerned with the refutation of this charge.[33] Not as though Settembrini and Naphta were in any way portrait likenesses of Heinrich and Thomas Mann respectively, even in their manner of arguing, despite the obvious similarity of Settembrini's and Heinrich Mann's ideology[34]: Settembrini has a warmth and generosity signally lacking in the literary personality of Heinrich

Mann, the master of the satirical grotesque; and Thomas Mann's reverence for continuity and tradition is certainly far removed from the nihilistic argumentativeness of the *déraciné* Naphta. Nevertheless, in making Naphta manifest an unbridled will to murder, Thomas Mann unquestionably makes him the exponent of impulses and emotions that clamored for release in his own heart when the feud with his brother was at its height. By letting the feud in the novel run its whole course to its ghastly but aesthetically satisfying conclusion; by overcoming, on the plane of aesthetic creation, the inhibitions that curbed his highly civilized self in actual life, Thomas Mann succeeded in "sublimating" the poison that festered in his system.

This was Thomas Mann's way of converting din into "music". It enabled him to envisage spiritual Germany, in contrast to the stark reality of the War, as steering its course between East and West, between vociferous individualistic liberalism and equally vociferous communistic radicalism, inclining its ear to both in turn, and learning from both alike, but selling its soul to neither. In so far as Hans Castorp represents spiritual Germany, then, his features correspond only in part to those of actual Germany; at the time of this writing certainly, and for all time possibly, they represent in large measure a wish projection of Thomas Mann's, an idealized expression of the direction of spiritual Germany's gropings and strivings through devious error. Thomas Mann would be the first to concede this, only qualifying his concession, I am convinced, by the reminder that a nation's ideal projections of itself, if made in a spirit of sincerity and humility, not by its official spokesmen but by its poets, are to that extent a revelation of its deepest self, and that, furthermore, the formulation of these wish projections is a step in the direction of their realization.

Let us now see concretely how the character of spiritual Germany, as interpreted by Thomas Mann, is mirrored in the person and the adventurings of Hans Castorp,—this young man whom, with his light ironic touch, Thomas Mann would fain introduce to us as altogether "mediocre", if the word were not barred by respect for his fate, "dem wir eine gewisse überpersönliche Bedeutung zuzuschreiben geneigt sind" [35] ("to which we are inclined to ascribe a certain over-individual significance").

To begin with, there is Hans Castorp's relation to music and, involved with it, his relation to language,—a double topic that might in itself amply fill a well-documented chapter. Music is the medium toward which he instinctively turns, as a flower does to sunlight. Music puts his whole being into a state of gentle vibration, stimulating all his faculties without making any precise demands upon any one of them, and inducing a general receptivity allied to that perfect equipoise of the aesthetic attitude described by Schiller in his letters "Über die aesthetische Erziehung des Menschen".[36] This intimacy of music's appeal remains the same for Hans Castorp throughout his sojourn at Davos and all the development it involves. There is no difference in kind, merely a difference in degree, between the somnolent nature of his response at the outset to musical harmonies however trivial, and the deep rapture of his absorption years later in the strains of his favorite records: "Aïda", "L'après-midi d'un Faune", "Carmen", "Valentin's Prayer", and "Der Lindenbaum",—records which express through the medium of a universal language of the emotions his own most intimate basic experiences, his "Urerlebnisse" of Loyalty, Death, Freedom, and Eros, with their varyingly blended ethos of reverence and boldness. There is no doubt about Hans Castorp being disposed toward the musical-contrapuntal way of responding to life that Thomas Mann regards as peculiarly German.[37] And with unerring instinct his Western mentor detects this disposition at an early stage of their relations and warns of its insidious dangers. Like Mephisto,[38] companion of another object of hermetic pedagogy, Settembrini feels a deep-seated aversion to music—for different reasons, naturally, which do not destroy the relevance of the analogy. In Settembrini's parlance, music is "politisch verdächtig",[39] politically suspect, because its stimulation is essentially vague and non-committal. As pure form, pledged to no specific content and idea, it is non-ethical; to the extent, therefore, that it acquires a dominating influence over man it is an obstacle in the path of activity and progress. From the point of view of a philosophy of life committed to action, music is a dangerous opiate, rightly to be classed with other drugs. "Bier, Tabak und Musik. Da haben wir Ihr Vaterland!" [40] ("Beer, tobacco, and music. Behold the Fatherland!")—that was Settembrini's opening shot in the first of his lectures on the subject. And he subscribes cordially to the observation, if not to the attitude of the author of the "Betracht-ungen", who remarked:

"Das Verhältnis der Musik zur Hu-manität ist so bei weitem lockerer, als das der Literatur, dass die musikalische Einstellung dem literarischen Tugend-sinn mindestens als unzuverlässig, mindestens als verdächtig erscheint",

"The relation of music to social idealism (Humanität) is so much less close than that of literature (with a purpose), that the musical outlook is eyed askance by literary virtue as unreliable, at the very least, as suspect",

and went on to say with regard to poetry (Dichtung):

"Es steht damit allzu ähnlich, wie mit der Musik; das Wort und der Geist spielen darin eine allzu indi-rekte, verschlagene, unverantwortliche und darum ebenfalls unzuverlässige Rolle." [41]

"In this regard poetry is altogether too similar to music; in poetry too, the word and the spirit play an all too indirect, furtive, irresponsible and unreliable rôle."

Music, taken in this its widest connotation; and intellect, political virtue:—the antagonism is fundamental. One thinks of Plato's ver-dict excluding the poets from his ideal republic. One thinks of Nie-tzsche's warning: "'Cave musicam' ist auch heute noch mein Rath an Alle, die Manns genug sind, um in Dingen des Geistes auf Rein-lichkeit zu halten" [42] ("'Cave musicam' is to this day my advice to all who are man enough to insist on cleanliness in matters of spirit"). And it is both amusing and instructive to compare Settem-brini's strictures against music with an almost identical utterance on the part of an arch-musician who was, paradoxically enough, an arch-propagandist at the same time, and who criticizes the short-comings of absolute music, that is music lacking the interpretive sup-port of words, as follows:

"Sie ist, in ihrer unendlichsten Steiger-ung, doch immer nur *Gefühl;* sie tritt im *Geleite* der sittlichen Tat, nicht

"Music, no matter how infinitely it soar, always remains mere feeling. It presents itself in company with

aber als *Tat selbst* ein; sie kann Gefühle und Stimmungen nebeneinander stellen, nicht aber nach Notwendigkeit eine Stimmung aus der andern entwickeln;—ihr fehlt *der moralische Wille.*" [43]

moral activity, but not as that activity itself. It can range feelings and moods alongside of one another, but it cannot evolve one mood as succeeding another by necessity:— It lacks moral will."

It is none other than Richard Wagner, the forty-eighter, who thus brands music as suspect in the best vein of the political moralist.[44]

While Hans Castorp's relation to music is intimate in the extreme, the converse is true of his relation to speech. If we search Lodovico Settembrini's life for the "Urerlebnis" that determines its pattern, we unquestionably find it in the magnetism of language, whereas in Hans Castorp's case articulate thought is conspicuously absent from the sphere of his "Urerlebnisse" of Loyalty, Death, Freedom, and Eros. What holds true of the small boy's earliest observations regarding the sphere of life represented by his venerable grandfather, applies to all these basic experiences of his; they were

"wortlose und also unkritische, vielmehr nur lebensvolle Erfahrungen, die übrigens auch später, als bewusstes Erinnerungsbild, ihr wort- und zergliederungsfeindliches, schlechthin bejahendes Gepräge durchaus bewahrten." [45]

"not phrased in words and therefore uncritical—they were merely vital experiences. And in later life too, persisting as the elements of a perfectly conscious memory picture, they defied expression in words and analysis, but they were none the less positive for all that."

And in this fundamental aspect Hans Castorp and his cousin are most closely akin. Both of them are intensely German in this respect, even though they come, in course of time, to represent two widely divergent manifestations of the German spirit, Hans Castorp's "civilian" temperament developing a staggering faculty of assimilation and expansion, while the "military" Joachim remains essentially static.

In Hans Castorp's realm of values the spoken word has a low rating. Logical analysis, articulate communication are matters of little moment in the young man's life. They belong to the social sphere, life's superficial layer, and do not touch the incommunicable core of individual experience.[46] He has given little thought to their use, and in matters that really count he feels silence to be a more expressive medium of communication. This instinctive valuation persists in large measure even after he has acquired facility in the use of language thanks to the stimulation of the hermetic pedagogy. Examples in abundance suggest themselves: After Hans Castorp has sat for the first time through one of Krokowski's psycho-analytic lectures, neither he nor his cousin alludes to the subject, "wie nach schweigender Übereinkunft" [47] ("as though by silent accord"), because the matter is one that affects them profoundly. When he goes to present himself for his first physical examination, Hans walks down the corridor with Joachim "in schweigendem Einverständnis" [48] ("in silent agreement").   When they visit the "moribundi" together, Joachim having first expressed his reluctance "durch Schweigen und Niederschlagen der Augen" [49] ("by silence and by casting down his eyes"), they observe that these people about to pass into the great beyond are all preoccupied with trifles, but their comment is a matter of silence. [50]   Up in the mountain cemetery, where they have taken Karen Karstedt for an outing, their eyes dwell on a little angel with a cap of snow, his finger held against his lip, and his figure impersonates to them the genius of silence, "und zwar eines Schweigens, das man sehr stark als Gegenteil und Widerspiel des Redens, als Verstummen also, keineswegs aber als inhaltsleer und ereignislos empfand" [51] ("a silence, moreover, that was very strongly felt as the opposite of speech, as an act of muteness, and by no means as insignificant and devoid of content"). Not a word passes between Hans and Joachim about the events of the night of the mardi gras, [52] or about Clavdia's departure and that of Marusya. [53]   After their first visit to Naphta, where they witnessed a disconcerting display of dialectics, we are told, as they start for home: "Sie schwiegen ein Stück Weges, aber ihr Schweigen handelte von Naphta" [54] ("They were silent for part of the way, but their silence spoke of Naphta"). Examples like these, easily multiplied, incidentally show "das Schweigen" to be one of the major themes of the "Zauberberg's" musical pattern.

But Hans Castorp's innermost feeling as regards the preciousness of silence in contrast to articulate speech is most convincingly revealed in his relations to Clavdia. The attentions he bestows on her are by gesture. He has no desire to speak with her or to enter into conventional social relations with her, such as involve speech, conventional speech at any rate. His daydreams about her are not built up around word nuclei. They are made of the incommunicable stuff of direct sense revery. In his mind he addresses her with the familiar "du", which has the value not so much of a word as of a caress. When they chance to meet in the waiting-room of the physician's office, it is to Joachim that Clavdia addresses her question, and it is he, and not Hans, who answers. On one occasion Hans Castorp trifles with his instinctive conviction and is promptly punished: Talking to Hermine Kleefeld he gives himself airs and affects a pointed eloquence and a modulation of voice copied from Settembrini,—all this for Clavdia's benefit, whose attention he would attract by this exhibition. And he finally succeeds; but the effect of her glance, which dwelt on his for a moment only to glide down deliberately to his shoe and remain fastened there, was such as to reduce him to abject misery for a full two days.[55] There comes a time, to be sure, when he talks to Clavdia, when the pent up passion of seven months pour from his half-paralyzed lips; but it is hardly as a vehicle of communication, rather as expression pure and simple, regardless of sense, that he employs language on that occasion. He is conscious of this, moreover; for in speaking he expresses his disdain of discourse as a sufficiently "republican" device, quite alien to the realm in which he feels at home, the realm of eternity, where there is no talking, where you do as when drawing little pigs: you bend your head backward and close your eyes. And for that reason he prefers to give utterance to his feelings in French, which is for him a make-believe language in which he can talk irresponsibly, just as he would in a dream.[56]

Settembrini's keen instinct detected Hans Castorp's native indifference to language during their very first meeting; and at once his pedagogical passion has found an object, and he concentrates on arousing him from his mental lethargy. By admonition, provocation, by example, most of all, Settembrini strives to make him exer-

cise his powers of analysis and logical judgment. His habitual slowness to take a decisive stand on new impressions Settembrini brands
as "Dumpfsinn"—mental apathy. "Urteilen Sie! Dafür hat die
Natur Ihnen Augen und Verstand gegeben" [57] ("Exercise your judgment! That's what nature has given you eyes for and understanding"), is his dictum. And at subsequent meetings he harps on the word
as the crowning triumph of humanity, the gist of his harangue being,

"das Wort sei die Ehre des Menschen, und nur dieses mache das Leben menschenwürdig. Nicht nur der Humanismus,—Humanität überhaupt, alle Menschenwürde, Menschenacht-ung und menschliche Selbstachtung sei untrennbar mit dem Worte, mit Literatur verbunden." [58]

"the word was the glory of mankind, it alone imparted dignity to life. Not only was humanism bound up with the word, and with literature, but so also was humanity itself, man's ancient dignity and manly self-respect."

To Settembrini's delight, Hans discovers in himself a remarkable
adeptness, hitherto dormant, in remembering and quoting Settembrini's finely chiselled phrases; and his own handling of speech derives an enormous incentive and stimulus from his mentor's illustrious example, although, in his rôle of novice, he refrains for a long
time from trying himself at connected discourse, overawed as he is
by the precise fluency of the Italian. But if Settembrini is overjoyed
to have found so apt a pupil, he also has reason to grieve at the use
his pupil makes of his talent: instead of using language to fashion
precise and cleancut judgments out of the material of his sense data,
Hans Castorp limits himself to formulations of a tentative and ex-
perimental sort. There is something slippery and elusive, something
decidedly mischievous about his way of hedging all his opinions with
reservations and his willingness to adopt every possible point of
view on a trial basis, and there is something of sly effrontery in his
adoption of Petrarch's motto: "Placet experiri". While acquiring
proficiency in the handling of his new tool, he obviously does not
attach the same value to it as his mentor. It is never admitted to
the sphere of his deepest reverence, it is never an adequate mirror
of his inmost self. And while in general he spars and feints with his
mentor-adversary, it may happen that when appealed to in a spirit
of intense seriousness and pressed to take sides on an issue of moment,

definitely and finally, he will again take refuge in a silence more expressive than any amount of talking. It is in considering a concrete instance of this sort that Hans Castorp's character as representative of spiritual Germany is brought home to us with peculiar force.

Settembrini has been haranguing Hans Castorp—by this time an old resident of Haus Berghof—on the great topic of politics. Speaking as a representative of free-masonry, he has summed up his stand in these sentences:

"Wir bekennen uns zur Politik, rückhaltslos, offen. Wir achten das Odium für nichts, das in den Augen einiger Toren—sie sitzen bei Ihnen zulande, Ingenieur, fast nirgends sonst—mit diesem Wort und Titel verbunden ist. Der Menschenfreund kann den Unterschied von Politik und Nichtpolitik überhaupt nicht anerkennen. Es gibt keine Nichtpolitik. Alles ist Politik." [59]

"We admit that we are political, admit it openly, unreservedly. We care nothing for the stigma that attaches to this word in the eyes of certain fools—they are at home in your own country, Engineer, and almost nowhere else. The friend of humanity cannot recognize a distinction between what is political and what is not. There is nothing that is not political. Everything is politics."

He has discoursed on the Protestant reformation in Germany, he has dwelt on the profoundly questionable composition of the personality of Luther, whose skull, cheek bones, and cut of eye, all of unmistakably Wendic-Slavic-Sarmatic cast, lead to the reflection that his career involved

"eine verhängnisvolle Überbelastung einer der beiden in Ihrem Lande so gefährlich gleichstehenden Schalen . . . , ein furchtbares Gewicht in die östliche, von welchem die andere, die westliche Schale, noch heute überwogen gen Himmel flattert . . ." [60].

"a fatal preponderance of one of the two scales which in your country hang so dangerously even, the scale of the East, so that the other even today is still outweighed and flies up in the air—"

And now a throb of deepest concern colors his voice, as he woos his pensive pupil with this direct appeal:

"Caro! Caro amico! Entscheidungen werden zu treffen sein,—Entscheidungen von unüberschätzbarer Tragweite für das Glück und die Zukunft Europas, und Ihrem Lande werden sie zufallen, in seiner Seele werden sie sich zu vollziehen haben.

"Caro! Caro amico! There will be decisions to make, decisions of unspeakable importance for the happiness and the future of Europe; it will fall to your country to decide, in her soul the decision will be con-

Zwischen Ost und West gestellt, wird es wählen müssen, wird es endgültig und mit Bewusstsein zwischen den beiden Sphären, die um sein Wesen werben, sich entscheiden müssen. Sie sind jung, Sie werden an dieser Entscheidung beteiligt sein, sind berufen, sie zu beeinflussen." [61]

summated. Placed as she is between East and West, she will have to choose, she will have to decide finally and consciously between the two spheres. You are young, you will have a share in this decision, it is your duty to influence it."

And with the utmost sincerity Settembrini pleads with him to awaken to his responsibility in contributing to a cleancut decision. And what is Hans Castorp's reaction to this plea?

"Hans Castorp sass, das Kinn in der Faust. Er blickte zum Mansardenfenster hinaus, und in seinen einfachen blauen Augen war eine gewisse Widerspenstigkeit zu lesen. Er schwieg." [62]

"Hans Castorp sat, his chin in his hand. He looked out of the mansard window, and in his simple blue eyes there was a certain obstinacy. He was silent."

Perhaps the most significant thing about this whole episode is Settembrini's comment on Hans Castorp's silence, being in essence a condensed recapitulation of the first two chapters of the "Betrachtungen eines Unpolitischen":

"'Sie schweigen', sprach Herr Settembrini bewegt. 'Sie und Ihr Land, Sie lassen ein vorbehaltvolles Schweigen walten, dessen Undurchsichtigkeit kein Urteil über seine Tiefe gestattet. Sie lieben das Wort nicht oder besitzen es nicht oder heiligen es auf eine unfreundliche Weise,—die artikulierte Welt weiss nicht und erfährt nicht, woran sie mit Ihnen ist. Mein Freund, das ist gefährlich. Die Sprache ist die Gesittung selbst . . . Das Wort, selbst das widersprechendste, ist so verbindend. . . . Aber die Wortlosigkeit vereinsamt.'" [63]

"You are silent. You and your native land, you preserve a silence which seems to cover a reservation— and which gives one no hint of what goes on in your depths. You do not love the word, or you have it not, or you are chary with it to unfriendliness. The articulate world does not know where it is with you. My friend, that is perilous. Speech is civilization itself. The word, even the most contradictious word, preserves contact—it is silence which isolates."

And he goes on to voice the concern of the Western world that this stubborn silence might be only the prelude to an act of war, in which there would be an equally representative rôle allotted to cousin Joachim as to Hans Castorp in time of peace. But here the ominous tension is relieved thanks to Settembrini's adeptness in the use of familiar quotations.

We are not left in the dark as to the content of Hans Castorp's silence on that occasion. At a later date, when Settembrini and Naphta are again sparring as usual for the young German's benefit and in order to provoke him to take sides, he makes the same face "voller Vorbehalt und Widerspenstigkeit" [64] ("full of reservation and obstinacy") that he had made on the former occasion and maintains silence,—a silence expressing the point of view of the German, the "Mensch der Mitte":

"Alles stellten sie auf die Spitze, diese zwei, wie es wohl nötig war, wenn man streiten wollte, und haderten erbittert um äusserste Wahlfälle, während ihm doch schien, als ob irgendwo inmitten zwischen den strittigen Unleidlichkeiten, zwischen rednerischem Humanismus und analphabetischer Barbarei das gelegen sein müsse, was man als das Menschliche oder Humane persönlich ansprechen durfte. Aber er sprach es nicht an, um nicht beide Geister zu ärgern, und sah, eingehüllt in Vorbehalt, wie sie weiter dahin trieben und einander feindlich behilflich waren, vom Hundertsten ins Tausendste zu kommen. . . ." [65]

"They forced everything to an issue, these two—as perhaps one must when one wants an argument—and wrangled bitterly over extremes, whereas it seemed to him, Hans Castorp, as though somewhere between two intolerable positions, between rhetorical humanism and analphabetic barbarism, must lie something which one might personally call the human. He did not express his thought, for fear of irritating them both; but, wrapped in his reserve, listened to the one goading the other on and being baited by the other in turn ad infinitum."

Once before, at the most critical moment of his life, he had put the case less charitably, when he had felt himself enshrouded in the primeval silence, the "Urschweigen" of the illimitable snow. Under its influence the two versatile debaters had shrunk to the rôle of mere "Schwätzer"—prattlers, both of them.[66] But had not his own character of mediator between extremes already been indelibly impressed upon him in that clinging memory image of himself as the youth in the boat, of a late summer evening, fascinated by the wonders of the western and the eastern sky equally, as he looked "aus der glasigen Tageshelle des westlichen Ufers vexierten und geblendeten Auges hinüber in die nebeldurchsponnene Mondnacht der östlichen Himmel" [67] ("with dazzled eyes from the glassy daylight of the western shore to the mist and moonbeams that wrapped the eastern heavens")?

"Sie lieben das Wort nicht oder besitzen es nicht oder heiligen es auf eine unfreundliche Weise" ("You do not love the word, or you have it not, or you are chary with it to unfriendliness"). With these words Settembrini had ruefully put his finger upon a difference of attitude as regards language that persisted throughout the give and take of the humanist's relations with the young German. Hans himself goes to the heart of the matter when he generalizes apologetically but with his tongue in his cheek all the same:

"Ich schwatze da Unsinn, aber ich will lieber ein bisschen faseln und dabei etwas Schwieriges halbwegs ausdrücken, als immer nur tadellose Hergebrachtheiten von mir geben,—das ist doch vielleicht auch so etwas wie ein militärischer Zug in meinem Charakterbilde, wenn ich so sagen darf. . . ." [68]

"I know I am talking nonsense, but I would rather make a stab at things in the hope of expressing something difficult half way incidentally, than always be spouting excellent platitudes.   Perhaps that is something like a military trait in my character, if I may say so."

—a sentiment to which Settembrini responds in his best style, with his inevitable rhetorical flourish, and quite unaware of the point directed at himself:

"Sagen Sie immerhin so.   Unbedingt wäre das ein Zug, den man loben dürfte.   Der Mut der Erkenntnis und des Ausdrucks, das ist die Literatur, es ist die Humanität. . . ." [69]

"You may say so. By all means a trait worthy of praise. The courage to discern and to express—that is literature, it is humanity."

It would be difficult to match this bit of dialogue for neatness and subtle humor in its expression of the fundamental difference between pupil and mentor.

But while this persistent difference is to be stressed, it must not lead us to overlook how enormously Hans Castorp's native reluctance to analyze his experiences in terms of speech has, after all, been modified.   By the time Peeperkorn enters upon the scene, Hans Castorp has acquired a fluency and control of language that does credit equally to pupil and mentor.   We not only hear him discourse like a past master of the art, but we are specifically told in connection with one of his verbal fencing matches:

"Neuerdings verwirrte und verhaspelte Hans Castorp sich nicht mehr bei solchen Expektorationen und blieb nicht stecken.   Er sprach seinen Part zu Ende, liess die Stimme sinken, machte Punktum und ging seines

"Nowadays, when Hans Castorp relieved his mind, he did not hem and haw, become involved and stick in the middle. He said his say to the end like a man, rounded off his period, let his voice drop and went

Weges wie ein Mann, obgleich er noch immer rot dabei wurde und eigentlich etwas Furcht hatte vor dem kritischen Schweigen, das seinem Verstummen folgen würde, damit er Zeit habe, sich zu schämen." [70]

his way; though he still got red, and at heart was still afraid of the silence he knew would follow when he had done, to give him time to feel mortified at what he had expressed."

Hans Castorp has learned not only to talk, but even to talk with a purpose; he has learned, that is, to forecast and calculate, in the act of speaking, the probable effect of his words upon his listener; to strike a judicious balance between the two foci of all speech: expression and communication. This is brought home to us on the night of Peeperkorn's bacchanalian party, where Hans Castorp has the brazen impudence of presuming to transform the half-articulated Dionysian emotions of the reeling colossus into civilized discourse, thereby provoking an access of choler that threatens to wreck the party; but as Peeperkorn's brow darkens and his fist is about to come down with the force of thunder, Hans Castorp's verbal adroitness succeeds in staying the outburst and effecting a perfectly harmless "abreaction" of the giant's wrath.[71] And in the tense bedside session where Hans brings to fruition his desire to make a clean breast of his intimacy with Peeperkorn's mistress, there is an admirably judicious—and calculated—blending of words striving to convey a situation down to its most fragile shadings of meaning, with silences equally expressive. Even the great Peeperkorn himself repeatedly condescends to pay tribute to Hans Castorp's skill in verbal expression: "Sie rühren, junger Mann, mit Ihrem gewandten kleinen Wort an heilige Gegebenheiten" [72] ("Young man, you are applying your adroit little phrases to the sacred conditions of our existence"), he begins on one occasion. "Ich lausche mit unwillkürlichem Vergnügen auf Ihr behendes kleines Wort, junger Mann. Es springt über Stock und Stein und rundet die Dinge zur Annehmlichkeit" [73] ("I listen with involuntary pleasure, young man, to your fluent little phrases. Your tongue runs on, it springs over stock and stone, and rounds off all the sharp corners"), he remarks a little later. "Sie haben das sehr artig—" [74] ("That you have very neatly—"), he says without finishing. And again: "Ich schätze die Artigkeit Ihres kleinen Wortes" [75] ("I appreciate the decorum of your little phrases"). All these disparagingly appreciative comments, however, leave no doubt as to the very restricted rating to which articulate speech is held down in the mystical realm of personality of the grand "format".

We are now in a position to summarize Hans Castorp's attitude toward language as reflecting that of spiritual Germany. During portions of this analysis the application to Germany was obvious. At times, however, the correspondence may have seemed doubtful. It is well for us to remind ourselves again that Hans Castorp, symbol of spiritual Germany, owes but some of his features to the long time trend of German character, while others are in the nature of anticipations and wish projections. The development of Hans Castorp is partly a record of achievement and partly a goal toward which spiritual Germany would be heading. Thomas Mann would not only have spiritual Germany contemplate Hans Castorp as its mirror image, but also read his career as a message.

Reading the "Zauberberg" with Thomas Mann's War Book, the "Betrachtungen" in mind, one finds the same fundamental intuition of the German national character in both, but one finds likewise that the emphasis of Thomas Mann's affirmations has perceptibly shifted. The War Book was based on the thesis that the German temperament inclines to a musically contemplative,—a "synthetic" way of embracing the world, and that "literary" expression, in so far as it uses language pre-eminently as a tool of analysis, is alien to it. Music and poetry are the characteristic German forms of expression, as prose literature is that of Western Civilization. In presenting us with the temperamental contrast of Hans Castorp and Lodovico Settembrini, the "Zauberberg" draws the same distinction; but here is the difference: Whereas in the War Book the German endeavored to entrench himself in the expressional sphere he claimed as his own and to combat the infiltration of Western influences, in the "Zauberberg" Thomas Mann subjects young Hans to the influence of the Western humanist and his logical discipline. Our author is acutely aware of the dangers inherent in the "musical" attitude; and, confident as he is that this musical attitude is too deeply ingrained to be easily supplanted, he would urge upon Germany the necessity—for her own sake and that of the world—of cultivating the virtues of her complementary opposite. Taking Hans Castorp as an example, Germany is not likely to succumb to the adoration of the word as a fetish, nor to abandon her music for the reverberating phrase; yet she is most seriously in need of modifying her native aversion to logical clarity and psychological analysis. For the sake of living up to her reputed universality, she needs to incline herself consciously to the rational pole without fear of endangering her irrational substratum. This is Thomas Mann's post-war message to Germany, and he has been tireless in his voicing of this conviction in the numerous essays that have flowed from his pen since 1922, thereby drawing upon himself the fire of all the irreconcilable elements of the old régime and that of the new nationalist movement as well. And it is due to this shifting of emphasis that the "Zauberberg", for all its German qualities, is tacitly or openly put upon the index by the conservative wing of the German intellectuals.

Yet to speak of this conviction of Thomas Mann's as if it were an altogether new phase of his post-war thinking would be to tell just one half the truth and to miss the other half. It would be much nearer the truth to say that it was also a part of his pre-war thinking and merely suffered an interruption during the War years. And only a partial interruption at that; for even in his most conservative German phase, when he strained himself to throw all his weight in the direction of the irrational pole, he knew and acknowledged that the drift of evolution was carrying Germany in the other direction, and that it could at most be retarded but not stopped. He knew and acknowledged furthermore that his own literary personality was one of the most outstanding symptoms of this drift: never before had Germany seen its own native genius of music so intimately wedded with the spirit of analytical prose. After a century of essentially "musical" expression Germany's course had been altered. There had been a new orientation in the direction of psychological analysis. Psychology had come to take the lead among the intellectual sciences, it had come to be regarded as the science par excellence.[76] This new orientation had been inaugurated by Nietzsche.[77] It was under the leadership of Nietzsche's spirit that German prose had been re-juvenated and fashioned into a supple and effective tool of psycho-logical analysis on a par with the prose of France.

Thus Hans Castorp's developing mastery of analytical prose, gradually superseding his native aversion to articulate utterance, reflects a novel achievement of the German spirit, an achievement deriving its impulse from Nietzsche and effected by Thomas Mann and his literary contemporaries. It is part of Germany's recent record and is chronicled symbolically in the "Zauberberg". This aspect of Hans Castorp's education to language we must keep in mind, with-out, however, losing sight of its other aspect, that of a summons and an imperative. And if, sensing a contradiction, we would differen-tiate between these two aspects by saying that Hans Castorp's record throws the emphasis upon achievement in so far as it reflects Thomas Mann's own development, whereas for Germany generally it represents an imperative and an ideal far from having found ful-filment, we have, I think, caught Thomas Mann's own meaning. Thomas Mann's genius is the genius of symbolic autobiography, and his exemplary sense of self-discipline and responsibility qualifies him to render a surpassingly objective appraisal of his own significance in the German world of letters,—in this respect like Goethe, who never stooped to false modesty.

We have seen Hans Castorp mirror Germany's relation to music and to language. We found his attitude toward these two spheres of expression to reveal a basic disposition of the national psyche, as inter-preted by Thomas Mann. In passing on now to the examination of other peculiarly German traits, we shall find them all bound up more or less with the temperamental trend manifested by this relation.

Such a correspondence is strikingly apparent in Hans Castorp's inclination to the theoretical as contrasted with the practical sphere. He has an enormous respect for work, but he feels more at home in contemplation. And this not only due to native inertia: his tranquil exterior often betrays by no sign the tremendous currents of sustained energy that circulate in his brain. As "phlegmatisch und energisch"

Settembrini characterizes the temper of Hans Castorp's country-men,[78]—a startling combination of qualities; and there is a distinct echo of this characterization in Hans Castorp's confession to Clavdia, years later: "Ich bin, offen gestanden, gar kein leidenschaftlicher Mensch, aber ich habe Leidenschaften, phlegmatische Leiden-schaften" [79] ("To tell the truth, I am not a passionate person, but I have passions, phlegmatic passions"). Hans is a philosopher, and by no means a pragmatist. Thought and speculation are endowed with value in his mental economy in themselves, regardless of any func-tional meaning attaching to them as impulses leading to action. In-stinctively he regards the world of ideas as a higher reality than the world of sense. He is so concerned with pondering man's relation to all the marvels of the cosmos—the unfathomable mystery of what is his environment and his heart tissue in one—that he cannot get excited over any practical schemes for refashioning one relatively insignificant domain of the great whole according to the desire of hearts like Settembrini's. This native inclination to high abstraction is even reflected in a certain haughtiness of his cast of features, re-peatedly dwelt upon. We do not grasp its significance when Hans Castorp is first introduced to us "mit seinem gut geschnittenen, irgendwie altertümlich geprägten Kopf, in dem ein ererbter und unbewusster Dünkel sich in Gestalt einer gewissen trockenen Schläf-rigkeit äusserte" [80] ("with his well-shaped head, which had about it a certain old-fashioned stamp, and his self-possessed, indolent bearing that expressed an innate, inherited, and perfectly unconscious self-esteem"); nor do we fully get the drift of a second hint to the same effect:

"Einsichtigerweise war Hans Castorp ganz ohne persönlichen Hochmut; aber ein Hochmut allgemeiner und weit hergeleiteter Art stand ihm ja auf der Stirn und um die etwas schläfrig blickenden Augen geschrieben, und aus ihm entsprang das Überlegenheitsge-fühl, dessen er sich beim Anblick von Frau Chauchats Sein und Wesen nicht entschlagen konnte noch wollte." [81]

"Hans Castorp was, for his own per-son, quite without arrogance; yet a larger arrogance, the pride of caste and tradition, stood written on his brow and in his rather sleepy-looking eyes, and voiced itself in the convic-tion of his own superiority, which came over him when he measured Frau Chauchat for what she was. It was this which he neither could, nor wished to, shake off."

It is reserved for the concluding pages to strike the theme of Hans Castorp's "Hochmut" once more, in explaining how the declaration of war struck him as a bolt from the blue. After recalling how Hans Castorp had all these years neglected to read the papers in spite of repeated admonitions to do so, Thomas Mann continues:

"Sein mittelländischer Freund und Mentor hatte dem immer ein wenig abzuhelfen gesucht und es sich angelegen sein lassen, das Sorgenkind seiner Erziehung in grossen Zügen zu unterrichten, hatte aber wenig Ohr bei einem Schüler gefunden, der sich zwar von den geistigen Schatten der Dinge regierungsweise das eine und andere träumen liess, der Dinge selbst aber nicht geachtet hatte und zwar aus der Hochmutsneigung, die Schatten für die Dinge zu nehmen, in diesen aber nur Schatten zu sehen,—weswegen man ihn nicht einmal allzu hart schelten darf, da dies Verhältnis nicht letztgültig geklärt ist." [82]

"His Mediterranean friend and mentor had ever tried to prompt him; had felt it incumbent upon him to instruct the problem child of his solicitude in what was going on down below; but his pupil had lent no ear. The young man had indeed, in his amateurish way, preoccupied himself with this or that among the spiritual shadows of things; but the things themselves he had been too haughty to heed at all, having a wilful tendency to take the shadow for the thing, and in the thing to see only shadow. For this, however, we must not judge him too harshly, since the relative value of shadow and thing has never been defined once and for all."

This time we understand—with the glint of a smile that fades into meditative silence.

On many an occasion the humanist had tried to counteract Hans Castorp's philosophical tendency; never more pointedly than when his pupil's laconic remark, "Kann ich mir denken" ("I can imagine"), provoked him to this sally:

"Sie können sich wenig denken, Ingenieur. Wähnen Sie nicht, sich von Haus aus viel denken zu können, sondern suchen Sie aufzunehmen und zu verarbeiten—ich bitte Sie darum in Ihrem eigenen Interesse, wie in dem Ihres Landes und im europäischen Interesse. . . ." [83]

"You can imagine little, Engineer. Don't fancy you can get very far by imagining things. Try rather to use your sense faculties and digest what they report—I say this in your own interest, as in that of your country and of Europe."

In many an amusing trifle Hans Castorp's love of theorizing betrays itself, as if the essential value of life lay in its affording a basis for theorizing, and as if the intellectual pleasure experienced in finding the individual fact express the general theory made the pleasant or

unpleasant character of the fact itself a matter of altogether subordinate moment. Thus part of his zest in the study of plant life
comes from this intellectual pleasure:—Hans Castorp "stellte die
wissenschaftliche Richtigkeit in dem Bau ihm bekannter Pflanzen
mit Befriedigung fest" [84] ("Hans Castorp felt a satisfaction in ascer-
taining the scientific correctness in the structure of the plants he
knew")—a delightfully characteristic German way, this, of reversing
the order of phenomena! The weather is abominable, and he dis-
courses to perfection on the confusion of the seasons prevailing in
these altitudes, prompting the gentle Joachim to remark caustically:
"Danke sehr. Und nun, wo du es erklärt hast, da bist du, glaub' ich,
so zufrieden, dass du unter anderm auch mit der Sache selbst zufrieden bist" [85] ("Much obliged. And now that you have explained it
you are so satisfied, I believe, that you are even satisfied with the
situation itself"). And the same humorous note is present during the
most critical moments of his skiing expedition, when he experiences
all the symptoms of a man who has hopelessly lost his bearings:

"So irrte man herum, so fand man nicht heim. Hans Castorp erkannte das überlieferte Phänomen mit einer gewissen Befriedigung, wenn auch mit Schrecken, und schlug sich auf den Schenkel vor Grimm und Staunen, weil sich das Allgemeine in seinem eigentümlichen, individuellen und gegenwärtigen Fall so pünktlich ereignet hatte." [86]

"You wandered about without getting home. Hans Castorp recognized the traditional phenomenon with a certain grim satisfaction—and even slapped his thigh in dismay and astonishment at this general law fulfilling itself in his particular case so punctually."

And is the honest and conscientious Joachim himself altogether
free from this German tendency to accept a theoretical substitution
for a practical end? He has no intellectual temptations, he has
only the one thought of getting himself fit to perform his "Dienst im
Flachland"; even so his meticulous observance of the prescribed
routine has at times all the characteristics of a satisfaction experienced in going through empty motions as if they were the coveted
end. Hans Castorp is quick to perceive this side of Joachim's "mili-
tärische Ehrbarkeit",—

"eine Ehrbarkeit, die, freilich ohne es gewahr zu werden, schon im Begriffe

"military propriety,—a propriety which, even though unconsciously,

stand, im Kurdienste Genüge zu finden, so dass dieser gleichsam zum Ersatz-mittel tiefländischer Pflichterfüllung und zum untergeschobenen Berufe wurde,—Hans Castorp war nicht so dumm, es nicht ganz genau zu bemerken." [87]

was on the point of finding satisfaction in the service of the cure, of substituting it for the service down below and making of it an interim profession. Hans Castorp was not so dull as not to perceive this."

But Joachim, infinitely lovable in his simplicity,[88] succeeds, thanks to his limitations, in breaking through the charmed circle at last, of his own will, while his cousin remains bound until released by the thunderclap.

A variety of other traits indicate Hans Castorp's theoretical, his scholarly temperament. He has a high degree of inbred tolerance. Thus he watches the grotesque antics of Adriatica von Mylendonck "mit all der bescheiden duldsamen und vertrauensvollen Menschenfreundlichkeit, die ihm angeboren war" [89] ("with all the modestly tolerant and trustful kindliness that was part of his nature"). He is in no hurry to pass judgment on phenomena that strike him as novel, such as the idea, for instance, of one's having for a grandfather a radical and an agitator, and of one's airing that fact with pride. In connection with his learning of Settembrini's ancestry we read: "Auch hütete er sich redlich, das Fremdartige zu verurteilen, sondern hielt sich an, es bei Vergleich und Feststellung bewenden zu lassen" [90] ("He honorably refrained from condemning what he did not understand, but simply made mental note of the contrast and let it go at that"). In general, his is the manner of one who lets "die Dinge an sich herankommen" [91]—things approach him at leisure, a phrase so often used in German in connection with Goethe's so-called "gegenständliches Denken" (objective thinking) as to stamp Hans Castorp's approach as very eminently German. Hans Castorp, while not interested in politics, has a strongly developed historical sense. Instinctively he thinks of the counterpart in his own country to Settembrini's grandfather, the radical barrister, as "ein grosser Rechtsgelehrter"; [92] for greatness in the field of law, if running at all true to the type of national genius manifested during the nineteenth century, would have been bound to take the form of passionate agitation in the one country and of profound historical scholarship in the other. Hans Castorp is a true German in his ingrained respect for authority and in his indifference to the political ideal of self-government. He and his cousin cannot even pay their weekly bill without instinctively feeling that the official window as such calls for an air of deference,—"wie junge Deutsche, die die Achtung vor der Behörde, der Amtsstube auf jedes Schreib- und Dienstlokal übertragen" [93] ("like young Germans, whose respect for authority leads them to be a bit overawed in the presence of pens, ink, and paper, or anything else which bears to their mind an official stamp"). The word "Dienst", in all its connotations, has the force of a veritable fetish upon the German mentality; in all its compounds and derivatives the word "Dienst" is probably more frequently met with in the "Zauberberg" than any other word, and with very conscious intent: in the first of his War essays Thomas Mann had hailed it as "das deutscheste Wort, das Wort Dienst".[94] Settembrini refers to this state of things very pointedly on more than one occasion. His first remarks on the subject, aimed at Joachim specifically, take their cue from the regularity of Joachim's attendance at the Sunday morning concerts:

"Nicht wahr, Leutnant, Sie betrachten es als zum Dienst gehörig. Oh, ich weiss, Sie kennen den Trick, in der Sklaverei Ihren Stolz zu bewahren. Nicht jedermann versteht sich darauf." [95]

"You regard it as part of the service, don't you, Lieutenant? Ah, yes, I know, you have the trick of hugging your pride, even in a state of slavery. Not everybody in Europe has the knack to take it that way."

And when, on a later occasion, he extols the spirit that will not kowtow before brute force, he is talking in the first instance of reason defying brute nature, but the fervor in his words is that of the political libertarian, and his protest is a thrust aimed at his pupil:

"Sehen Sie, Ingenieur, da haben Sie die Feindschaft des Geistes gegen die Natur, sein stolzes Misstrauen gegen sie, sein hochherziges Bestehen auf dem Rechte zur Kritik an ihr und ihrer bösen, vernunftwidrigen Macht. Denn sie ist die Macht, und es ist knechtisch, die Macht hinzunehmen, sich mit ihr abzufinden . . . wohlgemerkt, sich *innerlich* mit ihr abzufinden." [96]

"There, Engineer, you have the hostility the intellect feels against nature, its proud mistrust, its high-hearted insistence upon the right to criticize her and her evil, reason-denying power. Nature is force; and it is slavish to suffer force, to abdicate before it—to abdicate, that is, inwardly."

Settembrini's combination of the flaming gesture of revolt with passionate love of country is utterly alien to Hans Castorp's way of thinking, he and his cousin having always been accustomed, "vaterländische Gesinnung mit einem erhaltenden Ordnungssinn gleichzusetzen" [97] ("to regard patriotism as synonymous with a conservative love of order"); and in his "angeborene Achtung vor Gesetz und Ordnung jeder Art" [98] ("inborn respect for law and order of whatever sort") Hans Castorp is outstandingly German. Did not this sympathetic alignment with law and order form the first of his four "Urerlebnisse"—all of them German "Urerlebnisse", but none so marked with the stamp of national heritage as this? This experience had been "wortlos und unkritisch, nur lebensvoll—schlechthin bejahend" ("not phrased in words, and therefore uncritical, simply vital,—and for all that, positive"), but it has a name that has been one of the red letter words of the German language since the days of the "Nibelungenlied" and of Wolfram's "Parzival". That name is "Treue".[99] No other word has fired the German imagination like the word "Treue" since the rediscovery of the medieval German heritage got its great impetus a hundred and fifty years ago, and no word has been so uncritically exploited—and with such naïve good faith—in the interests of nationalistic propaganda as the word "Treue". Volumes could be written to show how the concept of "deutsche Treue", with Latin or—less frequently—Slavic slipperiness as its expressed or implied counterpart, has colored the thought of German intellectuals and poets from Schiller and Friedrich Schlegel to Conrad Ferdinand Meyer, to Wagner and to Wildenbruch;[100] and conversely, recent German satire has concentrated its heaviest fire on this vulnerable item of the national ideology.[101] Thomas Mann is acutely aware of the turgid emotionalism attaching to the word "Treue" in popular parlance; and while in his War Book he had again and again fallen back upon Richard Wagner's lapidary dictum: "Der Deutsche ist konservativ",[102] it is with the utmost reserve that he would attach the label "Treue" to Hans Castorp's "Urerlebnis" of conservatism and continuity. When he alludes for the first time to "Treue und Beständigkeit" as a characteristic quality of the young man's, he hedges this designation at once with the comment:

"Leider wohnt den Bezeichnungen von Charaktereigenschaften regelmässig ein moralisches Urteil inne, sei es im lobenden oder tadelnden Sinn, obgleich sie alle ihre zwei Seiten haben. Hans Castorps 'Treue', auf die er sich übrigens weiter nichts zugute tat, bestand, ohne Wertung gesprochen, in einer gewissen Schwerfälligkeit, Langsamkeit und Beharrlichkeit seines Gemütes, einer erhaltenden Grundstimmung, die ihm Zustände und Lebensverhältnisse der Anhänglichkeit und des Fortbestandes desto würdiger erscheinen liess, je länger sie bestanden. Auch war er geneigt, an die unendliche Dauer des Zustandes, der Verfassung zu glauben, worin er sich gerade befand, schätzte sie eben darum und war nicht auf Veränderung erpicht."[103]

"But alas, every characterization of this kind involves a moral judgment, whether favorable or unfavorable—though, to be sure, each trait of character has its two sides. Thus Hans Castorp's 'loyalty'—upon which, be it said, he was not prone to plume himself—consisted, baldly, in a certain temperamental heaviness, sluggishness, and quiescence, a fundamental tendency to feel respect for conditions of duration and stability; and the more respect, the longer they lasted. He inclined to believe in the permanence of the particular state or circumstances in which he for the moment found himself; prized it for that very quality, and was not bent on change."

Hans Castorp is well aware of being on the defensive with his temperamental "Treue"; he knows that his love of order and continuity has a very questionable side. In exposing the weakness attaching to it Settembrini stands not alone. There is humor in the fact that for once he finds an ally in the object of his pet antipathy, in the slant-eyed Russian siren. On the night of the mardi gras, when Hans and Clavdia engage in conversation for the first time, she refers to his cousin with bantering sarcasm as a young man "très étroit, très honnête, très allemand".[104] As Hans Castorp correctly gathers, the three epithets are in fact synonymous for Clavdia. He translates them into German for her in his rejoinder: "Du willst sagen, dass er pedantisch ist" ("You mean to say that he is pedantic"), adding the question: "Hältst du uns Deutsche für pedantisch—nous autres allemands?" ("Do you consider us Germans to be pedantic?"). In her reply, she fires point blank: "Nous causons de votre cousin. Mais c'est vrai, ihr seid ein wenig bourgeois. Vous aimez l'ordre mieux que la liberté, toute l'Europe le sait" ("We're talking about your cousin. But it's true, you are a bit bourgeois. You love order more than liberty, all Europe knows that"). Hans Castorp feels the force of this reproach, and it would not be his way to brush it aside with light banter. So he tells her that having heard the word liberty a great deal of late, he had been thinking about it. And as the upshot of his musings he expresses the thought that what Europe calls liberty is possibly a rather pedantic and bourgeois affair in comparison with the German need of order. The emphasis is on the word: need. Spiritually speaking, the Germans are "bedrohte Naturen"—of frail constitution. As a people, are they not possibly, as Settembrini had put his own case, just "Sorgenkinder des Lebens"? [105] What is this picturesque phrase but the artist's restatement of the conviction formulated by the author of the "Betrachtungen": "Der Begriff 'deutsch' ist ein Abgrund, bodenlos . . ." [106] ("The concept 'German' is an abyss, bottomless . . ."); and: "Die Deutschen (sind) das eigentlich problematische Volk" [107] ("The Germans are the essentially problematic people"); and:

"Wessen Bestreben es wäre, aus Deutschland einfach eine bürgerliche Demokratie im römisch-westlichen Sinn und Geiste zu machen, der würde ihm sein Bestes und Schwerstes, seine Problematik nehmen wollen, in der seine Nationalität ganz eigentlich besteht." [108]	"Whoever should strive to transform Germany into a bourgeois democracy pure and simple in the sense of Rome and the West, he would be trying to rob her of her best and weightiest quality, of her problematic endowment, which is the very essence of her nationality."

Why should the German feel a peculiar need of outward order at the price of political liberty? Hans Castorp does not explain in so many words what is in the back of his mind,—a certain delicacy doubtless contributes to his reserve; yet it is not difficult to guess his meaning. He affirms a conviction that practically every German intellectual has subscribed to since the days of Novalis. It is this: The German has a richer spiritual endowment than any of his brother Europeans. He has faculties of growth and development far surpassing those of the civilized West. His "Anlagen" contain in latent form the totality of what is human. His is the universal genius of Faust.[109]   Novalis and Friedrich Schlegel[110] had thrilled to this discovery as they perceived the first streaks of a new dawn breaking over Europe, in the personality of Goethe; and Fichte and Kleist had voiced it in extreme and aggressive terms when their patriotism re-volted against the yoke of Napoleon. And never since then had that conviction entirely subsided. But at all times this conviction—un-doubtedly a symptom of very genuine vitality—has been coupled with the sobering recognition of the fact that this superior endowment was unorganized and chaotic, that the Germans were still in a ferment of becoming, while their Western neighbors had advanced to a state of positive being. It was all very well to exult in Nietzsche's dictum: "Ich sage euch: Man muss noch Chaos in sich haben, um einen tanzenden Stern gebären zu können. Ich sage euch: ihr habt noch Chaos in euch" [111] ("I say unto you: One must have chaos within, to give birth to a dancing star. I say unto you: You still have chaos within"). But there is another side to the matter. The consciousness of such chaotic inner wealth carries with it a challenge and a summons to develop these latent riches and to reduce this chaos to order. And is not this the sense of Hans Castorp's apology for the German need of order: We need the outward order of political authority for the time being, because our best energies are entirely taken up with the struggle to master the wealth of our inner chaos?

This is no doubt Hans Castorp's and Thomas Mann's meaning. The German is engrossed with an inner task, a task that, charac-teristically, has a German name for which there is no adequate ren-dering in other languages. That name is "Bildung". The German has felt this as his peculiar task ever since Goethe gave articulate form to this ideal in "Wilhelm Meisters Lehrjahre". And this ideal is the central theme in the second of Hans Castorp's two intimate dialogues with Clavdia after her return, and we see in that connection how this ideal can be felt by alien temperaments as an exasperating irri-tant,—an irritant capable on occasion of contributing fuel to the flames of war.

"Es beruhigt mich ausserordentlich zu hören, dass Sie kein leiden-schaftlicher Mensch sind" ("It is exceedingly reassuring to hear that you are not a passionate man"), says Clavdia, piqued by the fact that Hans will not let any personal jealousy interfere with his objective appreciation of Peeperkorn's personality.

"Übrigens, wie denn auch wohl? Sie müssten aus der Art geschlagen sein. Leidenschaft, das ist: um des Lebens willen leben. Aber es ist bekannt, dass ihr um des Erlebnisses willen lebt. Leidenschaft, das ist Selbstvergessenheit. Aber euch ist es um Selbstbereicherung zu tun. C'est ça. Sie haben keine Ahnung, dass das abscheulicher Egoismus ist, und dass ihr damit eines Tages als Feinde der Menschheit dasteht en werdet?" [112]

"But how should you be—if running at all true to type? Passionate—that means to live for the sake of living. But one knows that you all live for the sake of experience. Passion, that is self-forgetfulness. But what you all want is self-enrichment. C'est ça. You don't realize what revolting egotism it is, and that one day it will brand you enemies of the human race?"

Here the dialogue is transparent. A fundamental antagonism of two national temperaments finds articulate expression. The German is not content to live for the sake of living, he wants to get something out of life, even though that something is an intangible spiritual value. He wants to fashion his life into a pattern and give a significance to the elements in relation to the whole which they do not possess taken singly. This is what he calls being true to himself. This is his morality, the morality of striving, as expressed in the ethical idealism of Kant, of Fichte, and of Nietzsche. And the Russian temperament, inclined to relaxation and self-indulgence, cannot but feel the German attitude as involving a reproach levelled against its own more easygoing ways. Clavdia's labelling of this German ethos as abominable egoism recalls to mind a wartime conversation between the Russian minister Sazonow and an English novelist, in which the ethos of "christenmenschliche Sünderdemut" (the Christian humility of the sinner) was pitted against "den unerträglich 'strikten Moralismus' des Preussentums" (the intolerably "strict moralism" of Prussianism). The author of the "Betrachtungen" chuckled to himself over the implications of this antithesis; [113] but even he asked the question, in another part of his War Book: "Ist nicht der Russe der menschlichste Mensch?" [114] (Is not the Russian the most human of men?), going on to the affirmation: "Es ist für mich keine Frage, dass deutsche und russische Menschlichkeit einander näher sind, als die deutsche und die lateinische" [115] ("To me it is beyond question that German and Russian humanity are closer to one another than the German and the Latin"). And as for Hans Castorp, he is weary of sparring, he loves Clavdia, symbol of Russia, and his whole development is keyed to the attempt to expand his own peculiar ethos so as to make it embrace, in a more neutral medium, both the infinite tolerance of the East and the precise self-assurance of the West. So Hans Castorp takes the sting out of Clavdia's reproach for his attitude as being abominably egotistic, by remarking:

"Ich meine, die Grenze ist fliessend. Da gibt es egoistische Hingabe und hingebenden Egoismus. . . . Ich glaube, es ist im ganzen, wie es in der Liebe ist." [116]

"I mean, the limits are fluid. There is egotistic devotion, and there is devoted egotism. I think, on the whole, that it is as it is in love."

And what Hans Castorp means specifically by this allusion to the dual nature of love, the author himself takes pains to explain at the end of this dialogue, when he refuses absolutely to make a precise distinction between carnal love as pitted against spiritual love, maintaining rather that in all love carnal and spiritual elements are commingled, and that to worry about this ambivalence would indicate "einen durchaus trostlosen Mangel an Verschlagenheit" [117] ("an absolutely hopeless lack of subtlety").

Whatever phase of Hans Castorp's development we examine, we find this peculiarly German striving for universality, for a synthesis of opposites. We find the German genius symbolized in his reconciliation of reverence and freedom, of adventurousness and responsibility, of self-respect and humility, of disease and health, of sympathy with death and all-inclusive affirmation of life. Wherever we probe, Hans Castorp's experience is fraught with symbolic significance. Take, for instance, the values he attaches to health and disease, to life and death. Here, certainly, the interpreter traces the course of nineteenth and twentieth century Germany. Just as the great spiritual experience of nineteenth century Germany was Romanticism, and Romanticism has been associated with disease since the days of Goethe, so whatever genius Germany has attained to in her arduous process of *Steigerung* she owes to her long intimacy with Romanticism as the cult of disease and death. To quote once again that key passage: "Zum Leben gibt es zwei Wege: Der eine ist der gewöhnliche, direkte und brave. Der andere ist schlimm, er führt über den Tod, und das ist der geniale Weg!" ("There are two paths to life: one is the regular one, direct, honest. The other is bad, it leads through death—that is the way of genius"). *Zum Leben!* Let us not overlook that disease and death function but as an approach to life. Accordingly, as in Hans Castorp's life, in the life of Germany, too, there came a time when the logic of development decreed a new orientation, away from Romanticism. "Gesünder werden und klüger werden—das muss sich vereinigen lassen" [118] ("To become healthier and to become wiser—there must be a way of combining the two"), became the new parole. And it is as the inaugurator of this new orientation that Thomas Mann hails Nietzsche. In Nietzsche nineteenth century Romanticism achieved its own self-conquest.[119] No one was so well qualified for this task as Nietzsche; for no one had come under the spell of Romantic disease more deeply, and no one had abandoned himself more utterly to Romantic "Sympathie mit dem Tode", to what Nietzsche calls "die ethische Luft, der faustische Duft, Kreuz, Tod und Gruft" [120] ("the ethical atmosphere, the Faustean scent, the cross, death, and the tomb"). If there is one conviction that the author of the "Betrachtungen" has not revised, it is this:

"Der *Lebensbegriff*, dieser deutscheste, goethischeste und im höchsten, religiösen Sinn konservative Begriff ist es, den Nietzsche mit neuem Gefühle durchdrungen, mit einer neuen Schönheit, Kraft und heiligen Unschuld umkleidet, zum obersten Range erhoben, zur geistigen Herrschaft geführt hat." [121]

"The concept of life,—this most German, most Goethean concept, conservative in the highest religious sense; it is this concept which Nietzsche impregnated with new feeling, invested with a new beauty, strength, and sacred innocence, and raised to a position of supremacy in the realm of the spirit."

It is because of this that Thomas Mann hails Nietzsche as the evangelist of a new covenant between Earth and Man. [122] In his recent centenary address on Goethe Thomas Mann again stresses the supremacy of the Goethean and Nietzschean "Lebensbegriff" [123] as the category reconciling within it all vital dissonances. In the light of this idea we grasp Hans Castorp's visionary affirmation of life, during that fateful skiing tour, as the axis around which the whole "Zauberberg" revolves, as the pivotal experience that endows all his spiritual adventures with ultimate meaning. If Germany's adventure in Romantic infatuation with death is not to go down in history as essentially aimless floundering, Thomas Mann would tell us, it is because of its inherent tendency to "other" itself; it is because, in the mad momentum of its course, it found itself, like Hans Castorp up in the snows, spun around in a circle; it is because at the end of its Romantic adventure there emerged a new vital synthesis, an infinitely enriched conception of life, embracing within its scope both the rational and the irrational pole, no longer as mortally antagonistic principles but held, rather, by a common bond of dynamic tension and equilibrium.

If these last thoughts have taken us rather far into the field of philosophic abstraction, may we not, in self-defense, once more quote Hans Castorp's plea: "Ich will lieber ein bisschen faseln und etwas Schwieriges halbwegs ausdrücken, als immer nur tadellose Hergebrachtheiten von mir geben" ("I would rather make a stab at things in the hope of expressing something difficult half way, incidentally, than always be spouting excellent platitudes")? And if Thomas Mann would seem to have lost the ground of reality from under his feet by crediting the German genius with the power to achieve so all-inclusive a synthesis, let us not forget that Hans Castorp has the intuitive clarity of his vision only for a few moments: an hour after his return to Haus Berghof it has already sunk below the threshold of his consciousness.[124] And let us remember, above all, that Thomas Mann is trying to give expression to an all-inclusive *human* ideal, and it would become us ill to chide him for seeing this ideal through the eyes of his national heritage. There is no trace of braggadocio about this. Pride and humility clasp hands in this earnest attempt to chart the course of man as the Homo Dei. Only recently Thomas Mann has stated that "die bürgerliche Lebensform" seems to him to find its completest expression in Germany.[125] But the bourgeois form of life, he amplifies his thought, seems to harbor within it an impulse and a faculty to outgrow its own peculiar limitations.[126] Thomas Mann's meaning is clearly this: If the star to which spiritual Germany hitches its wagon is the attainment of the universally human, it will achieve this ideal only in proportion to the steadfastness of its resolve to outgrow itself.

VII. MYSTICISM

Thomas Mann began his literary career as a writer of short stories and sketches. These are, for the most part, built around hypersensitive abnormal characters who come to experience life as a tiger that mangles its victims rather thoroughly. Life is exceedingly businesslike in its manner of despatching these unfortunates, who suffer excruciating agonies in the process, and there is an element of grim humor in the contrast between the inexorable tranquillity of the executioner and the convulsive writhings of the victims. The early Thomas Mann affects an objectivity in his pessimism that may cause the hasty reader to miss the depth of intuitive sympathy with which he has entered into the inner life of his characters. After these first concise productions, while still in his early twenties, Thomas Mann evolved the sustained genealogical epic "Buddenbrooks" that has remained unsurpassed in its field to this day. In the decade that followed, Thomas Mann was almost exclusively engrossed with the artist as a problematic phenomenon. The psychological analysis of the artistic impulse, especially in its literary manifestation, and the portrayal of the tension between art and life, between the aesthetic and the ethical imperative, form the avowed theme of a large number of the "Novellen" including "Tristan", "Tonio Kröger", "Der Tod in Venedig", and the dialogue "Fiorenza"; and the same problems, veiled under the playful disguise of an idyllic plot, endow the full-length novel "Königliche Hoheit" with its inner meaning. All these works, concerned with the artist, are autobiographical in a peculiar sense: While "Buddenbrooks" frankly chronicled the author's ancestry and social background through a succession of generations, these record the phases of his spiritual evolution and show him becoming progressively conscious of himself as a type, even when, as in "Der Tod in Venedig", the tragic collapse of the artist expresses only a presentiment of lurking danger on the author's part and the

delineation of this collapse has for Thomas Mann the effect of a
catharsis. After this long period of preoccupation with the artist
and his "Lebensform" no major work of the imagination issued
from Thomas Mann's pen for many a year:—the fragment of "Felix
Krull", the sketch "Herr und Hund", and "Gesang vom Kindchen"
(Thomas Mann's only attempt at versification) are minor diversions.
Instead, the essayist comes to the fore with an impressive array of
productions including the brilliant sketch of Frederick the Great,
the monumental "Betrachtungen eines Unpolitischen", and that
marvellous essay in literary counterpoint: "Goethe und Tolstoi".
Fourteen years after "Der Tod in Venedig", finally, the novelist
emerged again and exhibited the gigantic canvas of the "Zauberberg"
to the eyes of a startled world.

This was autobiography too, in a spiritual sense, as we have seen;
but how the personality of Thomas Mann had expanded in the interval, enabling him to lay so vast a record of experience before us!
For its greatness lies in the fact that the enormous wealth of fact and
thought in its pages has all been fused into living experience. Knowledge has been transmuted into "Erlebnis". Were it not so, the
"Zauberberg" might be a highly stimulating treatise but not the
supreme "Bildungsroman" of the world's literature. I need not re-
hearse in detail all those fascinating expositions from the realm of
the biological sciences, delving into dermatology, embryology, his-
tology, anatomy, and pathology—sciences the very names of which
make the layman shudder in bewilderment. Nor is it necessary to
make more than passing mention of the marvels of astronomy and
of molecular physics and the way they become linked in Hans Castorp's mind with the central mystery, the mystery of life. These
things occupy a large amount of space in the "Zauberberg", but
it would serve no useful purpose to expatiate on the panorama of the
natural sciences set forth there. To do so would be to overlook the
functional significance of this element of the "Zauberberg",—as if
it had been Thomas Mann's ambition to compete with the writers
of outlines of science! Hans Castorp's adventurings into the realm
of the various sciences do not yield him a neat stock of systematic

knowledge, to be stowed away in properly labelled compartments of his brain. He is not on the way to becoming a walking encyclopedia. His passion for knowledge is kindled by the flame of his Eros and in turn feeds this flame. Whatever phenomena his mind fastens upon it assimilates, and it fastens only upon that which is assimilable. The knowledge he absorbs ceases to be mere knowledge. It becomes completely integrated with the emotional core of his personality. It becomes part of his living tissue. Thus when Hans Castorp lies on his balcony under the stars and indulges in dizzying speculations that range the origin of matter, of living protoplasm, and of organic disease under one gigantic perspective after the manner of Schelling and Novalis, this intellectual orgy leads to a vision of Life personified, in the guise of Clavdia Chauchat.[1] And the fusion of his intellectual passion with his passion for Clavdia is so complete that each feeds the flame of the other. True, his intellectual passion represents a partial sublimation of his libido; but is not his libido, as centred upon this woman, itself but a symptom and manifestation of Eros as the divine principle of an all-embracing sympathy? Does not his libido itself become sublimated in due course into friendship, whereas Eros continues to rule? If there is a motto that can express the essence of the "Zauberberg" it is that line from the ecstatic song of the sirens in Faust, as they see the Homunculus throw caution to the winds, shatter the fragile vessel of his "hermetic" existence against the cliff, and mingle with the current of the universal element:

"So herrsche denn Eros, der alles begonnen!"
(Let Eros rule, prime mover of all!)

Everything about the human body becomes a living experience to Hans Castorp. Every one of its functions and its organic processes of growth and decay is impregnated for him with a sensuous flavor. And for him this flavor comes to attach to all forms of organic life, as being man's immediate kin, and thence to the inorganic environment that shares its substance and supports its existence. Thus Hans Castorp's sympathy focusses upon the pulse of his own heartbeat[2] and spans the remotest regions of the universe. His sympathy is the awareness of a mystic bond of unity between himself and the cosmos, an awareness of his self—infinitesimal mote that it is—as a node in which all the forces at work in the universe pulse in unison. Words are utterly inadequate, of course, to express the mystic religiosity of this experience; but it seems to me that in his most exalted moments Hans Castorp comes very close to attaining what Goethe's Faust despairingly formulates as the core of his strivings:

| "dass ich erkenne, was die Welt | "that I discern the innermost force |
| im Innersten zusammenhält" . . . | that holds the world together". . . |

Hans Castorp comes close to it, not by cognition in the abstract ("Erkenntnis")—an impossible approach—but by an intuitive sympathy in which the totality of his faculties responds to the great mystery that is both the self and the encompassing universe in one. And if that transcendental consciousness is restricted to a few exalted moments, a trace of it lingers, surely, to color the sobriety of Hans Castorp's everyday life.

Thus Thomas Mann's relation to life is that of a mystic, in the broader sense of the word. In this connection we must discuss Hans Castorp's weirdest experience, his adventure in the realm of the occult, characterized by the title of the section devoted to it ("Fragwürdigstes"), as questionable in a superlative degree. And such is surely its impression upon every reader who succumbs to the spell of the narrative for the first time. We have moved in a world of marvels all along, but the spiritualistic séance ends with a shock for which we were quite unprepared. The apparition of Joachim is felt to be a nightmare; but even that is nothing compared with the *guise* of his appearance. When the meaning of his accoutrement dawns upon us, when we—reluctantly—come to realize that his strange clothing and the inverted soup tureen on his head are the war uniform of 1914, the effect of this discovery is nothing short of ghastly:—No civilian of pre-war days could possibly have brought forth out of his subconsciousness a vision of a soldier in a garb like this![3] The moment we think of this obvious fact we are lost. The earth and its laws have slipped from under our feet and we are adrift in an unknowable void. We may refuse to believe our eyes, and reread the passage with microscopic care, only to find ourselves completely baffled. For up to this point, despite what shudders may have chilled our marrow, we had been sustained by the tacit conviction that the phenomena recorded must have their basis in the psychological situation, however imperfectly we understand the interaction of minds. We had been willing to stretch our ideas of mass psychosis, hallucination, unconscious suggestion to the utmost limit until our belief hung by ever so tenuous a thread; but now that thread has snapped, and all attempts to bring the laws of experience to bear upon the apparition of Joachim collapse like a house of cards. At this point Thomas Mann deliberately cuts adrift from psychology, in presenting us with a fact that is incommensurable with any knowable order.

But—the reader may be inclined to interpose—the appearance of Joachim in the unfamiliar coat and helmet is not the only inexplicable feature that confronts us in that dubious realm. On two previous occasions at least we were touched by a similar shudder: the first time when "Holger" pulled out of Hans Castorp's pocket the x-ray picture of Clavdia that he was positive of having left on his dresser; [4] the second time, when the record of Valentin's Prayer mysteriously turned up among the musical trifles that served to contribute a lighter note to these spiritualistic sessions. [5] It is certain that these two incidents are peculiarly startling and that they prepare the ground for the miracle of miracles. But they differ from the last, it seems to me, in that they at least harbor the possibility of a psychological interpretation,—leaving open the question whether such an interpretation is warranted in the light of the whole situation.

For if we scan the occultistic episode as a whole, we cannot fail to see that psychological laws are operative in this weird realm, and that personality is a dominant factor and has a decisive bearing on the quality of the phenomena produced. It suffices to recall that when a group of shallow and mediocre thrill seekers like Frau Stöhr, Hermine Kleefeld, Herr Albin, and others of the same calibre get together and experiment with Ellen Brand's faculties as a medium, the results are startlingly sensational, to be sure, but nothing more; the manifestations of the "spirit world" do not rise above the level of impish pranks and essentially meaningless stunts; they reflect the spiritual level of the minds that jointly produced them,—a "guazza-buglio" Herr Settembrini would rightly call it. When an integrated personality like Hans Castorp's joins this group, however, and an element of value leavens the "anonymous and common" working of the group mind, the results are correspondingly significant. Is it possible to read the prose poem about the sea, composed as it is by the Ouija Board method, without sensing Hans Castorp's dominant share in the performance? What a difference between this sustained chant—in the lethargy of its rhythm so similar to Novalis' "Hymnen an die Nacht"—and the usual quality of stunts in the repertory of little "Holger", who was smart enough to box people's ears and pull handkerchiefs out of their pockets, but evidently was "forbidden" to prompt Ellen when she did not know the answers to her questions at school! [6] And supposing that Hans Castorp had declined to take part in the session which had on its program the conjuring up of one of the dead, would anyone credit that giddy group of nonentities with the sustained concentration of will that succeeded in achieving the impossible? It is perfectly obvious that but for the compelling power of Hans Castorp's steady yearning, the medium's abortive convulsions would have ended in utter exhaustion long before the two hours were up, and it is equally obvious that what tipped the scale at last was the record of Valentin's Prayer: So deeply had Hans Castorp experienced this music as expressing his cousin's military ethos that the strains of this song, falling upon his ear at the moment of maximum tension, gripped his whole being as in a vise and caused the totality of his powers of suggestion to withdraw into one point, as it were, thereby generating a current of energy so intense as to fuse all the participants into one single psychic unit. It is impossible to talk of such phenomena at all except in terms of halting metaphors. My explanation, if it may be called such, aims at nothing more than showing that what happened at these séances has its analogy in the psychological manifestations with which we are familiar. Our initia-

tion into the mysteries of the occult is a matter of progressive stages. We are led along step by step. We feel that the terrific laboring of the medium in company with a group under the control of Hans Castorp's will must lead to a fearsome culmination. And when we see concentration rising to a height of intensity that projects an objective likeness of one of the dead into the room, we share in the experience despite ourselves. But our shudder is all the greater on that account, when the apparition departs so weirdly from what we and those who had known Joachim expected to see. It is here that Thomas Mann's occultism abruptly leaves the realm of psychology to enter upon a metaphysical flight.

Abruptly? Not quite so abruptly as it would seem. As a matter of fact, the ground had been prepared for this transition in a passage that we are all but certain to have passed over lightly. There was a point in the book when Thomas Mann, discussing the philosophical implications of occultism, had entertained the idea that what we call the subconscious is possibly connected with a super-consciousness that transcends the limits of the individual mind, an omniscient over-soul with which we may possibly enter into a fleeting and fragmentary rapport when occult phenomena manifest themselves. But the context in which this idea was broached was of such a nature that an element of ironic play seemed to hover about it, and it probably never occurred to us to entertain it more seriously than any number of possible standpoints with which the imagination may experiment. For this idea was broached in connection with the attempts of the highly ambiguous Krokowski to dignify his predilection for the occult, as for everything shady, by dressing it up in fine sounding technical language and then surrounding it by an aura of unctuous comment that drew equally upon logic, mysticism, and religion. We were not sure even whether Thomas Mann was sponsoring this idea in his own person, or whether he was merely lending to the character under consideration his own facility of expression, after his wont, when he accounted for Krokowski's taking up with this new hobby as follows:

"Immer schon hatten jene dunklen und weitläufigen Gegenden der mensch-

"The field of his study had always been those wide, dark tracts of the

lichen Seele sein Studiengebiet ausgemacht, die man als Unterbewusstsein bezeichnet, obgleich man möglicherweise besser täte, von einem Überbewusstsein zu reden, da aus diesen Sphären zuweilen ein Wissen emporgeistert, das das Bewusstseinswissen des Individuums bei weitem übersteigt und den Gedanken nahelegt, es möchten Verbindungen und Zusammenhänge zwischen den untersten und lichtlosen Gegenden der Einzelseele und einer durchaus wissenden Allseele bestehen. Der Bereich des Unterbewusstseins, 'okkult' dem eigentlichen Wortsinne nach, erweisst sich sehr bald auch als okkult im engeren Sinn dieses Wortes und bildet eine der Quellen, woraus die Erscheinungen fliessen, die man aushilfsweise so benennt. Das ist nicht alles. Wer im organischen Krankheitssymptom ein Werk aus dem bewussten Seelenleben verbannter und hysterisierter Affekte erblickt, der anerkennt die Schöpfermacht des Psychischen im Materiellen, —eine Macht, die man als zweite Quelle der magischen Phänomene anzusprechen gezwungen ist." [7]

human soul, which one had been used to call the subconsciousness, though they might perhaps better be called the superconsciousness, since from them sometimes emanates a knowingness beyond anything of which the conscious intelligence is capable, and giving rise to the hypothesis that there may subsist connections and associations between the lowest and least illumined regions of the individual soul and a wholly knowing All-soul. The province of the subconscious, 'occult' in the proper sense of the word, very soon shows itself to be occult in the narrower sense as well, and forms one of the sources whence flow the phenomena we have agreed thus to characterize. But that is not all. Whoever recognizes a symptom of organic disease as an effort of the conscious soul-life of forbidden and hystericized emotions, recognizes the creative force of the psychical within the material—a force which one is bound to claim as a second source of magic phenomena."

These reflections and others in a similar vein were calculated to make us realize how smoothly the wily Krokowski managed to link his new passion for the occult with the field of his specialty, psychoanalysis. The element of irony, as directed against Krokowski's ambiguous personality, could not escape us; but have we not found in Thomas Mann's irony a peculiar tendency to point both ways? And does it not seem now, in the light of Hans Castorp's experience with the occult, as if these speculations, put forward as rationalizations of a shady curiosity, had a validity of their own apart from and in spite of the use to which a Krokowski puts them?

This is a conclusion from which there is no escaping. If the apparition of Joachim in the World War uniform is indeed the work of a responsible poet-artist and not merely that of a surpassingly skilful manipulator of effects, it permits of only one interpretation: Thomas Mann, the mystic, believes in an omniscient over-soul. His thought identifies itself once again with a favorite conception of German Romanticism. Although the occult phenomena of the "Zauberberg" are, of course, fiction, nothing but fiction, the very make-believe of Joachim's apparition as a portent of the World War is predicated on the assumption that such revelations of the omniscient over-soul are at least within the realm of theoretical possibility. But it remains left for the reader to draw this conclusion, provided he feels justified in applying the criterion of ultimate seriousness to a work of fiction. It is an implication, no more. In contrast with the boisterous practice of expressionism that shrieked its metaphysical faith from the housetops, Thomas Mann is discretion itself in the matter of those convictions that are most intimate and incommunicable. "Ich darf nicht sagen, dass ich an Gott glaube" ("I dare not say that I believe in God"), he confesses in the War Book, only to add: "Es würde lange dauern, glaube ich, bis ich es sagen würde, auch wenn ich es täte" [8] ("And even if I did, it would be a long time, I think, before I would say so").

This is not the first time that an intimation of super-rational agencies confronts the reader in Thomas Mann's writings. Once before, in "Königliche Hoheit", substantially the same idea is set forth. There, however, it has all the earmarks of an idea to be experimented with, being only a functional element in a delicious satire aimed at the organs of modern enlightenment. Fifteen years lie, moreover, between the publication of "Königliche Hoheit" and that of the "Zauberberg". The interesting thing is, none the less, that already at that early date (and even earlier, as we shall presently see) Thomas Mann had begun to speculate upon the subject, and that his line of approach to that idea foreshadows one of the major features of the "Zauberberg". The situation in "Königliche Hoheit" is this:

When the little prince Klaus Heinrich is born, it is discovered that his left arm is partly atrophied. His father, the Grand-Duke, flies into a rage that vents itself upon the unfortunate physician who had the royal patient under his care. The tension is relieved when one of the Grand-Duke's ministers, Herr von Knobelsdorff, has the presence of mind to link the disability with the prophecy of a gypsy woman

who had foretold that the country was going to enjoy an era of un-
paralleled happiness under the rule of a prince with one hand. This
prince, the prophecy ran, would give the country more with one
hand than others with two. At the time of Klaus Heinrich's birth it
does not look as though he would ever come to the throne; but in due
course of time his elder brother abdicates in his favor and Klaus
Heinrich wins the love of an American multi-millionairess and is
thereby enabled to restore the credit of his bankrupt state. Now is
the time to recall that oracular prophecy: an officious press and the
savants of the local university vie with one another in the effort to
attach a providential significance to the old gypsy woman's words
and to find accommodation in their up-to-date enlightened philosophy
for such miraculous fore-knowledge. The account of these explana-
tions runs as follows:

"Äusserst fesselnd war es übrigens, zu beobachten, wie bei den publizistischen Erörterungen, die sich hierauf ent-spannen, unsere aufgeklärte und frei-geistig gesinnte Presse sich zu der volkstümlichen Seite der Sache, näm-lich zu der Prophezeiung stellte, die denn doch in zu hohem Grade poli-tische Bedeutung gewonnen hatte, als dass nicht Bildung und Intelligenz genötigt gewesen wären, sich damit auseinanderzusetzen. Weissagerei, Chi-romantie und dergleichen Hexen-wesen, erklärte der 'Eilbote', seien, soweit das Schicksal des Einzelnen in Frage komme, schlechterdings in das dunkle Gebiet des Aberglaubens zu verweisen, sie gehörten dem grauen Mittelalter an, und nicht genug zu belächeln seien die wahnbefangenen Personen, die, was freilich in den Städten wohl nicht mehr geschähe, sich von geriebenen Beutelschneidern die Grosch-en aus der Tasche ziehen liessen, um aus der Hand, den Karten oder dem Kaffeesatz sich ihre geringfügige Zu-kunft deuten, sich gesundbeten, homöo-pathisch kurieren oder ihr krankes Vieh von eingefahrenen Dämonen befreien zu lassen. . . . Allein ins

"It was exceedingly interesting, by the way, to follow the way this mat-ter was aired in public discussion, and to see the stand of our enlight-ened, free-thinking press with re-gard to the popular side of the issue, the prophecy, that is; for this side of the matter had come to loom as so important politically that the repre-sentatives of culture and intelligence could not affort to sidestep the question. Accordingly, the 'Cou-rier' spoke to the effect that sooth-saying, chiromancy, and the like were to be flatly relegated to the obscure realm of superstition, so far as the life of the individual was con-cerned. An indulgent smile was the only proper attitude to take toward such benighted folk—scarcely to be met with any more in our cities—as would let themselves be fleeced by sharpers in order to have their in-significant fortunes told by palmis-try, cards, or coffee-grounds; and faith-healing, homoeopathic cures, and the exorcising of sick cattle all belonged to the same class of non-sense. However, taking a broad view of things and considering de-

Grosse gerechnet und entscheidende Wendungen im Schicksal ganzer Völker oder Dynastien in Rede gestellt, so laufe einem geschulten und wissenschaftlichen Denken die Vorstellung nicht unbedingt zuwider, dass, da die Zeit nur eine Illusion und in Wahrheit betrachtet alles Geschehen in Ewigkeit feststehend sei, solche im Schosse der Zukunft ruhenden Umwälzungen den Menschen im voraus erschüttern und ihm gesichtsweise sich offenbaren könnten. . . ." 9

cisive turns in the fate of whole nations or dynasties, a philosophically schooled and scientific way of thinking would hesitate to repudiate the notion that coming events should be able to cast their shadows in advance and be heralded by prophetic vision,—this in view of the fact that time is only an illusion and that rightly considered the whole course of destiny is fixed in advance for all eternity."

The satirical broadside of this passage is aimed at the opportunistic face-about of our allegedly enlightened press. As for the *idea* contained in its last sentence,—barring the obviously satirical reference to dynasties—the passage affords us no hint in itself with regard to the author's own attitude toward the theoretical issue involved. But if we recall how deeply the author of the "Zauberberg" allows himself to become absorbed in the problem of time and its correlate eternity, we have a right to infer that the mystical conception of the movement of time as an illusion must have had an intimate appeal for him even when he wrote "Königliche Hoheit". (And now the first mention of the projected "Zauberberg" as "der Romanteppich 'Maja'"—in the language of Buddhism: the veil of illusion—appears fraught with a peculiar significance!) [10] But as a matter of fact, we can trace this mystical leaning all the way back to Thomas Mann's literary beginnings: For the hero of his fantastic "Novelle" "Der Kleiderschrank" (1899) time is at a standstill. He carries no watch; he has learned to ignore the calendar. In "Buddenbrooks" (1900) and again in "Tonio Kröger" (1903) the monotonous rhythm of the sea administers its most exquisite solace by effecting release from the fettering deceptions of time and space. [11]   And in his "Tristan" (1902) the ecstasy of the lovers reaches its acme as the tormenting illusion of individuality fades and the bars of space and time are lifted; [12] and while this is part of a condensed paraphrase of the second act of Wagner's "Tristan"—itself a transposition of Schopenhauer into poetry and music—it is at the same time a lyrical confession of Thomas Mann's own deepest yearnings. In the "Zauberberg"

time has the stamping rhythm of "geradeaus, geradeaus", whereas
eternity murmurs: "Karussell, Karussell"; time is the medium of
progress, whereas there is no progress in eternity.   Action is the
ethos of time; contemplation that of eternity.   Hans Castorp's surrender to eternity is expressly designated as "das Grundabenteuer
seiner Seele", a few pages before the end, where we hear that he has
long since discarded his watch and given up all measurement of
time

"aus Gründen der 'Freiheit' also, dem Strandspaziergange, dem stehenden Immer-und-Ewig zu Ehren, diesem hermetischen Zauber, für den der Entrückte sich aufnahmelustig erwiesen, und der das Grundabenteuer seiner Seele gewesen, dasjenige, worin alle alchymistischen Abenteuer dieses schlichten Stoffes sich abgespielt hatten." [13]

"for reasons of his 'freedom'. Thus he did honor to his abiding-ever-lasting, his walk by the ocean of time, the hermetic enchantment to which he had proved so extraordinarily susceptible that it had become the fundamental adventure of his life, in which all the alchemistical processes of his simple substance had found full play."

Unquestionably then, the conception of the omniscient over-soul
and the conception of time as an illusion when viewed under the
aspect of a changeless and motionless eternity, are bound up together in Thomas Mann's mysticism, and his philosophy of the occult
is anchored in both these conceptions.[14]   We have a right to speak
of a philosophy of the occult in Thomas Mann's case.   This must be
admitted by every reader who compares his essay "Okkulte Erlebnisse" (1923) with the subsequent treatment of the occult in the
"Zauberberg".   The one is a strictly factual piece of reporting and
presents an array of sense data that are admittedly at odds with all
rationally intelligible experience.   It gives us the raw material of
Thomas Mann's own experiences with a Munich medium.   The other
transforms this chaotic raw material and subjects it to the domination
of a metaphysical idea.   No one is probably more keenly aware than
Thomas Mann that the "Zauberberg's" philosophic and poetic version of these experiences is not put forward with dogmatic assur-
ance, and that it is but a faltering attempt to fit our materialistic
science into a cosmic scheme that will forever elude our understanding.   It was with this in mind, doubtless, that Thomas Mann

prefaced his narrative of Hans Castorp with the hint that it might turn out to have one or the other feature in common with fairy-tale.[15]

Our account of the occult, as it figures in the "Zauberberg", would be altogether onesided, if we failed to note how Thomas Mann regards experimentation in the realm of the occult, as a matter of principle. What possible value can attach to such experimentation, is the question; and Thomas Mann's way of answering it throws a great deal of light on his peculiar use of such basic terms of his ethical vocabulary as morality, virtue, and sin—terms that are familiar to everyone but in the context of the "Zauberberg" show a distressing tendency to "other" themselves and partake of the character of a special code.

A strong aversion to getting involved with so questionable a subject at all marks Thomas Mann's attitude from the outset. Taste and human pride alike find it repugnant to touch a subject that has to be handled with gloves. The results obtained by devices like the Ouija Board are bound to be

"eine innerlich bis zur Unreinlichkeit verwickelte Erscheinung . . . ein Mischprodukt ganz-, halb- und unbewusster Elemente, der wunschgetriebenen Nachhilfe Einzelner—ob sie selbst ein solches Tun sich nun eingestanden oder nicht—und des geheimen Einverständnisses lichtloser Seelenschichten der Allgemeinheit, eines unterirdischen Zusammenwirkens zu scheinbar fremden Ergebnissen, an denen die Dunkelheiten des Einzelnen mehr oder weniger beteiligt sein würden".[16]

"complex and contaminate, a mixed product of conscious, half-conscious, and unconscious elements; the desire and pressure of individuals, to whom the wish was father to the act, whether or not they were aware of what they did; and the secret acquiescence of some dark stratum in the soul of the generality, a common if subterranean effort toward seemingly impersonal results, in which the suppressed self of the individual was more or less involved."

Such phenomena by their very nature are outside the pale of rational interpretation. Thomas Mann is under no illusions, therefore, as to any quest for higher knowledge being served by experimentation in a realm which is spiritually inaccessible by definition.[17] The undertaking is concededly idle. In branding it as "müssig",[18] Thomas Mann echoes the keynote of Immanuel Kant's refutation of Swedenborg's alleged communications from the spirit world. The most reasonable thing, according to Kant, is to keep aloof from "dergleichen vorwitzigen oder müssigen Fragen" [19] ("such impertinent or idle questions"). And in coupling the epithet "müssig" with the epithet "sündig" and raising the question whether the two are not, in fact, synonymous in a case of this kind, Thomas Mann gives a twist to this problem of knowledge that summons it before a higher forum of ethics. The meaning conveyed by the word "sündig" in this context seems to coincide in a general way with the idea of the word sin as used by the Church, but it is arrived at by a devious route which we must retrace under pain of missing the point of Thomas Mann's ethical approach. As so often before, we shall find that a thought formulated in the "Betrachtungen" has assumed living form in the "Zauberberg". The most illuminating passage in the "Betrachtungen" on the theme of sin and its relation to "morality" versus "virtue" runs as follows:

"Der Moralist unterscheidet sich von dem Tugendhaften dadurch, dass er dem Gefährlich-Schädlichen offen ist; dass er, wie es im Evangelium heisst, 'dem Bösen nicht widersteht',[20]—was der Tugendbold allewege mit dem achtbarsten Erfolge tut. Was ist das Gefährlich-Schädliche? Seelenhirten nennen es die *Sünde*. Aber auch dies schwere, schaudervolle Wort ist eben nur ein Wort und verschiedentlich zu gebrauchen. Es gibt Sünde im Sinne der Kirche und Sünde im Sinne des Humanismus, der Humanität, der Wissenschaft, der Emanzipation des 'Menschen'. Auf jeden Fall ist 'Sünde': *Zweifel*; der Zug zum Verbotenen, der Trieb zum Abenteuer, zum Sichverlieren, Sichhingeben, Erleben, Erforschen, Erkennen, sie ist das Verführende und Versucherische. . . . Diesen Trieb unsittlich zu nennen, werden nur Spiessbürger sich beeilen; dass er sündig ist, leugnet niemand." [21]

"The moralist is distinguished from the man of virtue by being open to the dangerous and noxious, by following the gospel precept: 'Resist ye not evil', in contrast to the eminently successful practice of the paragon of virtue. What is the dangerous and noxious? Guardians of the soul call it sin. But even this grave and awesome word is only a word and subject to various uses. There is sin in the meaning of the Church and sin in the meaning of humanism, humanity, science, the emancipation of man. In any case sin is doubt: an inclination towards the forbidden, an impulse to go adventuring, to lose oneself, to yield oneself, to experience, explore, and discern; it is what tempts and seduces. . . . Only philistines will hasten to call this impulse immoral; that it is sinful, nobody would deny."

And a few pages later, taking issue with the humanist, who brands "jede abwegige Neigung und Stimmung als *Sünde*—und am

'Menschen'" ("every devious inclination and impulse as sin—sin against 'man'"), Thomas Mann writes:

"Wir fühlen mit ihm, dass es Sünde im Sinne des Humanismus *gibt*. Das Eine aber wenigstens bleibt darauf zu erwidern, dass Zweifel und Sünde fruchtbarer und menschlich befreiender sind, als Tugend, Vernunftwürde, der Besitzerstolz des Wahrheitsphilisters."[22]	"We feel with him that there is such a thing as sin in the humanist's sense of the word. But at least this one thing is to be said in reply, that doubt and sin are more fruitful and more humanly liberating than virtue, the dignity of reason, and the philistine's proud consciousness of possessing the truth."

It is evident that this conception of sin harks back to the myth of Genesis about the fall of man. There man jeopardized his status to eat of the tree of knowledge; and the passion to know, to question, to explore the unknown and forbidden at risk to body and soul, if need be, is the essential ethos of sin for Thomas Mann. But with that the tables are turned, and far from being a brand of shame, sin becomes a symbol of what is finest in man: his Faustean urge, his indomitable will to be the measure of all things in reckless disregard of ease and security. Thus Hans Castorp's receptivity to unfamiliar experiences, his willingness to experiment with unauthorized points of view is an affirmation of the ethos of sin from first to last. In this view sin becomes identified with the higher morality. The serene practice of approved virtue has its good points, without doubt; but it is more moral to plunge into sin, to lose oneself, even to abandon oneself to perdition, as Clavdia had put it in one memorable dialogue and Hans Castorp had had occasion to repeat more than once.[23] Taken in this symbolic sense, sin is the morality of the artist or, speaking more generally, of genius. That this morality has a highly sensitive consciousness of responsibility as its correlate has been sufficiently dwelt upon, I trust, to require no further comment.

It is obvious now, that when Thomas Mann applies the epithets idle and sinful to Hans Castorp's curiosity about the occult, he cannot be referring to this aspect of the case. Sin, as the will to know, is an ethical attitude; but when this will turns to a field that is in its very nature unknowable, is that not plainly an abuse of the cognitive impulse? Under those circumstances, does not sin, the Promethean heritage constituting man's glory, alter its nature and become just *plain* sin—an attitude of deliberate perversion from the point of view of any ethics concerned with values?

There seems to be no escaping this verdict, and Thomas Mann holds no brief for Hans Castorp in reporting on his paradoxical curiosity in the face of his better knowledge. He restricts himself to making us understand how an avid curiosity to explore this realm could coexist with a profound aversion to it on aesthetic, philosophical, and ethical grounds.

"Er begriff, dass 'Müssig oder Sündig', als Alternative schon schlimm genug, gar keine Alternative war, sondern dass das zusammenfiel, und dass geistige Hoffnungslosigkeit nur die aussermoralische Ausdrucksform der Verbotenheit war. Das *Placet experiri* aber, ihm eingepflanzt von einem, der *solche* Versuche freilich aufs prallste missbilligen musste, sass fest in Hans Castorps Sinn; seine Sittlichkeit fiel nachgerade mit seiner Neugier zusammen, hatte das wohl eigentlich immer getan: mit der unbedingten Neugier des Bildungsreisenden, die vielleicht schon, als sie vom Mysterium der Persönlichkeit kostete, nicht mehr weit von dem hier auftauchenden Gebiet entfernt gewesen war, und die eine Art von militärischem Charakter bekundete dadurch, dass sie dem Verbotenen nicht auswich, wenn es sich anbot." [24]

"He was aware that his alternative of 'barren' or else 'sinful', bad enough in itself, was in reality not an alternative at all, since the two ideas coincided, and calling a thing spiritually unavailable was only an a-moral way of expressing its forbidden character. But the *Placet experiri* planted in Hans Castorp's mind by one who would surely and resoundingly have reprobated any experimentation at all in this field, was planted firmly enough. Little by little his morality and his curiosity approached and overlapped, or had probably always done so; the pure curiosity of inquiring youth on its travels, which had already brought him pretty close to the forbidden field when he tasted the mystery of personality, and for which he had even claimed the justification that it too was almost military in character, in that it did not weakly avoid the forbidden, when it presented itself."

We might stop here and regard the matter as closed. But if we did so, I am sure that more than one reader would sense "einen durchaus trostlosen Mangel an Verschlagenheit" ("an altogether hopeless lack of subtlety") on our part. The issue is not so simple as it appears to be. The moralist's flatly negative verdict, too, has its ironic side. Whatever else it be, it is incidentally a most adroit tactical manoeuvre,—to belittle and disparage the occult from every possible angle and begin by reducing our expectations to the very lowest level, and then to expose us to a series of marvels with a graduated tightening of the tension until it reaches the limits of the endurable. That is the purely artistic irony lurking in the folds of these philosophical reflections. But this irony has a second aspect of much greater intrinsic significance. The approach that led to the condemnation of all tampering with the occult as idle and sinful was wholly speculative and proceeded along lines of a priori reasoning, very much after the manner of Kant in his "Träume eines Geister-sehers". For the philosopher, whose ultimate concern is abstract knowledge, that settled the matter. But if there is one thing our study has shown it is that "Erkenntnis" and "Erlebnis" are any-thing but interchangeable values. Logic is one thing, and living experience is another. And the ideal of "Bildung", the supreme concern of the "Zauberberg", finds its realization only in so far as it calls into play the totality of man's faculties in his every act of assimilating the sense data of experience. "Das Erlebnis" harbors a value of its own for which there is no substitute. And supposing that Hans Castorp's experiences with the occult had simply confirmed the conclusions of his a priori speculations and demonstrated the intrinsic hopelessness of any quest in that realm, this would have amounted to a positive gain nevertheless in respect to his ideal of "Bildung" as the integration of experience. Had he declined the challenge of that obscure realm, he would have renounced therewith the innermost principle of which his personality is the embodiment.

There is, of course, a third ironic aspect in the summary dismissal of the occult on a priori grounds. For far from turning out to be merely the blind alley of Hans Castorp's anticipation, it produces an upheaval that shakes the very foundations of his being and leaves him, we are certain, a different man. But the content of that upheaval has already engaged our attention above, and while we may continue to muse about its implications, further discussion of it would be idle.

In introducing a series of masterpieces of Russian narrative art to the German public, shortly after the War, Thomas Mann wrote:

"Zwei Erlebnisse sind es, welche den Sohn des 19. Jahrhunderts zur neuen Zeit in Beziehung setzen, ihm Brücken in die Zukunft bauen: das Erlebnis Nietzsches und das des russischen Wesens." [25]

"There are two experiences which link the son of the nineteenth century with the new epoch and build bridges into the future: the experience of Nietzsche and that of the Russian soul."

Thomas Mann attaches enough importance to this statement to quote it again verbatim in an open letter a year later.[26] It seems to me that this statement holds the key to Mann's relation to the occult, which is a dual relation and aims at reconciling two mental attitudes that are supposed to exclude one another. Nietzsche and Russia, or, to make the antithesis more pointed: Nietzsche and Dostoevsky, represent the ethos of pride and the ethos of humility in singularly pure form; the gesture of challenge rising to what the Greeks called "hybris", and the Christian mystic's gesture of resignation. Once more we must ponder the maxim which finds it more moral to plunge into sin, to lose oneself, even to abandon oneself to perdition, rather than to follow the straight and narrow path of certified virtue; for this maxim expresses at once the free spirit's reckless defiance of whatever barriers would limit his field of exploration, and the mystic's reverent awareness of his dependence upon the grace of God. It is Thomas Mann's aim to make us experience in Hans Castorp a vital synthesis of that freedom and that reverence.

Synthesis is the principle that governs the pattern of the "Zauberberg" from first to last. All its themes, beginning with the "Urerlebnisse" Loyalty and Freedom, Death and Eros, are grouped, as it were, in so many pairs of answering melodies that ultimately intertwine and blend their voices in patterns of a higher order. Whatever phase of the "Zauberberg" we study, we find this loving interpenetration of opposites. It even permeates the style, as we saw in the author's favorite method of "polarization" in the selecting and combining of epithets.[27] In the counterpoint of its ideas as in that of its artistic balance the "Zauberberg" transcends all ordinary categories. It blends the tradition of Romanticism with that of the most highly developed psychological realism. It depicts the world of

sense with unsurpassed exactness of observation and at the same
time makes every one of its elements a focus of psychic energies.
The mere Romanticist would have stopped short at making us experience nature, man's enveloping medium, as a sublime equilibrium
of dynamic forces. The mere realist would have been satisfied to
evoke by the power of his language images of things rivalling direct
sense perception in their vividness. Thomas Mann does both and
more. In presenting the environment of man's own making, the
mechanical artefacts of modern civilization in all their detail, he
humanizes them, he raises them from the rank of mere articles of
use to a level of expressiveness where they can function as symbols
of his deepest experiences. Not only such time-hallowed objects as
the Baptismal Bowl are admitted to the poetic realm and sanctified
by the loving play of the imagination, but also such things as a clin-
ical thermometer, a silver pencil, a watch, a cigar, a phonographic
disk [28] are embraced in the inner circle of sentiment where they
function as nodes for the crossing currents of association and link
the most commonplace features of everyday life with the problem of
eternity, the mystery of mysteries.

In concluding, let us observe how the principle of synthesis is em-
bodied in the "Zauberberg's" structural organization. The Germans
are fond of distinguishing books that grow from books that are
made, books that embody the freedom of organic life and books that
approach a geometric pattern in the calculated balance of their design. "Buddenbrooks" as clearly belongs to the first class as "Königliche Hoheit" does to the second, by Thomas Mann's own admission.[29] Organic freedom is said to embody the German ideal of
expression, while structural symmetry of design is supposed to be
a characteristically French quality. The German is apt to sin in the
direction of formlessness, whereas the Frenchman inclines to the
other extreme. The German tends to take a disparaging view of the
formal aspect of literature generally and to stress only the substance.
Vitality and form are often pitted against each other by German
writers, as though they must exclude each other. Echoes of this
way of thinking strike our ear in the first half of the "Zauberberg",

where Hans Castorp's reaction against his Western mentor's praise of "Apollonian" form—to use Nietzsche's term—finds expression in such "Dionysian" and orgiastic outbursts as: "Form ist etepetete" [30] ("Form is folderol") and "La forme, c'est la pédanterie elle-même!" [31] ("Form is in essence pedantry")—even if such a connection does not reveal itself to the casual glance. The first of these outbursts was Hans Castorp's cryptic rejoinder to Hofrat Behrens' definition of life: "Leben ist, dass im Wechsel der Materie die Form erhalten bleibt" [32] ("Life is, that the form is maintained through the change of substance"). To catch the meaning of that rejoinder one has to resort to paradox and recall that at this stage of Hans Castorp's development he felt Death as imbued with a "vitality" that made Life appear listless and sober in comparison. And as for the second, it is part of Hans Castorp's first, ecstatic dialogue with Clavdia which marks the culmination of his "Sympathie mit dem Tode".

If form and life are normally felt as antithetical by the German, the "Zauberberg" surely transcends the limitations of the national temperament by achieving a synthesis of these two principles. And if our study has been at all convincing in essentials, it is clear that this blending of vitality and form is not an accidental by-product of Thomas Mann's genius but a result striven for by the most conscious artist of our time. That the "Zauberberg" embodies the principle of form in a supreme degree no one can doubt after observing how deftly its themes are interwoven and how marvellously anticipation and recollection are forever brought into play in the unfolding of the author's avowed plan to make his narrative move along in time, as a succession of themes, and, in spite of this, to achieve the illusion of simultaneity at every moment. Superlatives should be used sparingly, but I see no reason to qualify the statement that of all the attempts ever undertaken to express life on a large scale through the medium of literary creation, the "Zauberberg" is the most highly integrated. But is it alive in a measure equal to its mastery of form? This whole study has tacitly implied an affirmative answer to this question. The secret of life, however, in literature eludes demonstration, and there is no recourse for the reader but to fall back upon his own feeling.

In his recent address in commemoration of the centenary of Goethe's death, Thomas Mann speaks of Goethe's "Faust" as "ein Standardgedicht der Deutschheit und Menschheit",—a sentiment that finds its echo not only in Germany. Does not the "Zauberberg" also bid fair to be remembered by successive generations as another such exemplary expression of the genius of Germany and of humanity in one?

NOTES

The paging of my quotations from Thomas Mann's writings refers to the edition of the *Gesammelte Werke* as published by S. Fischer 1922—. The following abbreviations are used:

Bud I; Bud II = Buddenbrooks vol. I and II
                (Buddenbrooks; A. A. Knopf, New York)
    K H = Königliche Hoheit
                (Royal Highness; A. A. Knopf, New York)
  Z I; Z II = Der Zauberberg vol. I and II
                (The Magic Mountain; A. A. Knopf, New York)
  N I; N II = Novellen vol. I and II
                (Contained for the most part in the three publications:
                  Death in Venice; A. A. Knopf, New York
                  Children and Fools; A. A. Knopf, New York
                  A Man and His Dog; A. A. Knopf, New York
    BeU = Betrachtungen eines Unpolitischen
    RuA = Rede und Antwort ⎰ (Contained in part in Three Essays;
    Bem = Bemühungen   ⎱ A. A. Knopf, New York)
    FdT = Die Forderung des Tages

Of works not yet included in the *Gesammelte Werke* the following are also quoted:

        L = Lebensabriss. Die Neue Rundschau 1930, pp. 732–69
        (A Sketch of My Life; Harrison, Paris)
        G = Goethe als Repräsentant des Bürgerlichen Zeitalters. Die Neue
        Rundschau 1932, pp. 434–62
        (Goethe. The Yale Review 1932, pp. 711–35. Abridged)

I. CLASSIFICATION

[1] Z II, 428–9
[2] Z II, 429
[3] Z II, 393, 419, 533, 573
[4] Tiecks Werke, Bong, III, 26–7
[5] An example showing that this is true despite occasional appearances to the contrary, is the section entitled "Herr Albin" (Z I, 133 f.) The scene takes place in the common rest hall in the garden. Hans Castorp is not present. He is lying on his private balcony above, within earshot of the voices below. The point of the scene is the emergence into Hans Castorp's consciousness of those school-boy experiences of his which he designates as "Vorteile der Schande" (Z I, 138). The scene has an incidental value, of course, in contributing to the *milieu* of Haus Berghof.

On the whole, Thomas Mann limits himself in this scene to the reporting of the dialogue that strikes upon Hans Castorp's ear. However, certain visual impressions are transmitted to the reader without Hans Castorp being in a position to share them. We get glimpses of Herr Albin's build, of his features, his movements, his revolver, whereas the other participants in the scene remain simply so many voices. This double point of view shows us that the "Zauberberg" does not aim at rigid observance of the canons of realism.

What I have said of the scene proper holds true also for those frequent and extensive portions of the narrative that give a condensed panoramic summary of developments. They all centre about Hans Castorp. The only exception to this principle that I am aware of is the *résumé* of Naphta's antecedents (Z II, 165–77), but even that purports to be the content of what Naphta told Hans Castorp about himself (ib. 177).

⁶ Z II, 521

⁷ I have developed this in detail in a paper entitled "Der Symbolisch-Auto-biographische Gehalt von Thomas Manns Romandichtung 'Königliche Hoheit'", Publications of the Modern Language Association, September, 1931, pp. 867–79.

⁸ Z I, 553–4

⁹ Z I, 101

¹⁰ Z II, 134. On casual examination it may appear as if it were the author who is speaking here, and not Hans Castorp. But the whole passage from which this is taken is cast in the stylistic mould known as "erlebte Rede". For an exposition of the term see O. Walzel: "Das Wortkunstwerk" 1926, pp. 207 ff.

¹¹ The section in which we make his acquaintance is entitled "Satana".— On the evening of the mardi gras the glitter of his conversational fireworks is all borrowed from the "Walpurgisnacht" and the "Walpurgisnachtstraum" of Goethe's "Faust". Eight times in all he quotes either Mephisto directly, or the witches, or the will-o'-the-wisps, or related voices, and he contemplates the masqueraders with the same proprietary air as Mephisto does his minions on the Blocksberg.—There is also a Mephistophelian undercurrent in his aversion to music. Arrived with Faust on the Blocksberg, Mephisto remarks:

> "Ich höre was von Instrumenten tönen!
> Verflucht Geschnarr! Man muss sich dran gewöhnen."
>   (4050–1)

¹² Aside from his noble gestures and rhetorical pathos generally, his way of wearing his eternally checked trousers and frayed coat "mit so viel *Anmut und Würde*" (Z II, 55) irresistibly reminds one of Schiller and his famous essay of that title. An interesting confirmation of the intellectual resemblance of Settembrini to Schiller is implied in the following passage from one of Thomas Mann's most recent essays:

> "Und nichts kann psychologisch interessanter sein, als zu sehen, wie Schiller hier, indem er das Verhältnis des Idealisten zum Menschen formuliert, das Französische seiner eigenen Natur hervorkehrt. Es ist der Charakter des

französischen literarischen Geistes, den er mit knappen Worten umschreibt, dieses eigentümliche Ineinander von humanitär-revolutionärem Schwung, von generösem Menschheitsglauben und tiefstem, bitterstem, ja höhnischstem Pessimismus, was den Menschen als Einzelwesen betrifft." (G 447)

[13] Settembrini's warnings addressed to Hans Castorp on the dangers of the ironical attitude (Z I, 372) and the use of paradox (Z I, 374) have their exact counterpart in similar utterances of the young Nietzsche. See Werke II, 292–3, and I, 398 respectively. All references to Nietzsche's writings in these notes are based on the large octavo edition in 19 volumes, edited by Elisabeth Förster-Nietzsche.—Nietzsche also utters the warning note, "Cave musicam" (III, 7) on pedagogical grounds akin to Settembrini's.

[14] Some of Settembrini's most brilliant phrases are echoes of early pronouncements of Thomas Mann's own, among them: "Schön schreiben, das heisse beinahe auch schon schön denken, und von da sei nicht mehr weit zum schönen Handeln" (Z I, 269); and "Das Absurde, das ist das geistig Ehrenhafte" (Z I, 421). Both of these are quoted in BeU 70–2 (written 1915–7), where Thomas Mann takes stock very critically of some of his earlier published opinions. Another very striking instance is this résumé of one of Settembrini's bursts of eloquence: "Die reinigende, heiligende Wirkung der Literatur, die Zerstörung der Leidenschaften durch die Erkenntnis und das Wort, die Literatur als Weg zum Verstehen, zum Vergeben und zur Liebe, die erlösende Macht der Sprache, der literarische Geist als edelste Erscheinung des Menschengeistes überhaupt, der Literat als vollkommener Mensch, als Heiliger: aus dieser strahlenden Tonart ging Herrn Settembrinis apologetischer Lobgesang." (Z II, 306) This passage—with the exception of the last line, of course—is lifted verbatim from "Tonio Kröger" (N II, 39).

[15] If we keep in mind that the following passage was written during the War, and that the character of Settembrini had ample time to mellow during the six years that elapsed between the end of the War and the publication of the "Zauberberg", we are certainly justified in regarding Mazzini as the model for Settembrini.

"Wenn ich etwas lesen will, wobei sich mir das Eingeweide umkehrt, wobei alles in mir sich in Widerspruch verwandelt (und das kann zuweilen nützlich sein), so schlage ich den Band Mazzini auf, der eines Tages, ganz ohne mein Verdienst und Zutun, wie vom Himmel gesandt, in meine Hände gelangte, und dem ich nicht nur mein bisschen Einsicht in das Wesen politischer Tugend ursprünglich verdanke, sondern der mich auch lehrte, woher der deutsche Zivilisationsliterat Stil, Geste, Atemführung und Leidenschaft seiner politischen Manifeste eigentlich hat. Hier habe ich den lateinischen Freimaurer, Demokraten, Revolutionsliteraten und Fortschrittsrhetor in Reinkultur und in seiner Blüte; hier lerne ich 'den Geist' als ein Ding zwischen Gross-Orient und Jakobinerklub begreifen, wie er heute, nach Rehabilitierung der Tugend, wieder begriffen werden will und muss. Hier kann ich den Anblick eines durch nichts gehemmten, von keines Zweifels

Blässe angekränkelten Aktivismus bestaunen, der bald, mit weitester Ge-
bärde, die Augen im Himmel, deklamierend vor seinem Volke steht, bald
mit eingestemmten Fäusten und zischenden Atems umherspringt, hetzend,
aufwiegelnd, agazierend. Hier werden die Barrikaden 'der Volksthron'
genannt, hier höre ich einen Menschen sagen: 'Sittlichkeit und Technik!'
'Christus und die Presse!' . . ." (BeU 395)

[16] The September massacres of the French Revolution, in 1792, after which
the verb "septembriser" came to be coined as a slogan for radical action.
Hans Castorp stumbles on the name when he is first introduced to the Italian,
and is cut off after the second syllable, with a humorous bow, when he tries to
address him as Herr Septembrini (Z I, 98).

II. ORGANIZATION

[1] This matter is repeatedly discussed in Percy Lubbock's fascinating volume:
"The Craft of Fiction", Traveller's Library Edition, 1926, Jonathan Cape,
London. See particularly pp. 49, 108–9, 226–30.

[2] Shakespeare's procedure is imitated by Tieck in his "Kaiser Oktavian",
where *Echo* and *Schlaf* appear as characters along with *Die Romanze*, who performs a function similar to that of Father Time. Werke, Bong III, 91 f.

In this connection I cannot resist the temptation to call attention to the
shockingly cavalier fashion in which a much greater writer than Tieck took the
hurdle of our problem a hundred years ago. Between Chapters VII and VIII
of Book Two of a famous novel there was an interval of several years to be
bridged, and the author proceeded to communicate this fact to the reader by
the following

ZWISCHENREDE:

"Hier aber finden wir uns in dem Falle, dem Leser eine Pause und zwar von
einigen Jahren anzukündigen, weshalb wir gern, wäre es mit der typograph-
ischen Einrichtung zu verknüpfen gewesen, an dieser Stelle einen Band abge-
schlossen hätten.

Doch wird ja wohl auch der Raum zwischen zwei Kapiteln genügen, um
sich über das Mass gedachter Zeit hinwegzusetzen, da wir längst gewohnt
sind, zwischen dem Sinken und Steigen des Vorhangs in unserer persönlichen
Gegenwart dergleichen geschehen zu lassen."

(There follows another paragraph)

With all due respect to Goethe—for it is "Wilhelm Meisters Wanderjahre"
from which I am quoting—the naïveté of this solution may strike the modern
reader as nothing short of quaint. As a matter of fact, it only illustrates the
sovereign license which the ageing Goethe at times felt privileged to indulge in,
when the multiplicity of unfinished projects threatened to swamp him.

[3] Z I, 91
[4] Z I, 169
[5] Z I, 100
[6] Z I, 321

[7] Z I, 538

[8] Z II, 51

[9] Z I, 80

[10] Z II, 620

[11] Bud I, Book One, Chapters 1 and 2.

[12] Z I, 76 f.

[13] Z I, 116 f. I have taken the liberty to anglicize the spelling of the Russian girl's nick-name for the same reason that I follow Mrs. Lowe-Porter's rendering of Clawdia's name as Clavdia in her English version of the "Zauberberg"— to preserve the phonetic values of the original.

[14] Z I, 123-4

[15] Z I, 127-33

[16] This is not the only subtle function to which indirect discourse lends itself in the hands of so expert a master of stylistic devices as Thomas Mann. A peculiarly humorous effect is at times achieved by rendering highly oratorical and impassioned tirades in indirect discourse. For a good example of this see Z II, 303.

[17] Z I, 140

[18] Z I, 141-2

[19] Z II, 336

[20] The first sign of articulate opposition on Hans Castorp's part occurs during their conversation, when Settembrini visits the patient put to bed for three weeks (Z I, 324 40). Here Hans has the effrontery to ask some embarrassing questions (331).

When they meet again (Z I, 372-7), he challenges the humanist by the question: "Was haben Sie gegen die Analyse?"

During their next conversation (Z I, 403-23) Settembrini once more solemnly counsels Hans to risk his health and depart. But Hans holds his ground, and the sparring ends with Settembrini's gracefully complimenting him on his skill as a verbal fencer.

Somewhat later we find Hans Castorp criticizing Settembrini's onesided insistence on the ethos of freedom, as against the ethos of piety (Z I, 495-6). This to Joachim. Settembrini is not present.

Next we find Settembrini reproaching Hans Castorp for playing the Christian charity worker among the "moribundi": "Lasst die Toten ihre Toten begraben." (Z I, 518-9) But Hans indicates by a gesture that he intends to follow his own counsel in this matter.

On the evening of the mardi gras, finally, Settembrini twice risks the prestige of his waning authority by addressing Hans Castorp in tones of peremptory command (Z I, 543; 552). Outspoken insubordination is the result.

[21] Z I, 146-8

[22] Z I, 297-8

[23] Z I, 572-3

[24] Z II, 130-1

[25] Z II, 141-65

III. SUBSTANCE AND EXPOSURE

¹ "Legitimität", if I am not mistaken, has only recently made its appearance in Thomas Mann's inventory of terms expressing his relation to the values of tradition. "Das Wichtigste, das Entscheidende ist Legitimität", he writes in his "Lebensabriss" (L 764). And the same statement, compressed into a clause, recurs on the first page of his essay: "Goethe als Repräsentant des bürgerlichen Zeitalters" (G 711).

² Z I, 366–9

³ Z I, 137–8

⁴ Z I, 155

⁵ See particularly Freud's "Drei Abhandlungen zur Sexualtheorie". 2. Aufl. 1910, Leipzig und Wien.

⁶ We should not overlook in this connection that these four experiences invite a different grouping by which they resolve themselves into two corresponding pairs: Continuity (loyalty to tradition) and Freedom (irresponsibility), on the one hand; and Death and Eros, on the other. Each pair expresses an opposition that may be antagonistic or complementary.

When we are introduced, toward the end of Volume II, to the most intimate favorites of Hans Castorp's select repertoire of phonograph records—Aida, L'après-midi d'un Faune, Carmen, Valentin's Prayer, and Der Lindenbaum, we may wonder on what basis they are selected. A little reflection will convince us that they are all felt by Hans Castorp as supreme expressions of one or more of his four "Urerlebnisse". Aïda and Carmen each embody all four. Valentin's Prayer embodies them all with the exception of Freedom (irresponsibility). Irresponsibility, i.e. "die Vorteile der Schande" is certainly the quiddity of L'après-midi. And Der Lindenbaum is the haunting song of Loyalty and Death.

⁷ Z I, 61

⁸ Z I, 60

⁹ Z II, 425

¹⁰ L 737

¹¹ "Über Königliche Hoheit" (1910), in RuA 347

¹² Z II, 428–9

¹³ Z I, 122

¹⁴ Hans Castorp pays tribute to love as "une puissance plus éducative que toute la pédagogie du monde". (Z I, 577)

¹⁵ L 754

¹⁶ But it must have begun to germinate even before 1912! Some vague plan for a novelistic work of immense scope was already taking shape while Thomas Mann worked on "Der Tod in Venedig" (1911). We infer this with certainty from what Thomas Mann tells us about the literary career of Gustav Aschenbach, the hero of this *Novelle*, who is definitely a projection of one of Thomas Mann's own possibilities of selfhood. In the list of Aschenbach's works as characterized in "Der Tod in Venedig" we positively identify the following among Thomas Mann's own literary creations: "Friedrich der Grosse" (N II, 356)—at that time planned as an extensive work, but condensed into an essay

during the first year of the War; "Buddenbrooks" (ib. 360), "Fiorenza" (ib. 361; 362); "Königliche Hoheit" (ib. 361); "Felix Krull" (ib. 361); "Tristan" (ib. 361; 362); "Tonio Kröger" (ib. 361; 362). This identification of Thomas Mann with Aschenbach is so far-reaching that when we read in "Der Tod in Venedig"

"Aschenbach hatte es einmal *an wenig sichtbarer Stelle* (italics mine) unmittelbar ausgesprochen, dass beinahe alles Grosse, was dastehe, als ein Trotzdem dastehe, trotz Kummer und Qual, Armut, Verlassenheit, Körperschwäche, Laster, Leidenschaft und tausend Hemmnissen zustande gekommen sei"

we are intuitively certain that this must be a verbatim quotation of one of Thomas Mann's own "buried" passages; and our search is rewarded when we find the identical passage in a two page essay "Über den Alkohol" (1906; RuA 376). To come to the point, now, which rests on this far-reaching identification of Thomas Mann with Aschenbach as its premise,—Aschenbach is introduced to us as "der geduldige Künstler, der in langem Fleiss den figurenreichen, so vielerlei Menschenschicksal im Schatten einer Idee versammelnden Romanteppich, 'Maja' mit Namen, wob" (ib. 356). That characterization certainly fits the "Zauberberg",—a "Romanteppich", if there ever was one! But to complete the proof, we read in the "Lebensabriss" that while at work on the "Zauberberg" Thomas Mann used to brace himself to the task by quoting to himself his favorite lines from Heine's "Der Dichter Firdusi":

> "Seines Liedes Riesenteppich—
> Zweimal hunderttausend Verse." (L 761)

[17] Werke II, 8
[18] Werke II, 8
[19] Werke XV, 11
[20] Werke XV, 31
[21] Thomas Mann defines "Passion" as "Hingabe zusammen mit Erkenntnis". BeU 40
[22] L 741
[23] "Goethe und Tolstoi" (1922), in Bem 56

IV. DISEASE

[1] Disease is a prominent theme in "Buddenbrooks", "Tristan", "Fiorenza", and "Der Tod in Venedig".

[2] Preface to "Saint Joan" lxxv, New York, Brentano, 1924

[3] That Thomas Mann finds not only disease interesting but also crime is evidenced by his fragmentary autobiography of a criminal: "Bekenntnisse des Hochstaplers Felix Krull", Deutsche Verlagsanstalt Stuttgart, 1923; now also available in the Inselbücherei.

[4] Novalis' Schriften (Kluckhohn), Bibl. Inst. IV, 424

[5] ibid. III, 232.—The philosophical speculations of the "Zauberberg", those of the section entitled "Forschungen" particularly (Z I, 450–82), are very close to the sphere of Novalis. Thomas Mann's intense preoccupation with Novalis

is also directly attested by his essay: "Von deutscher Republik" (1922), in Bem, which quotes Novalis liberally and is largely an exposition of his political views and an attempt to apply these to the German Republic and its post-war problems.

[6] ibid. III, 232

[7] ibid. III, 339

[8] ibid. III, 369

[9] "Lucinde", Inselbücherei #295, 79f.

[10] ibid. 81

[11] Z I, 164

[12] Heines Werke (Elster [1]), Bibl. Inst., III, 235

[13] ibid. III, 270

[14] ibid. IV, 132

[15] ibid. VII, 404

[16] ibid. I, 254

[17] Grillparzers Werke (Hock), Bong, I, 27

[18] The whole division called "Totentanz" is devoted to these matters. Z I, 482–541

[19] Z II, 425

[20] We first meet the word "regieren" Z II, 84, where it occurs three times. In the English translation it is rendered by "stock-taking", which strikes me as unfortunate, because it involves the degradation of a highly imaginative code word to an everyday expression with commercial associations.

[21] Z II, 77–8

[22] Z I, 121

[23] Z I, 122

[24] Z I, 130

[25] Z I, 237

[26] Z I, 575

[27] Z II, 265

[28] Attention is called in this connection to Thomas Mann's essay: "Die Stellung Freuds in der modernen Geistesgeschichte" (1929), in FdT, 196–224.

[29] Z I, 374

[30] Z I, 384

[31] KH 273–4, etc.

[32] Z I, 503–4

[33] "Brief an einen Verleger", RuA 318

[34] L 743

[35] Z II, 527

V. THE IRONIC TEMPER

[1] BeU 53

[2] BeU xxix

[3] The association of irony with *eros*, the principle of sympathy, is also developed in BeU 61.

4 Z I, 372

5 Z I, 373

6 See BeU 203–4

7 BeU 164

8 L 753

9 Athenaeum III (1800), 16

10 In the Lyceum der schönen Künste (1797) and in the Athenaeum (1798–1800). The most important of these, in the convenient numbering of Minor's edition of Friedrich Schlegels Prosaische Jugendschriften (1882) include the following *Fragmente* from the Lyceum: 7, 37, 42, 48, 87, 108; and the following *Fragmente* from Athenaeum I: 51, 121, 253, 269, 305, 418, 431

11 I think Novalis caught the ethos of Schlegel's doctrine of irony very happily as detachment, consciousness, sovereign play of the spirit, when he commented on it, in his "Blütenstaub" as follows: "Was Friedrich Schlegel so scharf als Ironie charakterisiert, ist meinem Bedünken nach nichts anderes als die Folge, der Charakter der Besonnenheit, der wahrhaften Gegenwart des Geistes. Schlegels Ironie scheint mir echter Humor zu sein." (Athenaeum I, 79)

12 Heines Werke (Elster 1), Bibl. Inst., IV, 288

13 Athenaeum I (1798)

14 Shakespeare und der deutsche Geist (1911), 327

15 Fragmente, Athenaeum I, numbers 116 and 121

16 There are novelists, of course, who waive the privileges of this convention and limit themselves strictly to the recording of what the author could plausibly have observed without resorting to a cloak of invisibility or to the magic of being able to share the unuttered thoughts of his characters. Such a procedure represents a further extreme tightening of the principles of realism. Where this method is applied without thoroughgoing consistency we become painfully aware of the convention and the illusion is destroyed, as, for instance, in Dostoevsky's "The Possessed", where the author begins by installing himself as an eye-witness and as the confidant of the principal character, and then proceeds to tell us scenically a great many incidents that he could not possibly have witnessed. In a similar way, Hauptmann's "Narr in Christo" suffers from a shifting of the point of view.

17 Z I, 58 f.

18 See Chapter III of this study, note 16.

19 Z I, 235–7

20 Z I, 239

21 Z I, 275

22 Z I, 347–8

23 Z I, 388

24 Z I, 398–9

25 Z I, 399–400

26 Z I, 391–2

27 Z II, 435

[28] Z I, 183
[29] Z I, 403–4
[30] Z I, 461
[31] Z II, 423 f.
[32] Z II, 145
[33] Z II, 10
[34] Z II, 14
[35] Z II, 14
[36] Z II, 17
[37] Z II, 18

[38] Throughout Volume One the reader's curiosity is teased in a similar way with regard to Clavdia's relations to Behrens. When Hans Castorp first learns of her being painted by Behrens, he at once experiences a stirring of jealousy. When Behrens shows the two cousins his paintings, no conclusions are to be drawn from the jargon he employs in describing Clavdia (Z I, 433 f.). But after reporting how Hans Castorp is enraptured by the fragrance of the painted skin, the author adds: "Es ist doch sachlich festzustellen, dass Frau Chauchats Dekolleté das bei weitem bemerkenswerteste Stück Malerei in diesem Zimmer war." (Z I, 435–6) That sets one thinking!

[39] Z II, 22
[40] Z II, 26
[41] Z II, 62
[42] Z II, 82–3

[43] The fact that Clavdia's image hovers just below the threshold of Hans Castorp's consciousness all the time is very subtly conveyed on a number of occasions by the turning up, in his conversation, of some of the French phrases that had figured in the dialogue on the evening of the mardi gras. (Z II, 77, 117, 125)

[44] Z II, 272
[45] Z II, 337
[46] Z II, 338–9
[47] Z II, 347
[48] Z II, 272–3
[49] Z II, 357
[50] Z II, 361
[51] Z I, 249; II, 156
[52] Z I, 562
[53] Z II, 321
[54] Z II, 110–11

[55] I mention only one or two of the most characteristic passages that impart, in each case, something of the intimacy of living things to these objects. Maria Mancini: Z I, 427; II, 617. The thermometer: Z I, 283–6. The pencil: Z I, 206–7; 560–1. The x-ray machine: Z I, 364. The x-ray picture: Z II, 16; 82–3. The watch: Z II, 341; 617. The phonograph disk: Z II, 495 f.; 504 f.

[56] Z II, 482

[57] Z II, 348. A few examples (that could be multiplied indefinitely) to show how Thomas Mann's will to see life in terms of a synthesis of opposites determines his way of combining characteristic epithets: "mit einem zugleich lässigen und heftigen Achselzucken" (Z I, 18); "vom Leben und seinem heilig-unreinen Geheimnis" (Z I, 462); " bewandert, aber fromm" (Z I, 493); "aske-tisch und witzig" (Z II, 90); "separiert und traulich" (Z II, 109); "forsch und melancholisch zugleich" (Z II, 149); "gleichsam räudig . . . jedoch elegant" (Z II, 190); "wüstlingshaft und asketisch" (Z II, 211); "ihre zugleich träge und heftige Huld" (Z II, 346); "Trägheit und Angeregtheit" (Z II, 457).

[58] Note how Thomas Mann conveys the illusion of the restless, ever changing play of the complex tracery of lines furrowing Peeperkorn's forehead, by an equally restless, ever-changing play of his descriptive phrasing. The one phenomenon is presented by all theser enderings: mächtige Stirnfalten, idolhaftes Arabeskenwerk, Stirnarabesken, monumentales Faltenwerk, lineares Falten-werk, die idolhafte Lineatur seiner Stirn, hochgezogene Arabesken, mit an-gezogenem Faltenwerk, hochgezogene Stirnlineatur, hochfaltige Königsmaske, idolhafte Stirnlineatur, angezogene Stirnlineatur, mit stirnfaltigem Erstaunen.

[59] Z II, 287

[60] Z II, 283

[61] Z II, 283

[62] Z II, 284–5

[63] Z II, 285

[64] In the field of contemporary literature I can think of only one other novel that attempts anything of this sort. I have reference to André Gide's "Les Faux-Monnayeurs",—it also a dual entity, presenting at once the created product and the creative process by which it comes into being.

[65] Z I, 436

[66] Bem 113

[67] Z I, 473

[68] Z I, 309

[69] Z II, 335

[70] Z II, 334

[71] Z II, 343

[72] I, 746

[73] Z II, 284

[74] Z II, 391

[75] Z I, 449

[76] Z I, 574

[77] Z I, 449

[78] Z II, 117

[79] Z I, 576

[80] Z I, 519

[81] Z I, 566

[82] Z II, 258

[83] Z II, 203

[84] Z I, 556

[85] Z I, 567

[86] Z II, 399

[87] Z I, 442 f.

[88] Z I, 83–4

[89] Z I, 489

[90] Z I, 190

[91] Z I, 524

[92] When we compare the ironic temper of the "Zauberberg" with that of Thomas Mann's early *Novellen*, the difference in emotional tone is very striking. There is an intense cruelty, a cold glitter about many of the early *Novellen*, such as "Der kleine Herr Friedemann", "Der Weg zum Friedhof", "Luischen", "Tristan", etc., contrasting sharply with the "erotic irony" of the "Zauberberg" and its all-pervasive "Sympathie mit dem Leben". The earlier tone is largely a youthful defense reaction against the encroachment of sentimentality, reinforced by literary influences, such as that of Wedekind.

VI. WHAT IS GERMAN?

[1] Bud I, 349, 458; II, 106, 286

[2] Z II, 118

[3] Z I, 219

[4] Z I, 104

[5] Z I, 154

[6] Z I, 250

[7] Z I, 514

[8] Z II, 618

[9] Z II, 622

[10] The converse, Thomas Mann is Hans Castorp, is also true, subject to certain reservations. To a much greater degree than the average reader would suspect, Naphta's love of casuistry portrays a phase of Mann's own personality.

[11] Z II, 522–5. Large portions of this analysis appear verbatim over Thomas Mann's own signature in his "Rede über Nietzsche" (1924) in Bem 331–5.

[12] See Chapter I, note 7, of this study.

[13] See Chapter IV, note 20, of this study.

[14] BeU 154–5. The "Betrachtungen eines Unpolitischen", written from 1915 to 1917 and published shortly before the end of the War, I quote throughout according to the slightly abridged edition that took its place in the "Gesammelte Werke" in 1922. In this edition the bulky volume, which still numbers xlvii + 630 pages has been reduced by somewhat less than six per cent. Some years ago the charge was raised against Thomas Mann and given wide currency in the conservative press that this abridgment had been undertaken in the spirit of a revision, in order to tone down the brusk conservatism of the original version and make Thomas Mann's change of front in 1922, when he espoused the cause of the young Republic, appear less radical. By direct statement and innuendo the impression was conveyed as though in place of the original

"anti-democratic" volume Thomas Mann had palmed off a "democratic" version upon the unsuspecting reader. When Thomas Mann repudiated the charge without mincing his words, pages of quotations and a long statistical table were marshalled to prove that in instance after instance the items deleted contained statements of points of view that must be embarrassing to the supporter of the democratic Republic. This was followed by a further exchange of polemics.

The charge is a serious one, and its sponsor seems to have made out a strong *prima facie* case in support of his contention. There is only one genuine way of testing its weight, namely, with the deleted pages in mind, to reread the whole of the 670 odd pages of the abridged version. Only then can one render any worth while opinion as to whether there has been any attempt to alter the spirit of the original by the abridgment.

I have made this test with an open mind (in so far as it is possible to have an open mind on the score of an author whose conscientiousness and sense of responsibility one has long regarded in the light of articles of faith). And I find this: Time after time, when the accuser delivers a thrust with the exultant announcement: "Gestrichen ist die Feststellung . . .", "Gestrichen ist das Urteil . . .", the same deleted idea, often phrased in the identical language, is found in half a dozen, a dozen, sometimes a score of passages throughout the volume. Consisting as it does of argument, discussion, polemics, the "Betrachtungen eines Unpolitischen" is a highly repetitive book, mulling over the variations of the one fundamental antithesis of Kultur and Zivilisation with a tenacity that may be felt as exhausting. "Die qualvoll-witzige Dauergrübelei über Charakter und Schicksal des Deutschtums" is Thomas Mann's own formula expressing its content. (FdT 184)

One of the items of the charge pressed with particular insistence is the claim that the most violently bitter conflict that rages in the Book—the polemic directed against Heinrich Mann, Thomas Mann's brother,—has been suppressed in the abridged version and replaced by a polemic "die ins Leere geht, die sich gegen keine scharf umrissene Persönlichkeit mehr richtet, sondern gegen einen verschwommen gezeichneten Typus, eine unbestimmte Personifikation von zersetzenden Kräften im deutschen Daseinskampf". (Süddeutsche Monatshefte XXV, 700.) The uninformed reader is bound to interpret this charge to mean among other things that the name of Heinrich Mann, present in the original version, has been deleted in the abridgment. But the fact is that Heinrich Mann's name does not appear in either version! In the abridgment, the section which is *exclusively* concerned with the reply to Heinrich Mann's attacks has been shortened by less than one fourth, still leaving some 33 pages (162–94). To claim, however, that the polemic has thereby lost one iota of its intensity and directness seems to me nothing short of wilful distortion. Already the "Vorrede" calls attention to "ein menschlich tragisches Element des Buches . . . jenen intimen Konflikt, dem eine Reihe von Seiten besonders gewidmet sind, und der auch sonst vieler Orten mein Denken färbt und bestimmt" (xxi), and justifies the inclusion of something so personal by remarking: "Dieser Konflikt spielt im Geistigen, und er besitzt ohne allen Zweifel genug symbolische Würde, um ein Recht auf Öffentlichkeit zu haben und folglich, dargestellt, nicht schimpflich zu wirken". (ibid.) The section devoted to Heinrich Mann strikes its keynote in the first sentence by quoting Shakespeare's "Mehr als befreundet, weniger als Freund" ("a little more than kin and less than kind"), and on the next two pages the references to "Bruderkriege"(163), to "brüderliche Kritik" (164), and again to "geistige Bürger- und Bruderkriege" (164) must give us pause. To anyone with a grain of insight it is perfectly clear that Thomas Mann's attacks are levelled at a specific individual related to him by bonds more intimate than those of friendship. The book abounds in clearly indicated quotations from his brother's speeches and essays, notably the essay on Zola, which is repeatedly mentioned by title so that the present-day reader, even if wholly ignorant of this war-time family feud at the outset, would have no difficulty in identifying the specific personality at which the attacks are aimed. No attempt was made, moreover, at the time of the War, to make a secret of this feud, and Eloesser's Thomas Mann biography of 1925—a tribute on the occasion of Thomas Mann's fiftieth birthday—discusses the feud with the utmost frankness.

Careful study will show that in the abridgment of the polemic Thomas Mann was guided by two principles: First, he rearranged and condensed in the interest of stylistic concentration; and secondly, he deleted such passages as reflected the jealous rivalry of two fellow-artists more than the super-personal issues involved,—passages felt by the revising eye as failing to measure up sufficiently to the criterion of publicity formulated in the preface. But in every essential point the bitter exchange of hostilities was left to stand as a matter of historical record, in keeping with Thomas Mann's conviction: "Europäische Kriege, sofern sie nur auch im Geistigen geführt werden, und das müssen sie immer, werden zugleich auch deutsche *Bruderkriege* sein, das bleibt das Schicksal dieses europäischen Herzvolks, und das ist bei aller Wucht seines Leibes seine innere, sittliche, seine politische Schwäche—es wird vielleicht sein Verhängnis sein." (163).

The real object of the charge levelled against Thomas Mann's abridgment of his War Book was unquestionably the desire to discredit his post-war political opinions by discrediting his character. On this fundamental point a foreigner is perhaps at an advantage over a German in the ability to consider the case without political bias, whereas it would be grossly improper to claim anything of the sort in discussing the political wisdom of Thomas Mann's change of front,—a matter obviously outside the scope of this study.

The documents bearing on the controversy are the following:

1. "Die überarbeiteten 'Betrachtungen eines Unpolitischen'". An article by Dr. Arthur Hübscher first published in 1927 in "Das Gewissen", designated by Thomas Mann (see #5 a) as "eine berliner faszistische Klubzeitung".

2. The same as the above, reprinted in the "Münchener Neueste Nachrichten" #228, 1927 under the title: "Die Metamorphose der 'Betrachtungen eines Unpolitischen'".

3. "Kultur und Sozialismus". Thomas Mann's reply to Dr. Hübscher's charges, published in "Preussische Jahrbücher", April 1928, 24–32.

4. "Offener Brief an Thomas Mann". A countercharge by Dr. Hübscher published in "Süddeutsche Monatshefte", June 1928, 697–706.

5. "Um Thomas Manns 'Betrachtungen'". In "Süddeutsche Monatshefte", July 1928, 769–72. This consists of

    a. A letter of Thomas Mann addressed to Dr. Hübscher.

    b. Dr. Hübscher's reply.

6. "Kultur und Sozialismus". In Thomas Mann's volume of essays "Die Forderung des Tages" (1930), 184–96. This is the same as #3 except for the first page, which is more restrained in tone than the original opening paragraph and omits certain statements which Dr. Hübscher had shown to be not strictly in accord with literal fact. It does not retract anything essential. The remainder of the essay shows a small number of minor stylistic changes that do not affect the controversy.

Coincident with Dr. Hübscher's attack there appeared another, more surreptitious, and perhaps more insidious on that account. In an article, " Thomas Manns 'Zauberberg'—ein Bildungsroman?", in the " Zeitschrift für Deutschkunde", 1928, 241–53, Wolfgang von Einsiedel summarizes his annihilating criticism of the later Thomas Mann in these words:

"Das letzte wesentliche Buch des Thomas Mann, den wir liebten, hiess: 'Betrachtungen eines Unpolitischen'. Das erste Buch des Thomas Mann, den wir noch respektieren, heisst: 'Der Zauberberg'.

Die 'Betrachtungen', mochte man sachlich im einzelnen zu ihnen stehen wie immer man wollte—sie waren das Bekenntnis eines, der noch fragte und rang, dem es noch um Erkenntnis ging und um Selbsterkenntnis; und also ein tiefes Buch. (Selbstverständlich gilt dies nur von der ersten Auflage der 'Betrachtungen', nicht von der untapferen und verwässerten Bearbeitung in der Ausgabe der gesammelten Werke.)" 252

To leave the epithet "untapfer" aside,—it is certainly a critical feat of note to refer to an abridgment and a condensation as "eine verwässerte Bearbeitung". Whether consciously or not, the slur was motivated by the principle, so effective in politics: "Semper aliquid haeret". The whole controversy is symptomatic of the violence of political antagonisms in post-war Germany.

[15] There is a wealth of well-organized material on this phase of the subject in Fernand Baldensperger's suggestive study: "La littérature. Creation, succès, durée" (1913). See particularly the section entitled: "Les synthétismes nationaux" (287–318).

[16] Werke III, 159

[17] Werke VI, 84–5

[18] As Korff points out in his "Geist der Goethezeit" (I, 150) Herder's essays "Von deutscher Art und Kunst" (1773) give to the following pairs of terms the value of synonyms: "deutsch und charakteristisch, deutsch und schöpferisch, deutsch und ursprünglich, ja auch deutsch und barbarisch". It is evident that

eighteenth century France was in the background of Herder's mind as the antithesis of all this.

[19] "Da es aber (gewiss ein Indizium gegen Deutschland!) eine beträchtlich heiklere und verwickeltere Sache ist, für Deutschland zu sprechen, als für die 'Zivilisation'". . . . BeU 23.

[20] BeU 17

[21] I don't know how far this idea can be traced back. The perspective that sees the German genius as one of mediation already marks the reflections of the young Kant on the subject of national character, in his "Beobachtungen über das Gefühl des Schönen und des Erhabenen" (Werke, Ernst Cassirer, II, 287, 291); and one does not get the impression that he is trying to say anything strikingly original on that subject.

[22] BeU 3, 11, etc.

[23] This is a war-time idea; and it is to Thomas Mann's credit that at no time during the struggle did he forget "dass wahre Gedanken nicht zu allen Zeiten gleich wahr sind" (BeU 7) and "dass Kriegsgedanken notwendig anders aussehen, als Gedanken im Frieden" (BeU 203). I wonder what he would have said if it had been pointed out to him at the time that none other than the imperialist Kipling had already expressed the peculiarity of the English temperament as consisting in this identical trait. From Kipling's poem, "The Puzzler" (Rudyard Kipling's Verse. Inclusive Edition, 1919, III, 54–5) keyed to this note in its entirety, I quote these lines characterizing the English:

"For undemocratic reasons and for motives not of State,
　They arrive at their conclusions—largely inarticulate.
　Being void of self-expression they confide their views to none;
　But sometimes in a smoking-room, one learns why things were done.
　　　　　- - - - -
In telegraphic sentences, half nodded to their friends,
　They hint a matter's inwardness—and there the matter ends.
　And while the Celt is talking from Valencia to Kirkwall,
　The English—ah, the English!—don't say anything at all!"

[24] Adam Müller: "Vorlesungen über deutsche Wissenschaft und Literatur", Dresden (1806).
Nietzsche: Werke VII, 209.

[25] BeU 85

[26] "Man kann in diesem Kriege mit Leib und Seele auf deutscher Seite sein . . . und dennoch in seiner stillsten Stunde der Meinung zuneigen, dass das gebildete, das wissende und problematische Volk zum europäischen Ferment bestimmt ist und *nicht* zur Herrschaft." BeU 530

[27] BeU 176

[28] BeU 32

[29] BeU 31

[30] The essay of that title was one of several that appeared together with the one on Frederick the Great in a volume entitled: "Friedrich und die grosse Koalition". Fischer, 1915, 7–32.

[31] BeU 203–4

[32] Z II, 597

[33] BeU 164–6

[34] In its *negative* aspects, Naphta's critique of Settembrini's ideology is an echo of Thomas Mann's own critique of his brother's position, in the "Betrachtungen". Substantially it reduces itself to the thesis that Western Liberalism, the political corollary of the enlightenment, at one time a living gospel, has ceased to be a genuinely vital force. It has degenerated into a clatter of rhetorical phrases, and with its glib oratory it glosses over all real problems. It stays on the surface of things and is blind to all the deeper realities. A few examples from the "Zauberberg" to illustrate this critique:

"Ich suchte Logik in unser Gespräch einzuführen", says Naphta to Settembrini, "und Sie antworten mir mit Hochherzigkeiten. . . . Das heroische Zeitalter Ihrer Ideale ist längst vorüber, diese Ideale sind tot, sie liegen heute zum mindesten in den letzten Zügen, und die Füsse derer, die ihnen den Garaus machen werden, stehen schon vor der Tür." (Z II, 99)

Settembrini and Naphta are discussing freedom, when Naphta takes occasion to remark: "Vorderhand wäre es mir eine Genugtuung, wenn diese Zusammenhänge Ihnen Veranlassung gäben, die Freiheit nicht so sehr als schöne Geste, denn als ein Problem zu begreifen." (Z II, 108)

"Die Philosophie seines Herrn Widersachers", Naphta is quoted as saying, "arbeite darauf hin, dem Leben alle schweren und todernsten Akzente zu nehmen; auf die Kastration des Lebens gehe sie aus, auch mit dem Determinismus ihrer sogenannten Wissenschaft." (Z II, 201) This passage is substantially identical with BeU 456.

In a bit of interior dialogue, Hans Castorp formulates his conflicting feelings regarding the two pedagogues by saying that he is really much fonder of Settembrini than of Naphta. "Du bist zwar ein Windbeutel und Drehorgelmann, aber du meinst es gut, meinst es besser und bist mir lieber als der scharfe kleine Jesuit und Terrorist . . . obgleich er fast immer recht hat, wenn ihr euch zankt." (Z II, 228)

The charge that Settembrini's mind feeds on worn-out phrases is symbolically expressed, of course, by his clothing—by his "gelber Flausch" and his "ewig gewürfelte Hosen". "Er trägt die alten Sachen übrigens mit hervorragendem Anstand", Hans Castorp remarks in justice to him. (Z II, 437) At all times he wears them with "Anmut und Würde", and on a specific occasion his appearance runs all the less danger of contrasting unfavorably with that of his more elegantly attired companions, as his checked trousers were freshly pressed, "so dass man sie auf den ersten Blick fast für neu hätte halten können". (Z II, 55) And there is his shabby winter jacket "deren Biberkragen und Ärmelrevers vermöge enthaarter Stellen gleichsam räudig wirkten, die er jedoch elegant zu tragen wusste". (Z II, 190) All this is pointedly brought home by Naphta's withering characterization of Settembrini's ideology as "diese ganze Mottenkiste klassizistisch-bourgeoiser Tugendideologie". (Z II, 278)

[35] Z I, 57

[36] See "Fünfzehnter Brief" in particular.

[37] BeU 529

[38] See Chapter I, note 11, of this study.

[39] Z I, 193

[40] Z I, 190

[41] BeU 12

[42] Werke III, 7

[43] "Das Kunstwerk der Zukunft". Wagners Gesammelte Schriften, Hesse und Becker, X, 100.

[44] To mention another paradoxical feature of Wagner's position, it is Wagner's music dramas, of course, that bear the brunt of the charge levelled by intellectuals against music generally, that it induces a narcotic effect.

[45] Z I, 45

[46] The "Betrachtungen" make a cleancut division between the social and the metaphysical sphere, between man's relation to his fellow-men and man's relation to the universe.

[47] Z I, 220

[48] Z I, 298

[49] Z I, 510

[50] Z I, 521

[51] Z I, 540

[52] Z II, 12

[53] Z II, 36

[54] Z II, 111

[55] Z I, 393

[56] Z I, 567

[57] Z I, 109

[58] Z I, 268–9. This passage is taken practically verbatim from BeU 12, where it serves to characterize the point of view of Western civilization.

[59] Z II, 290

[60] Z II, 294

[61] ibid.

[62] Z II, 295

[63] ibid.

[64] Z II, 304

[65] ibid.

[66] Z II, 258

[67] Z I, 271

[68] Z II, 410

[69] Z II, 411

[70] Z II, 408

[71] Z II, 378–81

[72] Z II, 439

[73] Z II, 443

[74] Z II, 448

[75] Z II, 452

[76] BeU 150

[77] BeU 263

[78] Z I, 333

[79] Z II, 425

[80] Z I, 54

[81] Z I, 242

[82] Z II, 618

[83] Z II, 291

[84] Z II, 49

[85] Z II, 124

[86] Z II, 243–4

[87] Z I, 349

[88] Of all the characters in the "Zauberberg" Joachim stands closest to his author's heart. The impersonally worded tribute, "dass er der Beste gewesen sei von allen hier oben" (Z II, 268) voices Thomas Mann's own feelings, and it is his own emotion that takes refuge with Hofrat Behrens behind a volley of puns at Joachim's deathbed. No reader familiar with Tonio Kröger's friendship with Hans Hansen—the affection of the marked man, the problematical individual, the biological sport, the morbid, "self-conscious" intellectual for his own opposite, for the sound, the perfect, the serenely unconscious representative of a general norm of animal life—no reader familiar with the leading rôle that this loving polarity obtaining between "Geist" and "Leben" plays in Thomas Mann's literary work can fail to detect the peculiar warmth of affection that has gone into the portrayal of Joachim. I mention this only because I have heard readers express the opinion that Thomas Mann in his treatment of Joachim had not been fair to the type.

[89] Z I, 281

[90] Z I, 260

[91] Z I, 264

[92] Z I, 261

[93] Z I, 221

[94] "Gedanken im Kriege" in "Friedrich und die grosse Koalition" (1915) 11.

[95] Z I, 190. We hear in this—negatively turned, of course—an echo of an observation of Thomas Mann's in the "Betrachtungen": "Stolz, Ehre und Lust des Gehorsams scheint heute eine deutsche Besonderheit und internationale Unbegreiflichkeit." (BeU 498)—"Der stolze Gehorsam . . . scheint heute etwas spezifisch Deutsches." (BeU 500)

[96] Z I, 422

[97] Z I, 258

[98] Z I, 345

[99] In medieval German literature "triuwe" (Treue) is the central concept of ethical idealism. The student will find an exceedingly fine exposition of this fact in Ehrismann's "Geschichte der deutschen Literatur bis zum Ausgang des Mittelalters". Significant allusions are to be found in abundance in Ehris-

mann's volume on the "Blütezeit", Erste Hälfte (2.2.1). See in particular pp. 103, 157, 183, 198–202, 205, 219, 225, 238, 257.

[100] The situation is expressed by proverbs like "Ein Mann, ein Wort" and by sentiments like the one in the second stanza of the German national anthem: "Deutsche Frauen, deutsche Treue, deutscher Wein und deutscher Sang . . .". To begin quoting the poets and intellectuals on the subject would be a hopelessly lengthy undertaking. I restrict myself to a few references that are typical:

Schiller: See his epigram "Deutsche Treue". Werke, Bibl. Inst. I, 145.

Friedrich Schlegel: Speaks of medieval France as "Jene altfranzösische Zeit, in der noch so viele Spuren deutscher Treue und Herzlichkeit übrig geglieben zu sein scheinen"; in "Grundzüge der gotischen Baukunst", Werke (1823) VI, 227.

Hebbel: See "Demetrius" lines 1879–82. For the Pole Ossip, the Germans are a people "die nur *eine* Zunge im Munde haben und nicht lügen können—so dumm als plump!"

C. F. Meyer: In "Die Hochzeit des Mönchs" Diana and her brother Germano, children of an Italian father and a German mother, exemplify a sense of "Treue" conspicuously lacking in the other, purely Italian characters.

Wagner: In the matter of "Treue", as in other respects, Wagner represents the culmination of the German Romantic Movement. "Treue" in all its forms is hailed as the central theme of Wagner's life work in one of the most dithyrambic passages of Nietzsche's "Richard Wagner in Bayreuth"; Werke I, 506.

Wildenbruch: Germanic "Treue" versus Norman-French treachery is, for instance, the theme of his "Harald".

[101] Heinrich Mann, for instance, in his novels "Diana", "Der Untertan", "Der Kopf"; also, with specific reference to Bismarck, in his essay on Zola, in "Macht und Mensch".

[102] BeU 97, etc.

[103] Z I, 204–5

[104] Z I, 564

[105] Z I, 566

[106] BeU 18

[107] BeU 530

[108] BeU 17

[109] For the author of the "Betrachtungen" the Germans are "das übernationale Volk", "das Volk das die höchsten universalistischen Überlieferungen, die reichste kosmopolitische Begabung, das tiefste Gefühl europäischer Verantwortlichkeit sein eigen nennt". BeU 179

[110] As early as 1791 Friedrich Schlegel had written to his brother August Wilhelm: "Ich sehe in allen, besonders den wissenschaftlichen Taten der Deutschen nur den *Keim* einer grossen herannahenden Zeit und glaube, dass unter unserm Volk Dinge geschehen werden, wie nie unter einem menschlichen Geschlecht. Rastlose Tätigkeit, tiefes Eindringen in das Innere der Dinge, sehr viel Anlage zur Sittlichkeit und Freiheit finde ich in unserm Volke.

Allenthalben aber sehe ich die Spuren des Werdens." Walzel: "Friedrich Schlegels Briefe an seinen Bruder," 26.

[111] Werke VI, 19

[112] Z II, 425

[113] BeU 9

[114] BeU 147

[115] BeU 449

[116] Z II, 425

[117] Z II, 434

[118] Z II, 78

[119] In his address, "Lübeck als geistige Lebensform" (1926) Thomas Mann alludes to Nietzsche as "jener Sohn und Enkel protestantischer Pfarrhäuser, in dem die Romantik des neunzehnten Jahrhunderts sich selbst überwand und mit dessen Opfertode am Kreuz des Gedankens unsäglich Neues sich anbahnte" (FdT 51–2). The same sentence recurs verbatim in his centenary address, "Goethe als Repräsentant des bürgerlichen Zeitalters" (G 460). The same idea, including the word "Selbstkreuzigung" applied to Nietzsche, is found in his little essay on Dürer, FdT 264.

[120] Quoted BeU 129

[121] BeU 52

[122] " Rede über Nietzsche" (1924), Bem 335

[123] G 453

[124] Z II, 262

[125] G 435

[126] "Die grossen Söhne des Bürgertums, die aus ihm hinaus ins Geistige und Überbürgerliche wuchsen, sind Zeugen dafür, dass im Bürgerlichen grenzenlose Möglichkeiten liegen, Möglichkeiten unbeschränkter Selbstbefreiung und Selbstüberwindung." (G 462)

VII. MYSTICISM

[1] Z I, 480–2

[2] Z II, 229

[3] There is a danger of the younger reader missing this point altogether, accustomed as he is to associating the soldier with the drab uniform of the World War, rather than with the color and glitter of his pre-war accoutrement. In telling of his own short term of military service—in 1900—Thomas Mann uses the characteristic phrase: "(Ich) liess mir bunte Kleider anmessen". (L 743)

[4] Z II 546

[5] Z II, 568–9

[6] Z II, 534

[7] Z II, 526–7

[8] BeU 563

[9] KH 426–7

[10] N II, 356. See Chapter III, note 16, of this study.

[11] . . . " in diesem irren, ewigen Getöse, das betäubt, stumm macht und das

Gefühl der Zeit ertötet." (Bud I, 179) . . . "dieses mühe- und schmerzlose
Schweifen und Sichverlieren der Augen über die grüne und blaue Unendlich-
keit hin . . . eine gedämpfte Betäubung, in der das Bewusstsein von Zeit
und Raum und allem Begrenzten still selig unterging . . ." (Bud II, 314)

"Zuweilen trug der Wind das Geräusch der Brandung zu ihm. . . . Er genoss
ein tiefes Vergessen, ein erlöstes Schweben über Raum und Zeit." (N II, 72)

[12] "O überschwenglicher und unersättlicher Jubel der Vereinigung im ewigen
Jenseits der Dinge! Des quälenden Irrtums entledigt, den Fesseln des Raumes
und der Zeit entronnen, verschmolzen das Du und Ich . . ." (N I, 351–2)

[13] Z II, 617

[14] An early expression of Thomas Mann's mysticism, revealing the autobiographical basis of Hans Castorp's experiences in this regard, is his essay "Süsser
Schlaf" (1909), where he dwells upon his intimate attachment to the bed,
"dies metaphysische Möbelstück", upon his love of the sea, his "Indertum",
and his "Neigung zum Ewigen". RuA 395–6

[15] "Zudem könnte es sein, dass die unsrige (Geschichte) mit dem Märchen
auch sonst, ihrer inneren Natur nach, das eine und andre zu schaffen hat."
(Z I, 10)

Another very interesting fairy-tale feature of the "Zauberberg" is the re-
current use of a mystic number, the number seven. Hans Castorp dwells in the
Magic Mountain for seven years. (Z II, 613) There are seven tables in the
establishment and, like Snow-White, Hans makes the rounds of them all during
his stay. (Z II, 579, 613) At the end of his first seven weeks he makes the
momentous decision involved in submitting to an x-ray examination. (Z I, 371)
It takes seven months before his passion for Clavdia reaches its climax. (Z I,
542) For seven minutes, four times a day, he listens to the pulse of his blood
with the thermometer in his mouth. (Z I, 284) The duration of Joachim's
stay exceeds seven times seventy days. (Z II, 137) The number of Clavdia's
room is seven. (Z I, 244) Joachim occupies number twenty-eight (seven times
four) on his return. (Z II, 266) Hans Castorp's own is thirty-four (Z I, 23),
and this number seems to have a double significance: First, it is also built up
on the principle of seven,—three plus four, as appears from "Holger's" cryptic
answer to Hans Castorp's question, how much the total duration of his time
at Davos would mount up to. "Geh quer durch dein Zimmer" is the instruc-
tion spelled out. (Z II, 544) No one knows what to make of this, but in the
light of the outcome it obviously amounts to a horizontal summation of the
elements of number thirty-four. But in the second place the number thirty-
four suggests the well-known "magic square" of four, as it appears in the upper
right-hand corner of Dürer's etching "Melancolia". It consists of sixteen equal
parts, and over these parts the numbers one to sixteen are distributed in such
fashion that when any four of them are added horizontally, vertically, or di-
agonally, the invariable sum is thirty-four. In this connection it is interesting
to note that Thomas Mann finds the rhythm of his own life yielding so definite
a numerical pattern as to make him venture to predict the year of his own
death. In his "Lebensabriss" he writes:

"Der Tag des Ehegedenkfestes steht unmittelbar bevor, herbeigeführt von einem Jahr, dessen Zahl rund ist wie alle, die mein Leben beherrschen. Es war Mittag, als ich zur Welt kam; zwischen den Mitten der Jahrzehnte lagen meine fünfzig Jahre, und inmitten eines Jahrzehnts, ein halbes nach ihrer Mitte, heiratete ich. Mein Sinn für mathematische Klarheit stimmt dem zu, wie er der Anordnung zustimmt, dass meine Kinder als drei reim- und reigenartig gestellte Paare—Mädchen, Knabe—Knabe, Mädchen—Mädchen, Knabe—erschienen und wandeln. Ich vermute, dass ich im Jahre 1945, so alt wie meine Mutter, sterben werde." (L 769)

[16] Z II, 537

[17] Z II, 532

[18] ibid.

[19] "Träume eines Geistersehers", Kants Werke, Ernst Cassirer, II, 332.

[20] This is another idea that Thomas Mann originally owes to Nietzsche. See Nietsches Werke VIII, 252.

[21] BeU 402

[22] BeU 405. Cf. also ibid. 41 and 390. This identification of sin and morality, as opposed to that of virtue and philistinism, is not merely a war-time idea of Thomas Mann's. It is at the bottom of all his reflections on the ethos of the artist. We already find it adequately formulated long before the "Betrachtungen" in his sketch of Schiller, "Schwere Stunde" (1905; N I, 250), and in the essay "Süsser Schlaf" (1909; RuA 397); and in briefer phrasing the same idea is voiced in the essay "Versuch über das Theater" (1907; RuA 35.—Its date is incorrectly given in that volume as 1910). Between the "Betrachtungen" and the "Zauberberg" we meet it again in "Brief an einen Verleger" (1920; RuA 318).

[23] Z I, 572; Z II, 77, 363

[24] Z II, 533.

[25] "Zum Geleit. Meisterwerke der russischen Erzählungskunst", Süddeutsche Monatshefte, Feb. 1921.

[26] "Russische Dichtergalerie" (1922), Bem 322–3

[27] See Chapter V, note 57, of this study.

[28] See Chapter V, note 55, of this study.

[29] BeU 67

[30] Z I, 449

[31] Z I, 574

[32] Z I, 449

UNIVERSITY OF NORTH CAROLINA
STUDIES IN THE GERMANIC LANGUAGES
AND LITERATURES

Publication Committee

FREDERIC E. COENEN, EDITOR

WERNER P. FRIEDERICH   GEORGE S. LANE

JOHN G. KUNSTMANN   HERBERT W. REICHERT

1. Herbert W. Reichert. THE BASIC CONCEPTS IN THE PHILOSOPHY OF GOTTFRIED KELLER. 1949. Pp. 164. Paper $ 3.00.
2. Olga Marx and Ernst Morwitz. THE WORKS OF STEFAN GEORGE. Rendered into English. 1949. Out of print.
3. Paul H. Curts. HEROD AND MARIAMNE, A Tragedy in Five Acts by Friedrich Hebbel, Translated into English Verse. 1950. Out of print.
4. Frederic E. Coenen. FRANZ GRILLPARZER'S PORTRAITURE OF MEN. 1951. Pp. xii, 135. Cloth $ 3.50.
5. Edwin H. Zeydel and B. Q. Morgan. THE PARZIVAL OF WOLFRAM VON ESCHENBACH. Translated into English Verse, with Introductions, Notes, and Connecting Summaries. 1951, 1956, 1960. Pp. xii, 370. Paper $ 4.50.
6. James C. O'Flaherty. UNITY AND LANGUAGE: A STUDY IN THE PHILOSOPHY OF JOHANN GEORG HAMANN. 1952. Out of print.
7. Sten G. Flygt. FRIEDRICH HEBBEL'S CONCEPTION OF MOVEMENT IN THE ABSOLUTE AND IN HISTORY. 1952. Out of print.
8. Richard Kuehnemund. ARMINIUS OR THE RISE OF A NATIONAL SYMBOL. (From Hutten to Grabbe.) 1953. Pp. xxx, 122. Cloth $ 3.50.
9. Lawrence S. Thompson. WILHELM WAIBLINGER IN ITALY. 1953. Pp. ix, 105. Paper $ 3.00.
10. Frederick Hiebel. NOVALIS. GERMAN POET - EUROPEAN THINKER - CHRISTIAN MYSTIC. 1953. Pp. xii, 126. 2nd rev. ed. 1959. Paper $ 3.50.
11. Walter Silz. Realism and Reality: Studies in the German Novelle of Poetic Realism. 1954. Third printing, 1962. Pp. xiv, 168. Paper $ 4.00.
12. Percy Matenko. LUDWIG TIECK AND AMERICA. 1954. Out of print.
13. Wilhelm Dilthey. THE ESSENCE OF PHILOSOPHY. Rendered into English by Stephen A. Emery and William T. Emery. 1954, 1961. Pp. xii, 78. Paper $ 1.50.
14. Edwin H. Zeydel and B. Q. Morgan. GREGORIUS. A Medieval Oedipus Legend by Hartmann von Aue. Translated in Rhyming Couplets with Introduction and Notes. 1955. Out of print.
15. Alfred G. Steer, Jr. GOETHE'S SOCIAL PHILOSOPHY AS REVEALED IN CAMPAGNE IN FRANKREICH AND BELAGERUNG VON MAINZ, With three full-page illustrations. 1955. Pp. xiv, 178. Paper $ 4.00.
16. Edwin H. Zeydel. GOETHE THE LYRIST. 100 Poems in New Translations facing the Original Texts. With a Biographical Introduction and an Appendix on Musical Settings. 1955. Pp. xviii, 182. 2nd ed. 1958. Paper $ 1.75.
17. Hermann J. Weigand. THREE CHAPTERS ON COURTLY LOVE IN ARTHURIAN FRANCE AND GERMANY. Out of print.
18. George Fenwick Jones. WITTENWILER'S „RING" AND THE ANONYMOUS SCOTS POEM „COLKELBIE SOW". Two Comic-Didactic Works from the Fifteenth Century. Translated into English. With five illustrations. 1956. Pp. xiv, 246. Paper $ 4.50.
19. George C. Schoolfield. THE FIGURE OF THE MUSICIAN IN GERMAN LITERATURE. 1956. Out of print.
20. Edwin H. Zeydel. POEMS OF GOETHE. A Sequel to GOETHE THE LYRIST. New Translations facing the Originals. With an Introduction and a List of Musical Settings. 1957. Pp. xii, 126. Paper $ 3.25. Out of print.
21. Joseph Mileck. HERMANN HESSE AND HIS CRITICS. The Criticism and Bibliography of Half a Century. 1958. Out of print.
22. Ernest N. Kirrmann. DEATH AND THE PLOWMAN or THE BOHEMIAN PLOWMAN. A Disputatious and Consolatory Dialogue about Death from the Year 1400. Translated from the Modern German Version of Alois Bernt. 1958. Pp. xviii, 40. Paper $ 1.85.
23. Edwin H. Zeydel. RUODLIEB, THE EARLIEST COURTLY NOVEL (after 1050). Introduction, Text, Translation, Commentary, and Textual Notes. With seven illustrations. 1959, Second printing, 1963. Pp. xii, 165. Paper $ 4.50.
24. John T. Krumpelmann. THE MAIDEN OF ORLEANS. A Romantic Tragedy in Five Acts by Friedrich Schiller. Translated into English in the Verse Forms of the Original German. 1959. Out of print.
25. George Fenwick Jones. HONOR IN GERMAN LITERATURE. 1959. Pp. xii, 208. Paper $ 4.50.